0

THE AMERICAN NEGRO
HIS HISTORY AND LITERATURE

THE NEGRO
IN
PENNSYLVANIA
A STUDY IN ECONOMIC HISTORY

Richard R. Wright, Jr.

ARNO PRESS and THE NEW YORK TIMES
NEW YORK 1969

General Editor
WILLIAM LOREN KATZ

"THE 'NEGRO PROBLEM'—THAT CONDITION WHICH IS peculiar to Negroes and common to them—is rather found in the attitude of the white race toward the Negro; an attitude of a majority which seeks to shut out a minority from the enjoyment of the whole social and economic life." So wrote Richard R. Wright, Jr. in 1912 in his book, *The Negro in Pennsylvania: A Study in Economic History,* as he argued for "open competition" between the races as a means of freeing blacks from the subtle indignities of "progressive" Pennsylvania.

Wright's book has much to say, while his life serves as a perfect model for C. Wright Mills's or Howard Zinn's idea of the involved scholar. Wright might well have lived out a life of quiet dignity and reflected glory as the son of Major Richard R. Wright, Sr. His father was thought to be descended from a Mandingo chief, and was one of the two highest ranking Negroes in the Spanish-American War, founder of the Georgia State Agricultural and Industrial Association, President of the Georgia State Industrial College, and later a bank president in Philadelphia. With a nod of the head he could have been McKinley's Minister to Liberia.

The younger Wright chose to follow the rigorous life of his father. At Chicago, while working for an M.A. degree, he assisted the local Teamsters in a strike and also maintained an A.M.E. pastorate. He managed to remain militant even while pursuing his doctorate at the University of Pennsylvania, challenging his white professor in a seminar on the Negro so frequently that eventually he was allowed to preview and dispute the lecture outlines before they were presented to the class. While in Philadelphia he helped form the Colored Protective Association and edited *The Colored Protector,* both activities aiding in exposing inequities and discrimination in the Philadelphia political machine and police department. He lived for two years in the Eighth Ward Social Settlement House, eventually forging it into an adjunct of the newly formed Urban League. Later in life he continued as an influential figure in the Republican Party, as President of Wilberforce University in Ohio, and finally as a Bishop of the African Methodist Episcopal Church.

Wright's books ranged from his dissertation on the Negro in Pennsylvania through church history, theology, the "Negro Problem," census studies for the Carnegie Foundation, a study of Pittsburgh Negroes for the Urban League, an autobiography, and with W. E. B. Du Bois and Monroe M. Work, a study of the Negroes in Lowndes County, Alabama.

The Negro in Pennsylvania was the result of a search by the University of Pennsylvania for a Negro scholar to broaden the base of Du Bois's famous pioneer study, *The Philadelphia Negro.* Wright's book briefly outlined the history of the black man from colonial servitude to the end of the nineteenth century. Then he abandoned his subtitle's stress on "economic history" for a broad social analysis of the plight of the ghettos and farms of black Pennsylvania. He exposed discriminatory labor conditions and wage structures while at the same time revealing the segregation patterns hidden behind the liberal rhetoric of Quaker Pennsylvania.

But most important for students of urban America and the Negro scene, he described the social creativity that grew out of the "air-tight cage" of ghetto life. When Pennsylvinia, for example, provided no training schools, private citizens formed the Association for the Protection of Working Women and the Home for Working Women as teaching institutions. He also noticed, as in all black ghettos, the fact that fraternal and benevolent associations provided insurance benefits. In addition to the work of such agencies, Wright leavened his study with reports of individual attainments such as the Negro doctor who made the highest score on the state medical examinations and the Negro barbers who struggled to hang onto their shops in the stations of the Pennsylvania Railroad.

Both as a necessary complement to Du Bois's study of Philadelphia and as a starting point for modern scholars, Wright's book deserves a wide audience.

Thomas R. Cripps
PROFESSOR OF HISTORY
MORGAN STATE UNIVERSITY

The Negro In Pennsylvania

❦ A Study In Economic History ❦

*A THESIS SUBMITTED TO THE UNIVERSITY OF
PENNSYLVANIA IN PARTIAL FULFILLMENT
OF THE REQUIREMENTS FOR THE
DEGREE OF PH.D.*

By Richard R. Wright, Jr.

Philadelphia
A. M. E. Book Concern
Printers
631 Pine St.

Contents

The Negro In Pennsylvania

SLAVERY IN THE COLONY OF PENNSYLVANIA

When the Colony of Pennsylvania was founded by
William Penn, Negro slavery was a recognized institution
in the New World. „The Dutch and Swedes, who settled
along the Delaware, had slaves. But whence these slaves
came and how many they were, or what was their exact lo-
cation, is not positively known. It is known, however, that
as early as 1639, an offender, named Coinclesse, was sentenced by the authorities of Manhattan for wounding a sol-
dier at Fort Amsterdam, to "serve along with blacks, to be
sent by the first ship to South River" (The Delaware).
And in 1677, one James Sunderlands, is said to have been a
slaveholder in the Delaware neighborhood.

When William Penn secured his charter and framed
the laws for the government of his colony, he intended to
give the greatest personal freedom to all who came to the
new land. To The Free Society of Traders, who purchased
some 20,000 acres of ground, Penn granted extensive privileges, and jurisdiction over their own land. In their articles
of settlement is the following: "It (The Free Society of
Traders) is a very unusual society; for it is an absolutely
free one and in a free country; a society without oppression,
wherein all may be concerned that will and yet have the
same liberty of private traffic as though there were no society at all." In this quite liberal description Negroes were,
however, not included; for in the following paragraph, the
society declared as a further inducement for colonists to
come to the Pennsylvania country, "Black servants to be

5

free at fourteen years, on giving the society two-thirds of
what they can produce on land allotted to them by the society, with stocks and tools; if they agree not to do this, to
be servants until they do." Thus, at the very beginning,
the founders of Pennsylvania sanctioned Negro servitude,
stating in very clear language the handicap under which
Negroes must live and labor.

The Penn Colony arrived in the country in 1682.
Though there is no record of any of them owning slaves at
this time, it is probable that slaves were early procured by
many. James Claypoole, of England, on deciding to come
to Pennsylvania in 1682, wrote as follows : "I have a great
drawing on my mind to remove with my family thither, so
that I am given up, if the Lord clears the way, to be gone
by next spring. Advise me in thy next, what I might have
two Negroes for **that they might be fit for cutting down
trees, building, plowing or any sort of labor that is required in the first planting of a country.**" In 1684, just two
years after the founding of the colony, one Cornelius Bonn,
is said to have had a Negro whom he "bought." In the
same year, among the goods of William Pomfret, of Bucks
County, which were levied on by Gilbert Wheeler was
"one man" supposed to be a Negro slave. There is
also evidence which seems to show that William Penn himself approved of slavery, that he used slaves, and probably
owned some. In his cash book, one "Dorcas," a colored
woman, is mentioned by him. In a letter to James Harri-
son, his steward, under date of August 25, 1685, he wrote
from England: "I have sent a gardener by this ship, or
he soon follows, with all requisites; a man of recommended
great skill. Let him have what help he can, not less than
two or three at any time; he will cast things into a proper
posture. He has his passage paid, thirty pounds at three
years, sixty acres of land and a month in the year to him-

self, not hindering my business, and he is to train two men and a boy in the art. **It were better that they were blacks for then, a man has them while they live.**" Two months later, October 4th, 1685, he wrote again: "The blacks of Captain Allen, I have as good as bought; so part not with them without my order." There are other evidences that he had slaves, but none that he ever possessed a large number of them at any one time.

It seems therefore that after the settlers of Pennsylvania began the actual work of settlement, they fell somewhat from the high ideals of human liberty as set forth by the Free Society of Traders, while they were still in London. Negroes were found to be useful in "cutting down trees, building, plowing, and any sort of labor that is required in the first planting of a country." Economic necessity thus forced upon the liberty-loving Pennsylvania community, human servitude, as it had also upon other colonies. And about 1700, slavery became a recognized institution in the Quaker Colony.

The Pennsylvania colonists procured their slaves chiefly from the West Indies and from the surrounding colonies on the mainland of America. Very few, however, came direct from Africa. Slaves were sold for from forty to a hundred pounds sterling. In 1700 slaves were numerous enough to call for special attention from the Philadelphia Monthly Meeting of the Society of Friends. The subject was brought up by no less a personage than William Penn himself, for "his mind had long been engaged for the benefit and welfare of the Negroes." Penn, with the consent of the Colonial Council, also recommended special legislation for Negroes. Slavery seemed to be taken as a matter of course. Nothing is heard of the emancipation after fourteen years' service, provided for in the plans of the Free Society of Traders. In 1683, Penn wrote a long letter to the Free Society of Traders, making mention of the important things relating to the Colony but said nothing of Negroes. For half a century the trade in slaves increased, not however without evoking some hostility from the Quakers and other anti-slavery colonists.

Newspapers contained frequent advertisements concerning slaves. Indeed, half of the advertising matter of the American Weekly Mercury, Pennsylvania's first newspaper, consisted of advertisements for the sale of Negroes, or for the apprehending of Negro slaves or other servants.

Slavery reached its height in Pennsylvania between 1750 and 1763 and from the latter date, began to decline. There are but few statistics of Negroes in the Colony; and in the literature of the early times there are but few references from which to form a trustworthy estimate of the number of slaves. But from the legislation of the times, the increasing number of protests of the abolitionists and other references, it is probable that slaves must have existed in the Colony in considerable numbers. In 1775, 2,000 slaves were held in the beginning by all classes, but became more and more characteristic of the English, Welsh and Scotch Irish settlements and less of the German and Quaker settlements.

On the whole it may be said that as compared with other colonies, the slavery which existed in Pennsylvania was mild. Yet there was a distinct status; first, on account of race and religion, and secondly, due to the influence of the general condition of slavery existing in the Colonies around Pennsylvania. The Constitution of 1682 recognized the status of the black servant as differing from that of the white servant in that the former was a servant for at least 14 years, while there was no specified time for the servitude of the white servant—the time being usually from four to six years. In the second place, the black servant might be freed, not however to become an independent member of the community but to remain under the patronage of some person, receiving tools, stocks, etc., from him and returning therefor, two-thirds of his produce. If the black servant refused this freedom he became a servant for life. On the contrary, the white servant, on working out his time, came into possession of a number of acres of land and became thereafter an independent member of the colony.

The first special legislative action with regard to Negroes in Pennsylvania was a law passed by the City Council of Philadelphia, in 1693 "against tumultuous gatherings of Negroes of the old town of Philadelphia on the first day of the week." By this law, constables or others were authorized "to take up Negroes, male or female, whom they should find gadding abroad, on the first day of the week, without a ticket from their master or mistress, or not in their company, to carry them to jail and there to cause them to remain that night and without meat or drink, or to cause them to be whipped publicly." In 1700, seven years later, colonial legislation looking toward separate treatment of blacks and whites was suggested by William Penn himself. This was the beginning of Pennsylvania's "Black Code." There were three laws proposed, two of which were enacted. The first and most important was "An Act for the Trial of Negroes," which was passed November 27, 1700. This Act stated that "some difficulties have arisen within this province and territory about the manner of trial and punishment of Negroes committing murder, manslaughter, buggery, burglary, rape, attempted rape, sodomy." It remained in force until 1705 when it was repealed by the law of January 12, 1705-6. The new law provided life imprisonment and thirty-nine lashes every three months during the first year of such imprisonment for any Negro convicted of sodomy or buggery; an attempt at rape or robbery of more than five pounds, sterling, made him liable to branding with a letter "R," or "T," and exportation. This act remained in force until slavery was abolished in 1780. In 1765, however, another "Act for the Trial of Negroes" was passed. This act provided that the exportation of the Negro convicted of robbery or rape, be at the expense of the master and also that the Negro convicted should "never return on pain of death."

The other act, suggested by William Penn and which was enacted by the colonial legislature, was for the "Better Regulation of Servants in the Province," etc., which was passed November 27, 1700. A third law was also proposed by him to regulate marriage among slaves but did not pass.

According to an act passed August 26, 1721, persons were prohibited from selling liquor to Negroes. The principal law in Pennsylvania's "Black Code" was that passed March 26, 1725-26, entitled "An Act for the better regulation of Negroes in this Province," which defined the status of the Negro not only as a slave but as a free man. This legislation provided for compensating the owner in case a slave was executed for crime; restricted the free Negroes and compelled them to work, forbade inter-race marriage, required slaves away from home to have passes and forbade the keeping or hiding of slaves without knowledge and consent of their masters.

The laws of the colonies discriminated very sharply between a Negro and a white person. The discrimination originating, perhaps, in an attempt to place the slave at the same time in two separate categories, that of a rational and responsible human being and that of property. Although the Negro slave was property, he was not to be treated as a horse or a cow, but as a person; still not as a white person. Later there were distinctions made between the slave and the free Negro, and between the free Negro and the white person. In the latter case, although the free Negro was no longer considered property, he was considered distinctly different from white persons.

Some of the discriminations were as follows; As to morals, it seemed to be taken for granted that the Negro had few and was only punishable for moral offences in which whites were involved. For adultery, a white person was imprisoned one year and fined fifty pounds and the injured party allowed to divorce, with heavier penalties for later offences. For adultery or fornication between Negroes, even free Negroes, there does not seem to have been any punishment whatever, but if a Negro and a white person were involved, the **Negro was to be sold as a servant for seven years.** The law against inter-race marriage provided that a white person, who may be convicted of such offence, shall be fined thirty pounds or suffer the penalty of being sold as a servant for seven years. But for a free Negro, there was no alternative but to become a slave for life. For rape a white man was publicly whipped, not exceeding thirty-one lashes and given seven years imprisonment. If unmarried, he forfeited all his estate; if married, he forfeited a third of his estate. For the second offence he was ostracised and branded with 'R" on his forehead. For the same crime by a Negro with "any white woman or maid" the black offender suffered death; and for attempted rape, a Negro was castrated. There does not seem to be any punishment for the rape of a Negro woman, whether the offender be white or black. Negroes were punished by death for murder, manslaughter, buggery, burglary and rape. Whites were so punished only for murder in the first degree. For sodomy or buggery a white man was imprisoned for life and whipped during the first year. Strict laws were made against Negroes drinking or remaining out later than nine o'clock at night or wandering through the country or competing with white men, etc. Whites were tried by a jury of their peers of freeholders, but Negroes by two justices and six freeholders. For punishment, whites were generally fined or imprisoned; Negroes were generally whipped. The law against trafficing with servants provided for a fine for the white master, a term of servitude for the white servant, but **"if the servant be black he shall be severely whipped."** For firing a gun or other arms, making or selling fireworks, in Philadelphia, the fine was five shillings or two days' imprisonment, but if such offender be a Negro or Indian slave, instead of imprisonment, he was publicly whipped.

So far as the laws of the colony go, there is evidence that Pennsylvania took but little legal notice of the fact that Negroes might be morally improved. There were laws on the statute books of the colony and state for nearly a hundred years, which were calculated only to inspire Negroes with fear, to discourage individual initiative on their part, to emphasize the difference between whites and blacks, to create a status of inferiority for the Negro, the effect of which was to put even the free Negro beneath the white servant. Although every protection was thrown around white women, there was no hint of protection of Negro women against white men or against men of their own race. So far as the laws of Pennsylvania were concerned the Negro woman was not recognized to have any virtue. The one effort made by William Penn, in 1700, to give moral standing to the Negroes by regulating marriage among them, was defeated in the Assembly and there the matter rested for many years. The beginning of the Negro race in this State was under a moral handicap as well as an economic handicap.

THE ABOLITION OF SLAVERY

Notwithstanding the fact that Pennsylvania drew sharp lines between Negroes and whites, and by her laws laid the foundation for a black caste and a white caste, yet to the people of this State is due much credit for instituting many of the most fruitful efforts against the slave system. This contradictory position may be accounted for by two things: first, to the favorable attitude of the British government regarding slavery in its colonies, and second, to the contrary attitude represented chiefly by the Quakers. In this contradictory position we see in bold relief the struggle between the economic and moral elements of our early colonial society. It was presumed economic necessity which caused slavery to take root and to flourish in the Colony of Pennsylvania. The moral sense of the colony, however, was never entirely crushed by its economic needs. Long before the economic advantage of free as against slave labor was clearly demonstrated, in this colony, for purely moral and religious reasons, vigorous protests against slavery were published. Pennsylvania might well be called the parent of the movement for the abolition of Negro slavery. For not only was the first protest against slave trade in this country made here, but here the underground railroad was probably started; here the first abolition society was formed; here the first anti-slavery society was organized; here was the first trial of gradual abolition by law, and here numerous pioneer movements for the emancipation of the slaves and the betterment of the condition of the freedmen found fertile soil and vigorous growth.

There were possibly three distinct factors which brought about the abolition of slavery in the colony. The

first of these was religious sentiment, represented chiefly
by the Quakers, who based their opposition to slavery on
the principle of brotherhood as taught by Jesus. They
made no excuse or allowance for economic needs and often
found themselves in direct opposition to the opinion of
the times. The first recorded protest against slavery in
America was that by the German Friends of Germantown,
near Philadelphia, in 1688, six years after the founding of
the Pennsylvania Colony. These Germans, a simple God-
fearing, liberty-loving people, were quick to see the utter
incompatibility of slavery and Christianity. For them, the
economic motive was not the ruling motive of life. The
original document containing the protest was lost and was
not discovered until 1846, when Nathan Kite found and
published it in "The Friend," the organ of the Society of
Friends. These Friends considered the Negroes as men
and brethren with a right of freedom to their bodies. They
concluded their protest with this exhortation, "Now consider well this thing, (slavery) if it is good or bad. And
in case you find it to be good to handle these blacks in that
manner, we desire and require you hereby, lovingly, that
you may inform us herein what at this time never was
done, viz: That Christians have such liberty so to do. To
the end, we may be satisfied and satisfy likewise, our good
friends and acquaintances in our native country, that men
should be handled so in Pennsylvania."

This protest was drawn up at a meeting held in Germantown February 18, 1688. The action of this and other
meetings showed that the protest was far in advance of
the times. The Monthly Meeting declared that the matter
was "so weighty" that it was "not expedient" to be handled
there. They referred it to the Quarterly Meeting which
also refused to take a definite stand regarding it, declaring that it was "a thing too great in weight for this

meeting to determine." The Yearly Meeting at Philadelphia found itself in the same predicament and refused to take action. At this time, it seems that not even the Friends as a body were strong enough to take a decided stand against slavery; for the slaves seemed necessary, to the majority of them, for the development of the new country. The next protest was that which George Keith, a Quaker, made at a meeting of Friends in Philadelphia about 1693. In 1696, "a minute of advice" was sent by the Yearly Meeting cautioning Friends as follows: "Whereas, several papers have been read relating to the keeping and bringing in of Negroes; which being duly considered it is the advice of this meeting that the Friends be careful not to encourage the bringing of any more Negroes and that such as have Negroes, be careful to bring them to meetings, have meetings with them in their families and restrain them from loose and lewd living as much as in them lies and from rambling abroad on first days and other times." William Penn brought to the attention of the Philadelphia Monthly Meeting the matter of Negroes and that meeting put it on record, "That Friends ought to be very careful in discharging good conscience towards them in all respects, but much more especially for the good of their souls." In 1715, the Yearly Meeting went on record against the importation of slaves declaring, "If any Friends are concerned in the importation of Negroes let them be dealt with and advised to avoid that practice." In 1716, the Quarterly Meeting at Chester tried to commit the Friends against buying and selling slaves, but without success. Nothing more practical was done until 1729, when the Chester Meeting again urged against Friends dealing in slaves; this after a year, was adopted as the advice by the Yearly Meeting of 1730, and was repeated from time to time. In 1743 a special query was adopted, "Do Friends observe the advice of the Yearly Meeting not to encourage the Importation of Negroes, nor to buy them after imported?" In 1754, a very urgent letter was circulated among the Friends by the Yearly Meeting advising against trading in slaves. In 1755 another step was made; the disciplinary question was asked, "Are Friends clear of importing or buying Negroes, and do they use those well that they are possessed of by inheritance or otherwise, endeavoring to train them up in the principles of the Christian religion?" In 1755, the Yearly Meeting also decided to disown all members of the Society who traded in Negroes. In 1766, it was decided to disown all those members who did not manumit their slaves.

This steady development in the attitude of Friends seems almost ideal, but it is always easier to pass resolutions than to act. The resolution to disown slave traders in 1755 was not followed by a wholesale disowning, though some Quakers did engage in the trade. After 1758, there were many who manumitted their slaves, but quite a large number still retained them, which led to the adoption of the severe measures in 1776. But even this could not be vigorously enforced. Some were holding slaves two years after the resolution of 1776. In 1777, the Friends Quarterly Meeting in Bucks County, reported that some of their number had liberated their slaves, but that others still persisted in holding them. The following year several members in Philadelphia were disowned for holding slaves. In this year also, Sarah Crowden and Joseph Lovett, members of the Falls Meeting, Bucks County, were dealt with for refusing to free their Negroes. As late as the registration of slaves in Bucks County, in 1782, slaves were retained by Quakers.

Some difficulties in the way of manumission often made it hard for persons of moderate means to free their slaves. Because a certain type of slaveholders, in some of the colonies manumitted the old and infirm slaves, who afterward became a burden upon the colony, several colonies had attempted to protect themselves by requiring the former master to give security for his manumitted slave, in case the latter should become a public charge. Pennsylvania adopted such a law in 1726. The difficulty under which one labored who desired to manumit his slaves may be illustrated by the following instance in Bucks County:

"Thomas Lancaster, Sr., a member of the Plymouth Meeting and the owner of a farm of 200 acres in Whitemarsh, having been prevailed upon by the Society, after several years entreaty, at length consented." The following were the conditions imposed upon him to carry out this measure legally, according to the royal requirements: "At a General Court of Quarter Sessions of the Peace, held for the city and county of Philadelphia, 6th of June, A. D., 1774, Thomas Lancaster of Whitemarsh township, in this county, yeoman, acknowledges himself to be held and firmly bound unto our sovereign lord, the King, in the sum of thirty pounds lawful money of Pennsylvania, to be levied on his goods, chattels, lands and tenements, to the use of our said lord, the King." "That, whereas, the said Thomas Lancaster hath manumitted and set free from slavery a certain Negro man named Cato, aged about forty-six years, and if the said Thomas Lancaster, his executors and administrators, shall do well and truly hold and keep harmless and indemnified the Overseers of the Bar, of the City and County of Philadelphia, respectively from all costs, charges and incumbrances whatsoever, which shall or may happen to accrue in case the said Negro man shall

2

be sick or otherwise rendered incapable of supporting himself; then the above obligation to be void, otherwise to be
and remain in full force and virtue, agreeable to an Act of
Assembly in such cases made and provided."

In time, economic necessity which helped to establish
slavery, also helped to destroy it. In the first few years,
while the Negroes were profitable for pioneer work, the
moral and religious arguments such as were advanced
by the German friends, Lay and Sandiford, and others apparently fell on deaf ears. Men devoted themselves in religion to other matters not so intimately associated with
their economic needs. But as years passed economic necessity did not favor an extensive system of slavery in
Pennsylvania such as existed in the South. Economic conditions reinforced the religious and moral forces and has-
tened the death of slavery, as a system, in Pennsylvania.
The quality of work which the colonists had for slave labor
was such as tended ultimately to discourage the development of a great slave system. In the early days, there
was great demand for slaves to do the heavy pioneer work
of clearing the forests, but as there was less and less of
this to do, and as the easy terms upon which white servants could be induced to come to the colony, caused the
number of white immigrants to increase, the actual demand
for Negro workers decreased. For white servants were a
better investment than Negro slaves. A white servant
could be secured for four or five years for the cost of his
transportation from Europe, while a Negro cost considerably more.

The colonist kept the white servants during these four
or five years, and at the end of this period his responsibility
ended. But with the Negro slave, his responsibility did
not end until the death of the Negro. For even if he manu-

mitted the Negro slave, he must still be responsible for him in case of sickness or extreme poverty. This, added to the fact that the white workmen were chiefly voluntary immigrants, were generally more intelligent than the slave, often spoke the same language as their employers, were of their race and religion, and above all, possessed what the Negro slave because of his servitude, could not possess, ambition to make their way in the new country—these things made the indentured servant or the redemptioner, far more profitable to the Pennsylvania colonists, after the first years of rough pioneer work were past, than the Negro slave. As white servants increased, slave labor became less and less profitable and the economists were the more and more in favor of a restriction on slavery.

The opposition of free labor to slave labor took definite form in the shape of a protest of white mechanics and day laborers against the practice of masters hiring out their slaves. The protest stated "That the practice of blacks being employed was a great disadvantage to them who had emigrated from Europe for the purpose of obtaining a livelihood; that they were poor and honest; they therefore hoped a law would be prepared for the prevention of the employment of blacks." In accordance with this the General Assembly put itself on record against the principle of masters hiring out their slaves, declaring that the principle was "dangerous and injurious to the republic and not to be sanctioned." And four years later, the legislature forbade masters to permit their Negro slaves from hiring their time. Up to 1726, the objection from the economic side was not as to slavery as a system, but as to the kind of labor slaves should do. It seems to be conceded that a slave should do the work of his own master but not, as in the early days, the work of others. This should be reserved for free laborers. This restriction was, however, a blow to the system, for it removed the temptation to increase the number of slaves beyond one's personal needs. It also tended to make slave labor more costly than free labor. For the fact that the slave must be kept the whole year and fed and clothed, without the privilege of being hired out, made him a burden in dull times.

The nature of the employments of the colony made slavery even less profitable as a permanent system. The work of the colony needed intelligence. There were no occupations, such as extensive cotton or tobacco growing, in which a large number of ignorant laborers could be used with profit. What farming was done must be intensive rather than extensive and could be carried on best by free labor. One person could not therefore keep a large number of slaves. The chief work which the slaves did was to help at gardening and in domestic service. Now and then they helped in skilled mechanical occupations. There is mention at a very early time of Negro blacksmiths. But the very nature of these employments which needed only a few persons, led to the restriction of slavery. It may be also that the climate had much to do with the death of slavery in the state. Though not so cold as New England, the winter is just cold enough and long enough to differentiate it from Virginia and other states further South. There is snow on the ground the greater part of the winter. The time for growth of agricultural products is comparatively short. But the climate had, possibly, another important influence. Although there are no serious complaints as to the death and sickness of the Negroes, it might be inferred that their sick and death rates were quite high, making it difficult for them to rear many healthy children. For most of the Negroes or their parents came from the west coast of Africa, between Senegal and the Congo, which is a part of the Torrid Zone, from ten degrees below to fifteen degrees above the Equator. Here, they had never known snow or cold climate. Many of those who came to Pennsylvania were born in Africa, or were the children and grandchildren of native Africans. In coming to Pennsylvania, they came to the North Temperate Zone, a distance from thirty to forty-five degrees. In making this migration, the Negroes were among the first peoples of the Torrid Zone to have done so successfully in historical times. But it took generations to adapt themselves, and during these first years, it is not unreasonable to suppose that they suffered from a very heavy death rate; all of which tended to make slavery less and less profitable.

Many of the most thoughtful men of the times saw that slavery was not only morally wrong but economically unprofitable and set themselves against it. Benjamin Franklin became a member of the Pennsylvania Abolition Society, and was its president at one time. Writing of the labor of slaves, he thus states the case in his characteristically practical way: "It is an ill-grounded opinion, that by the labor of slaves, America may possibly vie in cheapness with Britain. The labor of slaves can never be so cheap as the labor of workingmen in Britain. Any one may compute it. Interest is in the colonies from 6 to 10 per cent. Slaves, one with another, cost thirty pounds sterling per head. Reckon then the interest on the first purchase of a slave, the insurance or risk of his life; his clothing and diet, expense in his sickness and loss of time, loss by neglect of business (neglect is natural to a man who is not to be benefited by his own care or diligence), expense of a driver to keep him at work and his pilfering from time to time, almost every slave being a natural thief, and compare the whole amount with the wages of a manufacturer of iron or wool in England, you will see that labor is much cheaper there than it ever can be by the Negroes here."

A third obstacle to the development of slavery in Pennsylvania was the spirit of independence and the enthusiasm for the equality of all men, a spirit much akin indeed to the religious sentiment above referred to, which as one of the foundation stones of the philosophy of the times, came as a climax to the revival of learning. Toward the end of the eighteenth century men were taken with a positive and rather sudden zeal for humanity, for freedom, equality and fraternity. In France, the practical result of this was the revolt against monarchy, known as the French Revolution. In America, the result was a revolt against foreign rule and an assertion of political independence. The American Declaration of Independence declared, "all men are created equal;" and many of the signers of that document believed that this freedom and equality ought to extend to black as well as white men. Then, too, the part that Negroes took in the Revolutionary War made a profound impression on the minds of many. In Pennsylvania and in the North, economic conditions were such that this spirit of liberty could have its full effect so far as the Negroes' bodily freedom was concerned.

The legislative attempt to restrict slavery and the slave trade represents a politico-economic movement in which the politics was dominated by economic necessity. At first, the legislative attempt had but little success. One reason for this was, that the Legislature or General Council of Pennsylvania had but little power in itself. Its laws had to pass for review before the English Government and at that time it was thought to be advantageous to England to push the slave trade as far as possible. By the treaty of Utrecht, the British secured privileges which stimulated the trade more

than ever before. Up to the time of the Revolutionary
War, we have but one act in Pennsylvania, which was designed to prohibit the importation of slaves outright. But
this act, which was entitled, "An act to prevent the importation of Negroes and Indians into this province," was inspired by the fear of Negroes more than the love of freedom. It was passed June 7, 1712 and was repealed February 20, 1713, and was never enforced. In this same year,
1712, William Southbe, an ardent abolitionist, applied to
the Pennsylvania Assembly for a declaration of freedom to
all Negroes. To this, the Assembly resolved that it was
neither practical nor convenient to set them at liberty. A
series of duty acts was enacted between 1700 and 1780
which were designed more for the raising of revenue than
for prohibiting the slave trade. The first of these passed
November 27, 1700, was entitled, "An act for granting an
impost upon wines, rum, beer, ale, cider, etc., imported, re-
torted and sold in this province and territories." Section 2,
provided "for every Negro, male or female, imported, if
above sixteen, twenty shillings; for every Negro under the
age of sixteen, six shillings." Six years later, January 12,
1706, the duty was raised to forty shillings for each slave
except those who had lived two years in this country. In
1710, Section 28 of another act confirmed the duty of forty
shillings of the act of 1706 and made it general for all imported Negroes. Within two months of this last act, came
another act of February 28, 1711, under the same title, "An
impost act, laying a duty on Negroes, etc.," which affirmed
the duty of forty shillings on Negroes not imported for the
use of the importer. This duty was in force until February
20, 1713-1714, when it was repealed by a new "act for laying
a duty on Negroes imported into this province," which placed the duty at five pounds, and made the restriction that the

slaves of persons immigrating to the colony must not be
sold for twelve months. This was repealed July 21, 1719.
There were other acts laying duties and confirming previous acts. February 22, 1717-18, an act was passed continuing the duty of five pounds, but providing that the slaves
of immigrants should be entered free, if they be not sold
for sixteen months. This act was continued by an act February 24, 1725-26, and that in turn by an act May 12, 1722,
and again on March 5, 1725-1726, this time providing an additional five pounds to the duty. None of these acts was ever
considered by the Crown, and all were allowed to become
laws merely by the lapse of time. The last of this series
was in 1729, when the duty was fixed at two pounds. After
1729 there were no more "Duty Acts" in Pennsylvania for
thirty-two years until March 14, 1761, when, "An act for
the laying of a duty on Negro and Mulatto slaves, etc." was
passed. A duty of ten pounds was again provided for.
This was supplemented the next month, and continued to
February 20, 1768. The last act of the Colonial Government was, "An act for making perpetual of the acts entitled, 'An act for the laying of a duty on Negro and Mulatto slaves imported into this province, etc.'" This act increased the duty to twenty pounds and remained in force
until the act of gradual abolition in 1780. That there was
not much change when the English rule ceased is shown
by an act passed by the Legislature September 7, 1778, to
appoint an official to collect the duties accrued since July
4, 1776. At best, the legislative attempt was only feeble
and was more for the purpose of increasing the revenue of
the colony than diminishing the slave trade.

As late as 1775, a bill to prohibit the importation of Negro slaves was vetoed by the Colonial Governor. But the
spirit of equality and independence brought forth by the

Revolution showed itself in 1777, one year after the signing of the Declaration of Independence, when George Bryan, a representative in the Pennsylvania Assembly, introduced a bill to manumit all Negro infants. This bill failing to be passed, the next year, the author, being then Governor of the State, called attention to the same in his annual message November 9, 1778. And again, February 5, 1779, President Reid, of the Assembly, called attention to the subject in his message to the Pennsylvania House of Representatives; and on March 1, 1780, the "Act for the gradual abolition of slavery" was passed and Pennsylvania became forever a free State. It provided that those already slaves, should remain so to their death but that no children thereafter born within the State should be held as slaves for life, but in order that the economic change might not be too sudden, children born in the State might be held as servants until twenty-eight years of age. It prohibited the importation of slaves, with minor exceptions and abolished the duty acts of 1761 and 1763. It also abolished the act "For the trial of Negroes," passed 1705-6, and thus put Negro criminals on the same basis as whites.

One cannot read the act of gradual abolition of slavery without profound respect for those who drafted and passed it. The preamble shows how great was the influence of the "spirit of liberty" in combining with the religious and economic factors in bringing about its passage.

There were possibly not over 5000 Negro slaves in the State when the act of gradual abolition was passed and they were but a small proportion of the entire Negro population of the State. There is not much evidence as to the immediate effect of emancipation. There was no cataclysm. In an orderly way, Negro slaves gradually assumed the position of Negro servants, to eventually become free citizens. Some difficulties, however, arose over the interpretation of the act of March 1, 1760, and March 29, 1788, the Assembly passed an additional explanatory act, "in order to prevent many evils and abuses arising from ill-disposed persons availing themselves of certain defects in the act for the gradual abolition of slavery." This provided that all slaves brought into the State by persons, intending to reside therein, should be free; that slaves or servants for a term of years must not be removed from the State without their written consent, certified by two Justices, under penalty of seventy-five pounds. It reiterated that all children born in the State and liable to service for twenty-eight years must be registered. It provided against the separation of husbands and wives and of children from their parents without their consent, under penalty of fifty pounds. It positively forbade trading in slaves or equipping vessels for the slave trade under penalty of a thousand pounds. It forbade kidnapping under penalty of a hundred pounds and provided that the law abolishing slavery be read twice at each term of court.

In accordance with these two acts, slavery gradually disappeared. According to the United States Census of 1790, there were 3737 slaves in Pennsylvania; in 1800 there were 1706; in 1810, there were 795; in 1820, there were 211; in 1830, there were 386, and in 1840, slavery had finally disappeared from the State.

THE FREE PEOPLE OF COLOR.

Just when Negroes first became free in Pennsylvania is not known. If the original design of the Free Society of

Traders to liberate Negroes after fourteen years of service, was carried out, there must have been free Negroes in Pennsylvania as early as 1696. The first case definitely known, however, was in 1701, when Lydia Wade, the widow of Robert Wade, of Delaware County, manumitted her slaves by her will dated "30, 4th mo., 1701," probated August 8, 1701, and in which was stated, "16 ly, my will is that my Negroes, John, and Jane, his wife, shall be set free one month after my decease. 17 ly, my will is, that my Negro child called Jane, shall be set free after it has lived with my Negro John twelve years and after that with my kinsman, John Wade, five years." William Penn's will, made during the same year, provided for the emancipation of his slaves, but in his last will there is no mention of slaves. It is possible, therefore, that his slaves had been freed or otherwise disposed of. Janney in his "Life of Penn," says that the wishes of Penn were not fully carried out and gives as evidence a letter written by James Logan, Penn's secretary, to whom he left the matter of the slaves, to Hannah Penn, dated 11th of 3rd month, 1721.

Manumission by will was the chief method of granting freedom to Negroes and became more and more popular and as a result the class of free people increased gradually. Many, especially among the Quakers, had not reconciled themselves to perpetual slavery, and after they had had the service of their slaves for a term of years, set them free. William Bunson, one of the early settlers of Columbia, brought a number of slaves with him from Chester in 1727. When he died in 1746, he manumitted them. The descendants of the Barbers, among the first settlers of Columbia, "gradually quit owning slaves." In 1805, Sally Bell, a Quaker, manumitted between seventy-five and a hundred slaves. Now and then, the slaves were given a start in life by a donation of money or other wealth by their former masters. For example, in 1742, Jeremiah Longshore, of Bucks County, who possessed thirty or forty slaves, freed them by will, giving each of them ten pounds.

There were, however, other sources of freedom for Negroes. Many slaves gained their freedom by running away from their masters. The freedom thus procured, was a precarious and often temporary kind. Escaped slaves who were caught were frequently returned to their masters. It was not until the nineteenth century, when Pennsylvania had become a free State and considerable anti-slavery sentiment had developed, that runaway slaves could live within the State in anything like security. Yet there were many who ran away and thus secured freedom. The papers of the early times contained many advertisements for runaway slaves, often giving minute descriptions of them and offering rewards for their return. On account of the frequency of the running away, there soon developed throughout the colonies, special laws for the apprehension of Negroes. Any Negro found wandering abroad could be arrested. When a Negro was arrested it was his burden to prove his freedom.

There were also cases of manumission during the life of the owner, generally after his slaves or slave had rendered him long and profitable service. In the pioneer period, there were but few cases of this sort, owing to the scarcity of labor. Indeed, those who had promised to free their slaves after fourteen years' service, have left no record of living up to the promise.

During the Revolutionary War, freedom was given to Negroes who bore arms and who escaped from the British. There were also a few who hired out their extra time and thus gained their freedom, though hiring out, was early forbidden by law. There were also those who were brought into the state and liberated. This was, however, during the early part of the nineteenth century very largely after Pennsylvania had become a free State and the surrounding slave States of Maryland, Delaware, Virginia and others, had laws which were very harsh respecting the manumission of slaves and the residence of manumitted Negroes. In some of these States it was illegal for free Negroes to reside. Before the end of the Revolutionary War, a law was passed by the North Carolina General Assembly to apprehend and resell freed Negroes, and several years later, a bill was presented to the Tennessee Legislature to expel all free Negroes from the State. Especially after the African colonization agitation began, the presence of the free Negroes among the slaves in the South became obnoxious, and often masters were permitted to manumit their slaves only on condition of sending them out of the State. Thus, one' Israel Bacon, of Henrico County, Virginia, manumitted fifty-six slaves who were finally brought to Columbia, Pennsylvania, and settled in 1819. Two years later, about a hundred manumitted Negroes from Hanover County were settled in the same place. In Virginia and North Carolina, manumission societies, fostered chiefly by Quakers, were largely interested in sending Negroes out of the slave States into the free States. As early as 1740, there was correspondence between the Yearly Meeting of these two Southern colonies, and in 1776 the Eastern Quarterly Meeting of North Carolina advised the manumission of slaves. In 1814 more than forty Negroes were sent to Pennsylvania by the North Carolina Quakers, and from year to year, others were sent. Smaller numbers came from other States and counties and settled in different parts of Pennsylvania. In 1790 there were 6537 free persons of color out of a total of 10,274 colored people, and in 1800 there were more than twice as many; 14,564 of the 16,270 Negroes being free.

Prior to the year 1780, the free Negro had a distinctly lower legal and social status than the white, though not so low as that of the slave. The movement of the free Negroes was restricted, congregating by themselves was limited, their rights before the courts were but scantily recognized. Few in number and shut out as they were by the common society, it is but reasonable to suppose that they lagged behind the rest of their environment. The original reason for their presence in the State was to serve. When their servitude was over, they occupied an embarrassing position. In the preamble to the Third Section to the Act of 1725-26 it was declared that, "Free Negroes are an idle and slothful people, and often prove burdensome to the neighborhood and afford ill example to other Negroes."

In 1790 the Constitution of the State gave the right of elective franchise to all male citizens of the State twenty-one years of age, making no color distinctions. Whether or not Negroes voted before 1790, cannot be ascertained. But it is posssible that some of them voted and that the purpose of the attempt to introduce the word "white" was not only to provide for a probable future contingency, but to make an end of what some thought a civic evil.

The first attempt at anything like independent economic organization among the Negroes was the Free African Society, which was organized in 1787 for the purpose of looking after the sick and poor among them. This attempt became of great importance in the early history of Negroes of this part of the country. The following excerpts from the Constitution and By-Laws will illustrate its character:

Preamble of the Free African Society, "Philadelphia, 12th, 4th month, 1787. Whereas, Absalom Jones and Richard Allen, two men of the African race, who for their religious life and conversation, have obtained a good report among men, these persons, from a love to the people of their complexion, whom they behold with sorrow, because of their irreligious and uncivilized state, often communed together upon this painful subject, in order to form some kind of religious society, but there being too few under like concern and those who were, were different in their religious sentiments; with these circumstances, they labored for some time, till it was proposed, after a serious communication of sentiments, that a society should be formed, without regard to religious tenets, provided the persons lived an orderly and sober life, **in order to support one another in sickness and for the benefit of their widows and fatherless children.**

"Articles. (17th, 5th mo., 1787.) We, the free Africans and their descendants of the City of Philadelphia, in the State of Pennsylvania or elsewhere, do unanimously agree, for the benefit of each other, to **advance one shilling in silver, Pennsylvania currency, monthly and after one year's subscription from the date hereof then to hand forth to the needy of this society,** if it should require, the sum of three shillings and nine pence per week of said money; **provided, this necessity is not brought on them by their own imprudence.** And it is further agreed that no drunkard or disorderly person be admitted as a member, and if they should prove disorderly after having been received, the said disorderly person shall be disjoined from us, if there is not an amendment, by being informed by two of the members, without having any of his subscription money returned to him. And if any should neglect paying his monthly subscription for three months and no sufficient reason appearing for such neglect, if he do not pay the whole at the next ensuing meeting, he shall be disjoined from us by being informed by two of the members as an offender, without having any of his subscrpition money returned. Also if any persons neglect meeting every month, for every omission he shall pay 3 pence, except in case of sickness or other complaint that should require the assistance of the society, then, and in such a case, he shall be exempt from the fines and subscriptions during the said sickness. Also, we apprehend it to be just and reasonable, that the surviving widow of a deceased member should enjoy the benefits of this society as long as she remains his widow, complying with the rules thereof, excepting the subscriptions. And we apprehend it to be necessary that the children of our deceased members be under the care of the society so far as to pay their schooling, if they cannot attend the free school; also to put them out as apprentices, to suitable trades or places, if required. Also that no member shall convene the society together but it shall be the sole business of the committee and that only, on special occasions and to dispose of the money in hand to the best advantage for the use of the society, after they are granted the liberty at the Monthly Meeting, and to transact all other business whatever, except that of Clerk and Treasurer. And we unanimously agree to choose Joseph Clarke to be our clerk and treasurer; and whenever another shall succeed him, it is always understood, that one of the people called Quakers, belonging to one of the three Monthly Meetings in Philadelphia, is to be chosen to act as clerk and treasurer of this useful institution. The following persons met, viz, Absalom Jones, Richard Allen, Samuel Barton, Joseph Johnson, Cato Freeman, Caesar Cranchell and

James Potter, also William White, whose early assistance and useful remarks, are found truly profitable. This evening the articles were read and after some beneficial remarks were made, they were agreed unto." The society met in the house of Richard Allen until May, 1788, when it moved because his room was too small. From December 28, 1788, its meetings were held in the Friends' "free schoolhouse." January 1, 1791, the society began religious worship in another room. It seemed to have been at first purely beneficiary and included most of the free people regardless of religious affiliations. The following extracts from its minutes will give some idea of the work of this early organization: "The 17th, 7th mo., 1787. At a Monthly Meeting of Free Africans, Caesar Thomas, William White and Caesar Cranchell, were appointed to have the oversight of the members this month." "15th, 12th mo., 1787. At a Monthly Meeting of Free Africans, held at Philadelphia, Mark Stevenson, Caesar Thomas, William White, Moses Johnson, Absalom Jones and Richard Allen were appointed to visit the members and give such advice as may appear necessary." January 1, 1788, this committee reported: "There are daily applications to join." There was also a call for more funds—— "Our stock is small, considering the numbers of members—at present it is but 12 pounds and if a few sick members should now be supported from it, it would not last us six months." At this meeting a resolution, having as its purpose raising the morals of its members, was read and approved: "That no man shall live with any woman as man and wife, without she is lawfully his wife and his certificate must be delivered to the clerk to be put on record."

The committee reported on its first case of discipline, as follows: "Whereas, Samuel S., one of the members of

3

the Free African Society, held in Philadelphia, for the benefit of the sick, has so shamefully deviated from our known
rules, hath often unnecessarily left his tender wife and
child, and kept company with a common woman, some-
time quarreling, fighting, and swearing, for which he hath
been long and tenderly dealt with, but he not forsaking his
shameful practices, we therefore disown said Samuel S.,
from being a member of our society, till he condemns the
same in life and conversation, which is our desire for him.
Signed this 20th, of the 9th mo., 1788, on behalf of the society, by the Committee."

ABSALOM JONES,
RICHARD ALLEN,
WILLIAM WHITE,
MARK STEVENSON,
WILLIAM GRAY,
CAESAR CRANCHELL.
CAESAR THOMAS.

In the natural course of things, it became necessary
for this society to take the initiative in almost all things relative to the welfare of the free people of color; and we find
it taking under advisement a form of marriage. The marriage of slaves and even of free Negroes had been much
neglected and very grave conditions had therefore, developed. Early in the history of the society a committee was appointed to regulate as far as possible the matter of marriage and met with some success. As to the financial condition, the following excerpts from the minutes of the society
are of value: "On the 15th day of the 1st mo., 1790, the
balance in the treasury was 42 pounds 9 shillings and 1
pence, and as divers members think a propriety would attend a deposit of this balance in the Bank of North America, he (the Treasurer) is desired to lodge it therein on behalf of the society as soon as convenient and report his per-

formance of the business at the next meeting." Another step was to secure a burial place. Even though the Friends were as a rule, the best friends which the Negroes had, they did not care to be buried with them. In the record of the Friends of Middletown, in 1703 is written, "Friends are not satisfied with having Negroes buried in the Friends' burying ground, therefore Robert Heaton, and Thomas Stackhouse are appointed to fence off a portion for such cases." The same body of Friends declared in 1798 that, "Negroes are forbidden to be buried within the walls of the graveyard belonging to this Meeting." Negroes were buried on the edge of plantations, with unmarked graves. It therefore became the duty of the Free African Society to purchase a lot for burying purposes. In their minutes of March 20, 1790, the following "PETITION TO THE MAYOR," is recorded: "To the Worshipful Mayor, Aldermen and Common Councilmen of the City of Philadelphia, in Common Council: The petition of the Free African Society for the benefit of the sick, in the City of Philadelphia, respectfully showeth: That the burial ground called Potters Field, being in part appropriated for the benefit of black persons, and chiefly made use of for that purpose, and your petitioners being informed that the Common Council are about to let the same, are desirous to have said burial ground under the care of the said society and are willing to pay same rent that hath been offered by any other person and a year's advance as soon as ground is enclosed and they are put in possession thereof. They, therefore, pray that the said ground may be rented to them for one or more years on the terms that they propose and under

such regulations as the Common Council shall think prop-
or to make. And your petitioners shall pray."
    Signed on behalf of the society by

MOSE JOHNSON,
ABSALOM JONES,
Overseers.
CYRUS BUSTILL,
WILLIAM WHITE,
HENRY STEWART,
TOD FINCH,
ABRAHAM INGLIS,
JAMES CATON,
Committee.

    The endorsement on the back of the petition was as
follows:

    "We, the subscribers, having for some time past, been
acquainted with several of the members of the 'FREE AF-
RICAN SOCIETY, ESTABLISHED IN THE CITY OF
PHILADELPHIA FOR THE BENEFIT OF SUCH
AMONG THEM WHO MAY BECOME INFIRM,' do
certify that we have informed ourselves of the rules and orders established by said society and approve of their institution and can therefore recommend the members thereof,
as well as their humane design, to the notice and attention
of their fellow-citizens, they being worthy of a degree of
confidence and encouragement."
    (Signed)

GEO. WILLIAMS,
WM. ASHBY,
JOSEPH CLARK,
SAML. MAGAW,
TENCH COXE,
BENJAMIN RUSH,
NICHOLAS WALN,
WILLIAM WHITE,
CHAS. WILLIAMS,
JOSEPH JAMES,
WILLIAM SAVERY.

Societies similar to the Free African Society of Philadelphia existed in other cities. In Newport, Rhode Island, and in Boston, Massachusetts, were such societies among free people of color, and there is some interesting correspondence between them and the Philadelphia society. On October 17th, 1789, the Philadelphia society read a paper from the Newport and Boston societies, which was brought by Henry Stewart, a member of the Philadelphia society, who visited these two cities. The Newport letter (from the Union Society) stated its membership as 40, recited the woes of the Africans and twice expressed a desire that Negroes go back to Africa. It was signed by the president and seven members.

In reply the Philadelphia society wrote: "With regard to the emigration to Africa which you mention, we have at present, but little to communicate on that head, apprehending every pious man is a good citizen of the whole world."

Out of the African Society grew the independent Negro church organization. At first this society was opened and closed without any religious exercises, and not until it was several months old, did it have any religious or devotional opening. When the break came with St. George's Methodist Church, it was this society which was the center for the beginning of the real Negro church. The two leaders, Richard Allen and Absalom Jones, became the heads of the first two distinctively Negro churches in America. Richard Allen became the founder of Bethel African Methodist Episcopal Church, at Sixth, near Lombard Street, which was founded September, 1787, and afterwards (1816) formed a union of independent African churches into the African Methodist Episcopal Church.

Absalom Jones became the first rector of St. Thomas'

African Episcopal Church, now one of the leading Negro Episcopal Churches of America.

At the beginning of the nineteenth century, the Negro population was 16,270, of whom 14,564 were free and 1706 were slaves. The free Negro population increased from 14,564 in 1800, to 56,949 at the beginning of the Civil War, and was 65,294 in 1870. But the increase in this element of the population was considerably less than that of the white population of the State.

This period, especially prior to 1852, witnessed a great reaction in the attitude of the country at large, toward free Negroes. Their privileges were reduced almost to a minimum. Their rights of locomotion was greatly curtailed. Though some had done valiant service in the Revolutionary War; the right to bear arms was not given them by the Constitutions of most of the new States admitted into the Union during the first quarter of the new century. Ohio gave the privilege of the militia to the whites only. Indiana and Illinois did likewise. Although in some States the Negro could vote in earlier days, the franchise was in the first half of this century taken from the Negroes in several States. This happened in Pennsylvania in 1838.

One of the chief causes of the treatment of the Negroes was the agitation among the members of the American Colonization Society. Many of the members of this body were an earnest, well-intentioned people, who, however, knew but little of the real capacity of the Negroes and in spite of every argument against their own ideas, thought to benefit the Negroes by removing those who were freed, to Africa. It was organized in 1817, and included in its membership such men as Bishop White of the Episcopal Church, Dr. Benjamin Rush and others of their class, which is sufficient proof that the purpose was not wholly against the free people of color. The society grew rapidly. State branches were established in both Northern and Southern States. A local society was established in Philadelphia, and the Pennsylvania State branch was organized in 1827. The National and State Governments were called upon to aid the purposes of the society and gave liberal support. For a while it seemed that the North and South had agreed upon a common programme, at least as to the disposition of the free Negro. The society was instrumental in securing land in West Africa, where the Colony "Liberia" was established in 1821. Monrovia (named for President Monroe, who was a sympathizer), was made the capital and chief city. From 1821 to 1835 the society was active in transporting Negroes to Liberia, where the experiment of self-government was being tried by them. The Negroes who were transplanted to Africa to make this experiment consisted largely of the blacks manumitted in the South on the condition that they go to Africa and a few persons already free, who suffered the prejudice which their class had to undergo in the South. Few Negroes from the Northern States went. Only sixty-five were reported as going from Pennsylvania, from 1820 to 1833.

The Colonization Society was an organized expression of the sentiment that Negroes could not assimilate with whites and had no future in this country except that of slaves; but that they ought to have an opportunity to develop along their own lines. Having done duty as slaves the only hope for them and a great relief for the whites, was to have the Negroes carried back to Africa. This was apart from the idea, which no doubt strongly drew many of the Southern element into the society, namely, that it would relieve the South of a class of people who were a constant menace to the slave system and thus, by ridding the slaves of a bad example—the free Negro—and also by diverting the attention of the North from abolition of slavery, to colonization of free blacks, would make slavery in the South more secure.

From the first the society was bitterly opposed by the free blacks of the North. When the first attempt was made to organize in Pennsylvania, Richard Allen, one of the founders of the free African Society and the first Bishop of the A. M. E. Church, and James Forten, a prominent Negro merchant of Philadelphia, most strenuously opposed it. At no time and no place did the society secure a very strong following among the Negroes of this State; and it enrolled but few of the names of the most prominent Negroes in other Northern States. The first Annual Convention of Free Negroes in 1831, adopted a resolution recommended by the committee against "the operations and misrepresentations of the American Colonization Society in these United States." One of its direct influences was to make conditions extremely hard for Negroes. It painted a picture of despair for them, so long as they remained in this country. It busied itself in preaching the essential mental and moral inferiority of the Negro race. It told the whites that the free Negroes who were about one-tenth of the entire number of Negroes, would degrade them and that therefore, they must get rid of them. It told the Negroes that their only hope was in Africa. It preached despair. Legislators took its word and accordingly, laws were constructed against Negroes, in most wanton disregard of the spirit of the generation before.

Illustrating the state of public opinion brought about by the society, its organ, the African Repository, of March, 1827, printed from the Public Ledger, of Philadelphia, the following: "In consequence of his own inveterate habits and the no less inveterate prejudices of the whites, it is a sadly demonstrated truth that the Negro cannot in this country, become an enlightened and useful citizen. If then, they are a useless and dangerous species of population, we would ask, is it generous to our Southern friends to burden us with them? We think it is a mistaken philanthropy, which would liberate the slave, unfitted by education and habit for freedom, and cast him upon a merciless and despising world; for the Negroes' condition is not alleviated and an unkindly act is done to the free States" Another item in the same organ of the society was taken from the Ohio State Journal, as follows: "Columbus, Ohio, July 12. We are suffering under many pernicious effects incident to a slave population, without any of the few benefits which are derived from slave holding. Immense numbers of mulattoes are constantly flocking by tens and hundreds into Ohio. Their fecundity is proverbial; they are worse than drones to society and they already swarm in our land like locusts. This State calls loudly for legislative interference." A correspondent from Maine, a clergyman, wrote the Repository: "The colored population of this country can never rise to respectability and happiness here." The weaknesses of the free Negroes were exaggerated and their failures were widely advertised, to convince them and the whites that they had no place in this country.

Pennsylvania did not go quite so far as other States but the reaction showed itself even here. The first attempt made in the State to get obnoxious laws in operation, was in July, 1832, just after the Nat Turner insurrection in Virginia, when a bill was introduced in the Legislature to require all free Negroes to carry passes and to exclude all others from the State. This bill was defeated. Five years later, however, the Supreme Court of the Commonwealth in the case of Hobbs et al., v. Fogg, declared that a Negro was not a free man in the sense of being a voter. The following year, 1838, the Constitutional Convention limited the franchise to "free white male" citizens; and until 1855, for a period of seventeen years, the Negroes of the State were disfranchised.

Under these discouragements, it would have been quite natural for the Negroes to have sunk into even a lower position than they were. What they needed was encouragement and inspiration and not discouragement and ostracism. They were but an extremely small minority of the population and at best, they would do but little. They were lately enslaved and generally ignorant. The Colonization agitation was one of the most unfortunate occurrences which entered into the life of the Northern Negro.

Contrary to the above opinions, the Negroes of Pennsylvania were generally progressing, notwithstanding the fact that the period from 1820 to 1855 was for them, the darkest in the history of the State. With the aid of Quakers and abolitionists, who as a body, were never very enthusiastic over the colonization scheme, they had established schools, churches, and other institutions of helpfulness and uplifts. Between 1820 and 1855, there were established at least a dozen schools taught by Negroes, largely under the patronage of Friends.

Philadelphia Negroes organized during this period, various literary and debating societies. In 1833, the "Philadelphia Library Company of Colored Persons" was organized and in 1841 had a hundred members notwithstanding the entrance fee was one dollar and the monthly dues, twenty-five cents. The Rush Library Company and Debating Society of Pennsylvania was organized in 1836. The Demosthenean Institute was organized in 1839, and the Gilbert Lyceum in 1841. Among the women were the Minerva Literary Society and the Edgeworth Literary Association. Out of one of these societies grew a Negro newspaper—The Demosthenean Shield, which was started in 1841. This paper had a subscription list of a thousand at its first appearance.

The Institute for Colored Youth was established for the special purpose of extending to Negroes "the benefits of a good education." In this period, Negro minstrels began to attract attention in Philadelphia. This period also saw the organization of the churches. In 1816, the African Methodist Episcopal Church denomination was organized in Philadelphia; and in 1820 the African Methodist Episcopal Zion Church in New York. These were the first attempts of Negroes to secure co-operation in church matters on a large scale. During this period the African Methodist Episcopal Church, with headquarters at Philadelphia, sent its black missionaries as far west as the Mississippi River and north into Canada to organize the church life of the blacks of these sections. This period also witnessed the rise of the independent secret orders among Negroes, which have become so powerful among them throughout the country. The strongest of these in early days was the Odd Fellows, which was introduced from England in 1843 and 1846. During this period we have from time to time, sketches of Negroes of Philadelphia and Pennsylvania. The chief ones were made in 1837, 1848 and 1856. In 1837 there was made a registry of the trades of Free People of Color, which gave the names of a large number of Negroes doing business on their own account. In 1838 there was published a pamphlet on "The Present State and Condition of the People of Color of Philadelphia," in which it was reported that whereas the taxable real estate of 229 persons was $112,464; it was in 1838, $322,532, with encumbrances amounting to only $12,906. The personal property amounted to $667,859, making a total of $990,391, for both real and personal property. It was reported that Negroes paid $161,008 in house rents, $5491 in ground rents and $464.50 in water rents.

In 1849 another report was made on the "Condition of the People of Color of Philadelphia." The value of real estate was put at $531,809, and the amount of encumbrance by mortgage and ground rent at $130,442, making a net real estate valuation of $401,367. The total number of families in the city was reported as 4262, and the total number of property owners as 315, about 7.4 per cent. of the total. The value of personal estate was estimated as $630,886, of which all except $194,318 was owned by persons living with white families. Forty-three persons were said to own property worth from $1000 to $2000; ten from $2000 to $5000, and two between $10,000 and $20,000. The property holders were, 78 laborers; 53 females, of whom 46 were widows; 49 tradesmen, 41 mechanics, 35 coachmen and hackmen, 28 waiters, 20 hairdressers, and 11 professional men. Besides the above, they were reported to have had $200,000 in banks. In 1849, the report showed that there were 15,532 Negroes in the city, of whom 8900, or 57.5 per cent. were natives of Pennsylvania, and 6632, or 42.77 per cent. were immigrants; 1077 were born slaves, of whom 767 were manumitted by their masters; 275 bought their freedom themselves, paying $63,034 for the same; and the freedom of 256 was purchased by others; the remaining 39 not reporting. In the "Statistics of Colored People," published in 1856, there is the following statements: "We (of Philadelphia) possess $2,685,693 of real and personal estate and have paid $9766.42 for taxes during the past year, and $396,782.27 for house and ground rent. We have had incorporated 108 mutual beneficial societies, having 9762 members, with an annual income of $29,600 and a permanent invested fund of $28,366, which is deposited in various institutions among the whites, who derive large profit therefrom. One thousand three hundred and eighty-five families were assisted by these societies to the amount of $10,-292.38 during the year 1853. Again as to crimes among us, by a letter from Judge Kelly, written in answer to certain questions put to him, it is shown that for the three years up to 1854, the commitments of colored persons to the Philadelphia County prison have gradually decreased, while those of the whites for the same period have markedly increased."

This period witnesses the rise of Negro business. As early as 1810, there was a Negro fire company in Philadelphia. About this time, the Negro people began to go to Pittsburg, largely from Virginia and West Virginia. The Negro engaged in hairdressing and barbers' business. One of the oldest Negro businesses owned by Negroes in the State of Pennsylvania is in Pittsburg. During this period, the Negro caterers were the most prominent in Philadelphia. Smith & Whipper was one of the largest lumber firms in South Central Pennsylvania. Both men were among the wealthiest Negroes the State has produced. Another development was the beneficial society. The Free African Society was the pioneer among them. This had become identified mainly with St. Thomas' Episcopal Church, but other societies had grown out of it. The condition of these societies in 1831 is given in the following advertisement in the Public Ledger, March, 1831: "To the Public: Whereas, we believe it to be the duty of every person to contribute as far as is in their power towards alleviating the miseries and supplying the wants of those of our fellow-beings who through the many misfortunes and calamities to which human nature is subject, may become fit objects for charity. And whereas, from the many privations to which we, as people of color are subject and our limited opportunity of obtaining the necessaries of life, many of us have been included in the number dependent on the provisions made by law, for the maintenance of the poor; therefore, as we constitute a part of the public burden, we have deemed it our duty to use such means as was in our reach to lessen its weight, among which we have found the forming of institutions for mutual relief, the most practical and best calculated to effect our object." "Some have misunderstood the object and the benefit of these societies, therefore, this report is given." To these institutions, each member pays a sum varying from one to eight dollars as an initiation fee, and from 12 to 25 cents monthly. These funds are exclusively appropriated to the relief of such of its members as through sickness or misfortune are unable to work; to the interments of the deceased members and the relief of their widows, orphans, etc. The records show a total of $5,819 paid out in the years 1830-31.

Negroes were not without interest in their country, notwithstanding the country at that time gave them but little to inspire patriotism. When the war with England began in 1812, Pennsylvania Negroes offered their services. The committee which had charge of the defense of Philadelphia, declined the services of a "Black Legion" because of lack of arms; but Negroes helped in the fortification of Philadelphia, and later a Negro battalion was recruited in that city.

One of the growing signs of racial self-consciousness was the conventions of free people of color. It was found necessary about the middle of this period for the free people of color to consult one another about their welfare in this country, and in the North. Accordingly, several conventions were called. The first one of them was in Philadelphia in 1831, when there were forty delegates and honorary members from Pennsylvania, New York, New Jersey, Massachusetts, Connecticut, Rhode Island and Maryland. Pennsylvania had the largest number of representatives, eighteen in all. The session lasted four days and various topics were discussed. One of the chief of these was education. It was proposed to establish a school of manual labor, where students could go and work their way. New Haven, Connecticut, was chosen as the place for such a school. In accord with the spirit of the times, however, the citizens of New Haven very greatly objected to any such institution. At a meeting held in New Haven, the white citizens expressed themselves as greatly opposed to such schools, and gave notice that the Mayor, Aldermen, Common Council and freedmen of New Haven would resist its establishment by every lawful means.

The manual labor school was never established. So far as the evidence goes, this was the first attempt of Negroes to establish an industrial school. The subject of emigration also received a lengthy discussion before the convention, and it was recommended that the emigration to Canada be encouraged as a measure of relief from the prejudice and persecutions which Negroes suffered in many places in the North. But "strong resolutions against the American Colonization Society were adopted."

The second convention was held June 4 to 15, 1832.

There were thirty delegates representing eight States, Pennsylvania having nine delegates. At this convention, the American Colonization Society was vigorously condemned, abolition of slavery in the District of Columbia urged and a proposition to purchase lands in Canada for an asylum for Negroes emigrating from the United States was discussed. It was reported to this convention that eight hundred acres of land had already been secured, five hundred of which were under cultivation, two hundred log houses had been erected, and two thousand persons had emigrated there from their native country, despite the hostility of the Canadians. The convention appointed an agent to investigate the whole Canadian situation. At the third convention, June 7, 1833, there were fifty-eight delegates, representing seven States and the District of Columbia. This convention condemned the law passed by the Legislature of Connecticut, designed to prohibit the establishment of any school in that State for colored persons. William Lloyd Garrison's effort to obtain funds to establish a manual labor school was endorsed; the Colonization Society's schemes condemned, and a committee on the Canadian settlement was appointed. An effort was made to find out the exact status of the free people of color, their number, churches, Sunday Schools, temperance societies, benevolent societies, day schools, mechanics and storekeepers. It was further recommended that "free labor stores" be established from which the products of slave labor should be debarred.

The next convention was held in New York, June 8, 1834, at which there were about forty delegates, representing ten States. The principal action discussed this year was the foundation of moral reform and total abstinence from intoxicating liquors, which was recommended. It was further urged that all boarding houses where gambling was permitted be discontinued.

The next session of the convention was held in Philadelphia, June 1 to 5, inclusive, 1835. Forty-four delegates were present. In 1836 and 1837, a "Convention of the Moral Reforms" held sessions in Philadelphia, and from time to time, other conventions were held. Philadelphia was always the center for these early movements and Pennsylvania Negroes always took a prominent part in them. Among the representatives of Pennsylvania in this convention, were such men as Bishop Richard Allen, of the African Methodist Episcopal Church; William Whipper, James Cornish, Frederick Hinton, Richard D. Johnson, James Forten, Sr., James Forten, Jr., Jacob C. White, Sr., Joseph Cassey and Robert Purvis.

The history of the Negro in the movement for the freedom of the slave has hitherto received all too slight mention and except in a few rare instances, even the names of Negroes who gave valuable services have perished. Without the presence and help of the free Negroes in Pennsylvania, that great and mysterious system known as the Underground Railroad, would never have operated so successfully. The homes of Negroes were the stopping places of slaves. When whites dared not keep a Negro in their homes for fear of discovery, Negroes could hide the escaping slave among those of his own race. Not only did Negroes do work of sheltering, but much of the actual work of rescuing was largely done by Negroes. Some of them were able to go into the very heart of slave territory and bring their brethren out. Thus Harriett Tubman is said to have led scores of Negroes out of slavery into freedom.

4

Negroes did much of the hauling from place to place and the ferrying across rivers, the watching during the night, and general patrolling so necessary to the safety of the fugitives. One of the greatest and most active agents of the Underground Railroad, was a Negro in Gettysburg. Daniel Ross, colored, was active in Norristown; another "colored man," in York; a colored man assisted William White, of Columbia; Cato Johnson, colored, drove a team which hauled cars over the bridge and brought all "baggage" safely across, where the agents had another trusty colored man to receive it.   *   *   *

The fugitives were then taken through Black's hotel yard to another portion of the town and concealed over night, when William Wright, of that place, generally took them in charge and sent some to Daniel Gibbons and some direct to Philadelphia, in a false end of a box car, owned by Stephen Smith and William Whipper, colored men and lumber merchants of Columbia. "Thomas Bessick, a colored man who ran cars in Columbia, was one of the boldest and most useful agents there." "Robert Loney, colored, ferried slaves over the Susquehanna to Columbia." "Samuel Mifflin, gave an escaped slave named Perry, over to the care of Robert Loney;" "two slaves from Cecil County, Maryland," early in the night, they with their sister and her child, fled to that well known colored man on the Susquehanna, Robert Loney, who ferried fugitives across the river in the night, at various places below Columbia, and gave them to the care of William Wright, who distributed them to other agents. Many other cases are cited.

Not only in the actual work of the abolition movement, were Negroes concerned, but they had part in the planning of the movement in Pennsylvania. It has been said that

the first twenty-five dollars that William Lloyd Garrison
secured for his "Liberator" came from a Negro. It was
true that even before the first issue of the Liberator was
published, a Philadelphia Negro, James Forten, Sr., sent
fifty-four dollars, payment in advance, for twenty-seven
subscriptions. Forten afterward contributed over a thousand dollars to Garrison and his cause. Negroes contributed liberally of their scanty means. "In one case, as far
back as 1836, the colored people of Philadelphia raised over
seven thousand dollars in twenty-four hours to purchase a
runaway slave." William Whipper, a lumber merchant,
said that he contributed $13,000 to the anti-slavery cause;
a thousand dollars, each year from 1847 to 1860; and gave
$5000 during the war. Robert Purvis and William Still
were two most useful members of the Philadelphia Vigi-
lance Committee; the former at one time its president, and
the latter for many years, its secretary. This committee
was composed of the most prominent of the anti-slavery ad-
vocates of Philadelphia.

It received the escaping slaves from all parts of the
country, cared for them, found them work or shipped them
on toward Canada. This committee investigated cases of
kidnapping of Negroes and instituted proceedings for their
recovery. It also helped to raise funds to purchase Negroes whom the fugitive slave laws had delivered out of
their hands. Much of the clerical work with regards to
these matters was done by a Negro, William Still, the
secretary, who wrote a very interesting and comprehensive
description of its work.

THE NEGRO POPULATION SINCE THE CIVIL WAR.

The Civil War marks a distinct break in the history of the Pennsylvania Negro population. This break is noticed in the character of the population. During the period before the Civil War, though the native Negroes were barely a majority, they were made of a desirable sort, while the immigrant Negroes were not altogether of an undesirable character. In fact this period as compared with later periods, witnessed the migration of many of the best of the Southern Negroes to the North. There were several distinctive groups. One of the most important of these, is the South Carolina group, composed of several score of Negroes who came chiefly from Charleston and vicinity. Most of them were free born; many of them were well educated and some of them were comparatively wealthy. Among these were the Purvises, the Adgers, Daniel A. Payne, afterward, Bishop of the A. M. E. Church. Many of them were skilled mechanics, such as the Vennings, the Casseys, the Mains and others. There was another group not quite so distinguished as the Charleston group, from Delaware. Most of these were mulattoes, as were many of the Charlestonians. They formed their own beneficial society and to a large extent, attended their own church. Then there were the Maryland and Virginia groups, composed largely of ex-slaves, but a selected class, being those who had been manumitted by their masters, or who had bought their freedom, and a few who escaped from slavery. Another important group was the West India group, nearly all of whom were skilled in some kind of art or craft.

Among these, were the LeCounts, of Negro-French extraction, the Cuyjets, Rolands, Montiers, the Dutertes, the Dutrieuilles, the Augustines, the Baptistes, and others who became active in the affairs of their people.

With the Civil War there began a less selected kind of immigration. For, whereas before the war, there was but small opportunity for self-expression on the part of the intelligent and skilled Negroes in the South, the end of the war suddenly left them with opportunities which far excelled even their preparation. When the slaves were freed, this skilled group naturally assumed the leadership in politics, religion, business, and otherwise. Thus was cut short to a large extent, the migration of the intelligent and skilled Negroes to the North. Indeed, many in the North, went South. On the other hand, many of the exslaves of the more ignorant type migrated North.

There was also another change which was not however, so sudden as that in the character of the Negro immigration and that was in the attitude of the whites. The Negro before the war, had served in the family of the white Pennsylvanian so far as to gain their respect and largely their confidence. The Friends especially, felt themselves much concerned about the Negroes; for four times at least, between 1820 and 1860, they published statistical sketches of the Negroes. But after the war, the interest in the Negroes in the South far overshadowed that of those at home. Then, too, an entirely new group began to congregate in the cities and to overshadow the old group.

Philadelphia and Pittsburg attracted the greatest number of Negroes. The Negro population which increased but very slowly from 1820 to 1860, began after 1860, to grow rapidly and was in 1900, 156,845, an increase of 175 per cent. during forty years. In 1860, there were 56,949 Negroes in the State; in 1870, 65,294; in 1880, 85,535: in 1890, 107,596, and in 1900, 156,845. This increase is due almost solely to the immigration from the South. From 1870 to 1880 it was greatest, being 34.9 per cent. At present there is a rapid increase of Negro immigrants from the South, in spite of the fact that the economic conditions in the North are presumed to be harder than in the South.

The large plantations of the South are being broken up, and much land is being neglected for the want of labor. The head of the Department of Agriculture in Virginia writes: "The farmers are not able to gather crops at the proper time on account of lack of labor." The head of the Department of Agriculture in North Carolina writes: "From all over the State comes the complaint of the scarcity of labor." There can be no doubt of the fact therefore, that the particular part of the South from which the Pennsylvania Negro immigrants come, has great need of the kind of labor furnished by Negroes. Not only is there great demand for laborers to remain at home but the resources of the South are quite undeveloped as compared with those of the North.

The South is, to a large extent, as the West was forty years ago, a country of opportunity, where land is comparatively cheap, the cost of living is comparatively low, improvements are easily made; the climate is not so rigorous and the returns from the lands are often better than in the North; in some places two crops may be made during a year. On the other hand, the opportunities of the North, and especially in the cities to which Negroes go most rapidly, do not seem so inviting to the small investor; here the cost of living is high and tends to rise;

the land is practically outside the reach of most wage-earners and the taxes and repairs, connected with the unsteadi-
ness of employment, are such that it appears of but little
advantage for a wage-earner to own a home. Here competition is keenest and, for the Negroes, a climate different
from that in which their ancestors for thousands of years
lived, as well as the indifference and even hostility, of organized labor toward the Negro. Here is also a higher
standard of efficiency and a more systematic method of
labor. It seems therefore, a **priori** that for the Negro to
leave the South and come to the North, is to go contrary to
sane economic philosophy. Still, the migration goes on,
and for this reason, its causes must be carefully sought.

In order to find out why the Negroes leave the South,
a personal canvass was made among them. Five hundred
and twelve Negroes filled out blanks answering the questions: "Why did you leave the South?" "Why did you
come to Philadelphia?" etc. The answers are arranged as
nearly as possible in the exact language of the immigrant
in the following table:

CAUSES ASSIGNED BY PHILADELPHIA NEGROES FOR LEAVING
THE SOUTH

Causes	Males		Females		Total	
	Number	Percent	Number	Percent	Number	Percent
Desire for higher wages	120	44.6	96	39.5	216	42.2
Higher wages and travel	12	4.5	10	4.1	22	4.3
Higher wages and protection.......	14	5.2	6	2 5	20	3.9
To better conditions......................	25	9 3	31	12.8	56	10.9
Tired of the South........................	9	3.3	13	5.4	22	4.3
Wanted to make change................	27	10	22	9	49	9.6
Came with parent or guardian.....	29	10.8	40	16.5	69	33.5
Old persons to be with their children...	3	1.1	6	2.5	9	1.3
Parent died; left home to work.....	2	.7	5	2	7	1 3
Had position in North..................	3	1.1	3	1.2	6	1.2
Run away from home	1	.4	....	....	1	.2
Brought away by soldiers.............	1	.4	....	....	1	.2
To attend school................	3	1.1	....	....	3	.6
Not given......................................	20	7.5	11	4.5	31	6
Total........., ...	269	100	243	100	312	100

According to this table 54.3 per cent. of the males and 46.1 per cent. of the females came chiefly for the higher wages which they expected. If those who came "to better their condition" are included among those who came for higher wages and those who came with parents or guardians, and elderly persons who came with their adult children are excluded from the count, as having come without any particular choice of their own, it is clear that the great majority of Negroes who came to the State, came for the money wages they expected to obtain.

There can be no doubt that the economic motive is the chief one but just why, it seems hard to understand, since the economic advantages of the South seem to be so great. There are secondary causes, which will be discussed before, and preliminary to, the chief economic cause. The first of these remote causes is the change of the whole Southern situation. Slavery was abolished, in the 60's, and as a system became illegal. But the sentiments of the whites and the capacity of the Negroes did not thereby become much altered. The Negro, indeed, freed from servitude had time to follow his own inclinations, and the best of them had opportunity to cultivate their capabilities along some new lines. But the whites—even those who were kind—never believed that Negroes were capable of self-initiative, or of independently carrying on their own business. Trained in this belief by the school of actual conditions for generations in this country, it is easily explained why the whites did not readily accept the situation. Though the Negroes were nominally free, the first attempt of the white South was to re-enslave the Negroes, by a system of black laws, contract laws, lien laws, etc.

Although in the main, these laws have been repealed

or changed in the Southern States, still the spirit which
called them forth is not entirely dead, so far as a large proportion of the whites of the South are concerned, and the
Negro laborer still finds himself hedged about by a multi-
tude of laws and customs which bind him practically to
serfdom. It is the attempt to force Negro laborers to work
by outside pressure, rather than appeal to their economic
sense and economic needs, that causes unrest among the
blacks in all parts of the South. For throughout the South
the interests taken seriously into consideration are the interests of the white employer and not of the black laborer,
as such.

The Southern white man does not seem to have yet
reached the point where he differentiates between racial
and economic problems. He often refuses to listen to the
Negroes' economic demands, because he mistakes them for
demands for racial and social equality.

On the other hand, Negroes are acquiring property,
intelligence, and a larger view of the world, which is not
retarding the growth of their self-respect, nor their desire
for a larger share of the product of their labor. Because
the whites of the South are not realizing this rapidly
enough, the vexing problems of that section are increasing.

The increase of intelligence and wealth is creating
more discontent among a large class of Negroes, as respects
many economic conditions. This discontent is felt most by
those who are most intelligent and who possess the most
wealth. But this class, however, does not emigrate from
the South, chiefly because of their position. Generally,
they are situated socially and economically better than they
might be if they should leave. But the Negro who does not
own property, who has no high position among Negroes

either socially or economically sees but little reason for remaining, and when opportunity affords, he leaves. The
wages paid in the South to the 512 Negroes above mentioned were as follows, as compared with wages they now
receive:

NUMBER OF NEGROES RECEIVING SPECIFIED WAGES
PER WEEK IN THE SOUTH AND NORTH.

Weekly Wages.	South. Males.	Females.	Tot.	North. Males.	Females.	Tot.
Board and clothes only..	6	4	10	..	..	..
50c. to $1.99	8	26	34	..	1	1
$2.00 to $2.99	22	48	70	..	11	11
$3.00 to $3.99	26	34	60	..	16	16
$4.00 to $4.99	12	11	23	10	46	56
$5.00 to $5.99	21	14	35	11	31	42
$6.00 to $6.99	47	6	53	23	12	35
$7.00 to $8.99	24	1	25	35	9	44
$9.00 to $11.99	5	..	5	64	7	71
$12.00 to $13.99	1	..	1	23	4	27
$14.00 to $15.99	1	..	1	3	..	3
$16.00 and over	1	..	1	7	..	7
Working for self	5	..	5	5	19	24
Not working	19	24	43	5	19	24
Not reported	71	75	146	83	68	151
Total	269	243	512	269	243	512

More than 50 per cent. said that they left the South because they wanted higher wages, and this comparison
seems to corroborate their statement. The wages generally paid the women in the South were $6 per month ($1.50
per week), to $3 per week in the small towns, and from $2
to $4 per week in the cities; while the men in the South re-
ceive $2 to $3.50 per week in the small towns and on the
farm, from $5 to $9 in the cities. These wages are bettered
by from 75 per cent. to 150 per cent. in the North. Domestic service pays women in Philadelphia from $3 to $6 per
week, averaging about $4.50, while men receive from $6 to
$12 per week, averaging $9.

According to the "Wages of Farm Labor in the United States," Bulletin No. 26, of the Department of Agriculture, Negro labor in ordinary times in Pennsylvania, received in 1902, 92 cents per day with board, or $1.30 per day without board, while in Virginia the same labor received 56 cents and 76 cents respectively; in North Carolina, 49 cents and 62 cents. If hired by the year the Negro farm labor in Pennsylvania received $14.31 with board, or $24.29 without board, per month, while in the South the wages are as low as $7.61 with board and $10.79 without board, less than half what is paid Negroes in Pennsylvania.

According to the testimony before the Industrial Commission, many Negroes have migrated from Prince George County, Maryland, for shorter hours and larger pay. Many of these came to Pennsylvania. Many thousands of Negroes have been brought to Pennsylvania by the employment agencies.

One Philadelphia agent claimed to have given positions to more than 15,000 Southern girls and women during the past eighteen years. Some of the new industrial opportunities have been the asphalt paving in Philadelphia, Pittsburg and other cities, which is done largely by Negroes from the South. The filter plant in Philadelphia, the Subway in the same city, have employed thousands of Negroes, more or less regularly, and at better wages than they could have gotten at home. Street railways, railroads and steel works, the coal mines, needing sturdy, rough workers have brought many. Such companies as the Midvale Steel Company, the United States Steel Corporation, and other great industrial plants, employ hundreds of Negroes, most of whom are immigrants from the South. Domestic service is the chief inducement for women, and brings not a few men. The brilliancy of the city, the desire for excitement; for fine clothes and unrestrained amusement, undoubtedly bring many, but there are comparatively few who are not attracted by the prospect of a better social situation, and increased earnings, and freer self-expression.

Many Negroes have come away from their homes in the South because of the fear of mob violence. While this has not been by any means the chief cause of emigration, yet a sufficient number have come to warrant attention being paid to this factor. This is especially important because some of the Negroes driven North by this cause, are rather above than below the average. Perhaps no instance of race conflict in the South has had more effect upon the Negroes in Pennsylvania, than the riot at Wilmington, North Carolina, which occurred during August, 1898. The occasion for the riot was an editorial or series of editorials in the Record, a Negro daily paper in Wilmington, accusing white men of greater immorality than Negro men are guilty of. This was sufficient to stir the anger of the whites. The editor was seized and beaten and would have been killed had he not left the city. His property was destroyed and the building burned to the ground. His assistant editor and business manager, traveling agent, foreman and general manager were also sent away. As a result of this riot which came just at the time when the political fight against Negro enfranchisement was bitterest in North Carolina, hundreds of Negroes left the city of Wilmington and country round about, and scattered themselves through the North. To Pennsylvania a large number of them came, and there are possibly a thousand of them in the State to-day. The editor himself became a janitor in Philadelphia.

As a result of the friction of race, another immigrant was a former member of Congress from North Carolina. The Atlanta, Georgia, riot of 1906, caused many Negroes to come North, some of whom stopped in Philadelphia. As in the case of the editor from North Carolina, so the editor of "The Voice of the Negro," then the most widely circulated Negro magazine in the country, was forced to leave Atlanta, Georgia, and give up his business. He is now in Philadelphia, an exile from home, and his magazine has been crushed.

The major portion of Pennsylvania's Negroes are immigrants from other States. The census gives the birthplace of Negroes living in the different States; and from this it is possible to find the birthplace of the Negroes who help to make up the Pennsylvania population. The census also enables us to find the place of residence of the Negroes who were born in the State of Pennsylvania, thus to show the immigration and the emigration. According to the census of 1900, there were 85,014 Negroes living in the United States who were born in Pennsylvania. Of these, 70,365 still live in the State, while 14,649 had moved out of the State and lived in other parts of the country. There were but few Negroes who were born in other Northern States who had immigrated to Pennsylvania. On the other hand, there has been considerable emigration to other Northern States. Pennsylvania has given more liberally of her Negro population to the New England and Middle Atlantic States, than she has received from them, although the excess is small, the largest being only 1297 for New Jersey. On the other hand, there has been comparatively little emigration to the South, excepting Maryland and Delaware.

Virginia has given to Pennsylvania more than ninety times as many Negroes as it has received from this State; Pennsylvania received from Virginia 40,870 immigrant Negroes and gave 848; from North Carolina, 5206 and gave 137; from South Carolina, 1009 and gave 32. The stream of migration to-day has kept up steadily. During the year 1906, the Philadelphia Association for the Protection of Colored Women reported more than 1600 cases of women met at the docks. Most of them came by boat and were probably of the poorer class. Perhaps a larger number came by rail. Of those reported by the association above referred to, 757 came from Virginia, 598 from Maryland, 30 from the District of Columbia, 46 from Pennsylvania, 2 from New Jersey, 5 from New York, 2 from South Carolina, 6 from Jamaica, 2 from Colorado.

The population of Pennsylvania is thus kept up by immigration chiefly from the South. This is not wholly abnormal considering the fact that the Negro population of Pennsylvania is chiefly and increasingly urban; for not only in the case of Negroes but in the case of the whites as well, it is a question if our large cities are increasing in population by natural growth, exclusive of immigration.

The Negro population in Pennsylvania in 1900, was 76.7 per cent. urban and 23.3 per cent. rural; 120,285 of the 156,845 Negroes of the state lived in cities of at least 100,-000 inhabitants; 15,004, in cities of between 25,000 and 100,-000 inhabitants; 10,184 in cities of between 8,000 and 25,-000; 7,155 in cities of from 4.000 to 8,000; and 4,453 in cities from 2,500 to 4,000 inhabitants. A much larger percentage of the Negroes than of the whites live in cities of Pennsylvania. The following table will show the percentage of Negro population in cities of different sizes at the last three censuses:

PER CENT. OF NEGRO POPULATION IN CITIES OF DIF-
FERENT SIZES, 1880, 1890, 1900.

	Negro Population		
Cities of at least 100,000 inhabitants.	1880.	1890.	1900.
At least 100,000	41.8	46.2	53.2
25,000 to 100,000	7.2	6.9	9.6
8,000 to 25,000	6.6	8.0	6.5
4,000 to 8,000	6.3	7.4	4.6
2,500 to 4,000	...	3.0	2.8
At least 4,000	61.9	68.5	73.9
At least 2,500	...	71.5	76.7
Country	38.1	28.5	23.3

The Negro city population has been steadily increasing; while the rural population has actually decreased,
there being 10,000 less Negroes in rural districts than in
1860.

Forty years ago there were less Negroes in the large
cities, largely because there were fewer large cities. In
1860 five cities in the state had 100,000 or more inhabitants: viz.: Allegheny, Harrisburg, Philadelphia and Reading, having a total population of 680,011, of whom 25,835
were Negroes. At the same time, only one city had as
many as 10,000 Negroes; two cities having between 1,000
and 10,000 and only eight places in the state contained more
than five hundred Negroes. They were as follows: Allegheny, 690 Negroes; Pittsburg, 1,154; West Chester, 561;
Carlisle, 509; Harrisburg, 1,321; Chambersburg, 524; Columbia, 648; and Philadelphia, 22,185. In 1900 there were
forty-three places in the state which had five hundred or
more Negroes.

While the total Negro population of the cities has
grown much more rapidly than the white population in
the past forty years, it has not spread over so many communities as the white population. More than half of the

Negroes of the state are in Philadelphia and Pittsburg, while these cities contain only a fourth of the total population. Excepting Pittsburg and Philadelphia, the Negro population is scattered over the state in small aggregations, chiefly in the southern and eastern sections.

Philadelphia increased during the forty years from 22,185 to 62,613 or 182 per cent.; Pittsburg increased from 1,154 to 17,040, which is more than 1,372 per cent.; Harrisburg increased 211 per cent.; Allegheny, 379 per cent.; Chester City had 417 Negroes in 1860 and West Chester had 561. In 1900, Chester's Negro population had increased to 4,403, or 950 per cent.; and that of West Chester to 1,777, or 247 per cent. during forty years. Some few communities had made but slight increase. Carlisle, York and Washington just a little more than doubled their Negro population, while Norristown and Reading lacked a little of doubling theirs. Chambersburg's Negro population increased less than fifty per cent. and that of Columbia actually decreased thirty-five per cent. Some towns which in 1860 had no Negroes whatever or a very few had a considerable Negro population in 1900; Scranton had only one Negro in 1860, but 521 in 1900. No Negroes were returned in 1860 for Braddock. Lancaster had 29 in 1860, and 777 in 1900. For Homestead, McKeesport, Steelton, Uniontown, Wilkes-Barre or Williamsport, no Negroes are returned in 1860, while in 1900, two of these cities, Williamsport and Steelton, had more than 1,000 Negroes, and each of the others more than 500 Negroes.

Within the cities the Negroes are more or less segregated. In Philadelphia, the largest groups of Negroes are in the 7th and 30th wards, which contained in 1900 10,462 and 5,242 Negroes respectively. The segregated communities were formed naturally; the first Negroes who settled for themselves settled in the places which they could secure employment. Others moved near them and so on, until there was a so-called settlement of Negroes. Race feeling, common interests, common bearing of racial prejudice, were among the things which tended to keep the Negroes together. But the home-owning and the more prosperous Negroes are, as a rule, moving out of the distinctively Negro neighborhood. In Philadelphia, west of 15th street and south of Bainbridge, in Elmwood and Germantown, a large number of the better class of Negroes have settled within the past ten years. The largest number of home-owners is outside of the most densely settled Negro neighborhoods. All except one of the large churches have moved from what was once the largest Negro district, but which is now chiefly inhabited by foreigners. The only one of the old churches which holds its original position is Bethel, A. M. E. Church, which is now entirely surrounded by Jews.

In the various cities the Negro population is fairly well distributed. There are wards which have a large proportion of Negroes, but in no city is there a ward which is composed principally of Negroes. Often, however, the Negro population is cut into by a ward line, and the segregation does not appear as much as it really is. In Philadelphia, the second, third, fourth, fifth, seventh, eighth and thirtieth wards are contiguous and form the largest Negro settlement. In this district there were 25,317 Negroes in 1900. This district includes a part of the central business district of the city. The next largest district includes contiguous portions of the fourteenth, fifteenth, twentieth and twenty-ninth wards, which in 1900 had a population of 10,365 Negroes. There are other smaller districts included, principally within a single ward. It is worthy of notice that in none of these wards do the Negroes comprise a majority of the population. The seventh ward had 10,462 Negroes in 1900, but also 28,137 whites; the other wards had a larger proportion of whites.

But one can get a very hazy idea of the segregation of Negroes if he depends upon the figures given by the wards as Hoffman does in his treatise on the Negro. For in wards the distribution of the Negro population is often very regular. In the eighth ward in Philadelphia, one of the richest resident wards of the city, the whites are generally in the western part and the Negroes in the eastern. This eastern section is generally referred to as the Negro section, yet Negroes are in a minority, and there are only three of the seventeen voting divisions where the Negro vote is larger than the white vote. In the seventh ward, the Negroes are more generally distributed, but by no means evenly so. In 1906, there were 2,687 Negro voters in this ward, an average of about one hundred voters to a political precinct. But in eleven of the twenty-seven divisions the number of Negroes who vote was below the average, and in nine of these there were less than fifty Negro voters. All of which goes to show that although the seventh ward has the largest population of Negroes, it is not necessarily a "Negro ward."

The extent of the segregation of the Negro population cannot be shown by wards, but is as to streets or parts of streets. For example, the Negro population is densest in Philadelphia on Lombard and South streets, from Seventh to Twenty-third, and on the cross streets between these two; in Pittsburg, on Wylie Avenue, Webster street and Bedford Avenue, from Washington to Herron Avenue, and in Harrisburg, the neighborhood of South and Short streets. These are rightly called Negro settlements.

Throughout the larger cities there are often found from half a dozen to a score of Negro families in one block, or on adjacent streets, while there are many blocks in the neighborhood in which no Negroes live. This partial segregation of Negroes is not, however, a thing peculiar to them. On the one hand, they live in nearly every ward in the cities above named and in no one do they constitute a majority, though probably the next census will give the Negroes a majority in the seventh ward in Philadelphia.

They are not more segregated than the Jews, and the Italians in Philadelphia. On the other hand, it seems to be the tendency for the incoming Negroes to settle in those parts of the city where the older members of the race have already settled. This tendency has been aided much by the real estate and renting agents who find that whites do not care to live next door to Negroes, as a rule, just as native Americans do not like to live next door to Italians, or Jews, or Slavs. There is no evidence that the Negro will spread over a greater area of the cities, but at the same time, the Negro districts will continue to grow.

The largest section in which the race is said to be segregated is, however, more characteristic of poverty than of race. Negroes and Jews; Irish and Italians; and other classes composing a large proportion of the poor, live more or less together. In Philadelphia, the real poverty quarter, so far as the Negroes are concerned, is really from Front street to 16th street and west; from Pine to Fitzwater. But only the eastern part of this was included in the "Slums" in the Seventh Special Report of the Commissioner of Labor. The slum district of Philadelphia was, according to this report on the "Slums of the Great Cities," in 1894, as follows:

Philadelphia.—(1)

Starting from the corner of Front and South streets, along South to Fourth, along Fourth to Bainbridge, along Bainbridge to Front and along South to Ronaldson, along Ronaldson to Bainbridge, along Bainbridge to Eighth, along Eighth to Fitzwater, along Fitzwater to Fallon, along Fallon to Christian, along Christian to Eighth, along Eighth to Marriott, along Marriott to Fifth, along Fifth to German, along German to Passyunk Avenue, along Passyunk Avenue to Bainbridge, along Bainbridge to Fifth and along Fifth to South.

In this slum district of Philadelphia were 17,060 persons, as follows: 16,612 whites or 97.38 per cent.; 348 blacks or 2.04 per cent.; 84 mulattoes, quadroons and octoroons, or 0.40 per cent.; and 16 Chinese, or 0.09 per cent. The great majority of the Negroes of Philadelphia do not live in the typical slum district, notwithstanding Negroes in a measure are segregated and many of them do live in the slums. As a rule in these slums, the Negroes do not live in the worst sections. Gradually they have moved from the lower eastern side further toward the banks of the Schuylkill River and many hundreds of them to-day occupy houses which a few years back were occupied by well-to-do whites. Many of these houses are old and old-fashioned but most of them are better than those in which the Negroes formerly lived. On the other hand, the houses nearer the Delaware, about Fourth, Fifth, Sixth, Seventh, and Spruce, Pine, Lombard, South and the smaller streets and courts and alleys, in which the generations of Negroes before the war, and the first generation after the war lived, have been taken by the Italians and Jews, who therefore, live in the main, under worse conditions than the blacks now live. The same is practically true in Pittsburg.

There is also a peculiar kind of segregation in blocks where the better-to-do classes live. For many years the Negroes have been a servant class, and have lived in the houses of the employers or very close to them. So, in Philadelphia to-day, while on Spruce street and Walnut street, many of the wealthiest Philadelphians live, just behind them the Negroes are on Pine, Addison and Lombard streets in parallel lines. In West Philadelphia, the well-to-do whites live on Walnut and Chestnut streets, the Negroes live on the small streets just behind them. Sometimes the Negroes are completely surrounded by the whites as in the Eighth ward, where the whites live on the wide outside streets and Negroes on the smaller inside streets.

The Negro rural districts: The rural population of Pennsylvania in 1900 was 2,315,932 or 36.7 per cent. of the whole. The rural population of Negroes was 26.1 per cent. as against 38.1 per cent. twenty years before. In some of the counties, especially those where there is no large city, such as Clarion, Cumberland, Franklin, the Negro population is falling off.

In more than half the counties of the state, the Negro population has fallen off in the last twenty years, and the increase of the population has been mainly in the cities. In many places where Negroes were settled on farms before the war, there has either been a large death rate or heavy immigration to the cities. Columbia county was one of the counties in which many Negroes were largely settled before the war. In 1900, there were only 125 Negroes in the county. Negroes who formerly owned farms have given them up to move to the city.

As to sex, there is in this state an excess of Negro males over Negro females. There were in 1900, 79,384 Negro males and 77,497 Negro females in the state, or a pro-

portion of 977 females to 1000 males. The excess of males
in Pennsylvania is in accord with the condition of the
country at large. In Philadelphia there is an excess of
females; in Pittsburg of males, due chiefly to the economic opportunities of the sexes in the two cities.

OCCUPATIONS OF NEGROES.

What is the status of the Negro laborer in the North in
general, and in Pennsylvania in particular? Upon the answer
to this question depends very largely the view we shall be
forced to take as to whether or not the Negro will be able to
survive the competition of free labor. The North is the
severest testing place for the Negro, not simply because of
its climate but also because of its labor traditions and organizations. In the South, the Negroes have had a practical
monopoly of certain forms of labor, but in the North they
find the field already occupied by the world's best and most
aggressive workmen; they find higher standards in nearly
all lines of work and tremendous organizations for the purpose of reducing competition and controlling workmen and
apprentices.

Slavery, no matter what its industrial benefits were, did
not demand of its workmen accuracy of detail and quickness
in execution; nor did it cultivate that creative imagination so
necessary in highly organized communities for successful competition. It left the laborers illiterate, largely dependent, and
shiftless, except under outside pressure. It was therefore, to
be expected that such a class of laborers would be found among
the least efficient of a country's workingmen. If in the North

any of them or their children have been able to rise to skill
and self-direction; to success as business men, professional
men, skilled artisans, organizers and promoters, this, of itself is a hopeful omen for the industrial future of the race.

The Negroes are truly a working people. Of the entire 8,833,994 Negroes in the country, 3,992,337 were engaged
in gainful occupations in 1900; that is, 452 out of every 1,000.
Of the 6,415,581 Negroes ten years of age or more, 622 out
of every 1,000 were gainful workers. On the other hand,
373 of every 1,000 whites in the country, and 486 of every
1,000 whites ten years of age and older, were engaged in
gainful occupations. Though the Negroes compose but 11.4
per cent. of the country's entire population, they are 13.7 per
cent. of its entire working force.

In the country at large a greater percent of Negro males
than white males, are engaged in gainful occupations in every
age period, except from 25 to 44. For the period from 10 to
15 years more than twice as many Negro children are at work
proportionately as whites. Among the females there is a
very striking contrast, proportionately two and a half times
as many Negro females being in gainful occupations as white
females. Of female children more than four times as many
Negroes as whites proportionately are engaged in gainful occupations, and about the same proportion holds good for the
females between 55 and 65 years of age, and for 65 years and
over.

Negro workers in Pennsylvania: According to the census
of 1900, there were in the State of Pennsylvania 4,885,479
persons of ten years of age and over. Of these 2,448,589 or
50.1 per cent. were engaged in gainful occupations. The Negroes of Pennsylvania, as the Negroes of the country at large,
furnish a larger proportion of workers than their number
would indicate; for while they are only 2.5 per cent. of Penn-

sylvania's total population, they were 3.3 per cent. of the total gainful workers in this State.

According to the census in 1900, 80,429 Negroes who were engaged in gainful occupations in the State of Pennsylvania were distributed by sex as follows:

TABLE FROM THE CENSUS OF 1900.

	Males.		Females		Total.	
Occupations.	No.	%	No.	%	No.	%
Agricultural pursuits ..	3,656	6.6	40	0.2	3,696	4.6
Professional service ...	936	1.6	276	1.1	1,212	1.5
Domestic and personal service ...	33,030	59.2	22,830	92.7	55,860	69.4
Trade & transportation .	9,033	16.2	201	.8	9,234	11.6
Mfg. & mech. pursuits ..	9,150	16.4	1,277	5.2	10,427	12.9
Total ..	55,805	100.0	24,624	100.0	80,429	100.0

Ninety-three out of every hundred females, and fifty-nine out of every hundred Negro males of the State are in domestic and personal service. Among the occupations most largely followed by Negro unskilled laborers who comprise 65 per cent. of this entire group, are servants and waiters, barbers, and janitors. These four classes of labor comprise more than 96 per cent. of all the Negro domestic and personal service workers. While most of this service is unskilled an increasing amount of skill is being required; and in some cases, an apprenticeship must be served, as in the case of barbers, cooks, nurses, stewards. Some, however, require capital, and though the service is personal, often a lucrative business is conducted, as in the case of barbers, caterers, hotel and boarding house keepers, restaurant and saloon keepers.

The specific occupations chiefly followed by Negro females are those of servants, waiters, laundresses and house-keepers. These comprise more than 93 per cent. of the whole body of Negro females in domestic and personal service. Servants and waitresses alone are 78 per cent. of the total. Domestic service is occupied largely by the newcomers from the South. What is true of domestic service, commonly so called, is true of common unskilled labor. There are more than forty employment agencies in Philadelphia, which make a specialty of supplying Negro domestic servants, some of them having representatives in the Southern cities and towns who secure women and men of all descriptions and send them to the North. These agencies supply the city and the surrounding country with a large proportion of the servants. Most of these agencies agree that the vast majority of the people whom they supply are immigrant Negroes; that the native Negroes do not care to work in domestic service; and also that the average house-holder prefers a Southern Negro, because she is cheaper and more docile. The twelve per cent. of native Negroes who are in domestic service are generally in a higher grade of service than the immigrant Negro.

There are many kinds of this service in which a high grade of intelligence is needed. Several Negroes in the State have invented and patented devices for improving the labor of the household worker. A young Philadelphian, named Booker, has taken the lead in this, having invented and patented a dish washer which has an extensive sale; also devices for cleaning windows and scrubbing floors. He has organized a cleaning company, which employs from ten to fifteen persons regularly cleaning windows, marble fronts, etc. Another Negro, George Frank Hall, has invented and patented what he calls the "Kitchen King," combining in a single utensil the functions of the whip and bowl, puree brush, sieve and potato masher. Among other devices invented by Negroes in Pennsylvania for domestic service are an apple and potato parer, and a refrigerator by Alfred Cornell, a caterer; a device for keeping fumes of a cooking stove from spreading over the kitchen, by P. C. Slowe.

There has been but little attempt to train Negro servants. The oldest institution doing work of any kind in this line is Avery Institute, of Allegheny, which reaches a very few persons. Some sporadic work is done by organizations of women but there is nothing effective in the State. The Association for the Protection of Colored Women, in Philadelphia, started in 1905, and the Home for Working Women, in Pittsburg, reach a few servants, but because of the very limited resources they are able to do but little in the way of effective training of household workers. They do more on the moral and social sides than on the educational and economic sides. In more skilled grades of domestic or personal service, such as catering, barbering and hair-dressing, there is some training given to apprentices in shops and private businesses conducted by members of the race.

Since the Civil War there have been many changes in the relation of the Negro to domestic service. Time was when the most lucrative occupations open to Negroes were in domestic service, in which were most of the best Negroes in the State. With enlarging opportunities this is no longer true. The Negroes of best training and circumstances are going into this kind of service to a much less extent than formerly. Many of the sons and daughters of those who held most prominent places as domestic servants are now in business or in professions. The native born Negroes of Philadelphia comprise about 37 per cent. of the total Negro population, while they are only about 12 per cent. of Negro domestic

servants. The first Negro lawyer of Philadelphia is the son
of a successful Negro caterer, and his son is a successful
physician, and one of the largest property holders among
Negroes in the State. The son of another caterer is a successful physician, and a daughter of a barber has won more
than a local reputation as an artist, having studied several
years in Paris. Her design of the Negro historical group
for the Jamestown Exposition attracted wide attention and
won for her a medal of honor.

The economic changes during the past generation have
brought new opportunities to the Negroes of Pennsylvania,
and have helped to raise many of them from domestic service, which has caused an apparent loss in this field. In the
barber's trade it is often asserted that the Negro has lost
ground. This is true if it means that they have lost proportionately; for there are proportionately fewer Negro barbers than
formerly. In no large cities do Negroes have a monopoly of
this trade. There has been no absolute loss in numbers however, but rather a gain. There is now a greater demand for
Negro barbers than existed a generation ago. Shaving and
hair-cutting are now a necessity even to many laborers, as
well as to the business and professional men. That being the
case, a great many more persons are needed in the barbers'
trade which is made a business, that whites as well as Negroes have entered. To-day Negroes have a monopoly of the
Negro trade, which alone supports in the State more than one
hundred and fifty shops, which is probably larger than the
whole number of shops conducted by Negroes before the
war. Negroes also have a fair proportion of the patronage
of whites. In nearly every large city in the State there are
first-class shops conducted by Negroes exclusively for whites.
In the Pennsylvania Railroad Station, at both Philadelphia
and Pittsburg, there are Negro barbers. The rise in the stan-

dard of the barbers' trade has been great within forty years.
To enter the business now requires more than mere knowledge
of the art of shaving and hair-cutting.   Much capital can be
invested in the business.   There has also been large improvement in the sanitary standards.

What is true of barbers is true of caterers.   When catering was merely a species of house service, the competition with
whites was not great.   The caterer was the cook and butler to
the fashionables, and largely had the monopoly of a trade,
which others did not very greatly desire. But to-day, catering
is not house service in the common sense; it is a business
which requires not only skill and capital but business ability
and connections.   The great cook is not the caterer of today,
but he may be hired by the monied man who knows how to
organize and advertise a catering business.   Thus Negroes
have lost much of the prestige they once had in Philadelphia,
but they do more catering today than they ever did.   There
are more Negro caterers in this city than ever before—over
100.   They now have practically the monopoly of a growing
trade among Negroes (though not as exclusively as the barbers), and have been able to hold much of the other trade.
The best caterers have survived the changes in their trade and
have opened business on a large scale, as represented by
Augustine and Baptiste, and John S. Trower, in Philadelphia;
and Spriggs and John T. Writt & Co., in Pittsburg.   These
men do a much larger business than any of the ante-bellum
caterers in their best days.   But they are less conspicuous
and have less of a monopoly.

If it is true that the Negroes are in domestic service
proportionately less today than formerly, this is not a loss
but a gain and is significant of a wider range of economic
opportunities for the race.

The Professions: The professions may be classed among

the new occupations for Negroes. Although there have been individual Negroes in different professions for many years, yet, as a class, the Negro professional group in Pennsylvania is the growth of the present generation.

As to the particular professions there were at the census of 1900, in Pennsylvania, 91 actors and professional showmen and women; 411 clergymen; 20 dentists; 24 lawyers; 258 musicians and teachers of music; 12 government officers; 60 physicians and surgeons; 222 teachers and professors in schools and colleges; and 114 miscellaneous professions. To every 1,000 Negroes in the State there were 6.3 actors and actresses, 26 clergymen, 1.2 dentists, 1.5 lawyers, 16.4 musicians, .8 government officials, 3.8 physicians, 14.2 teachers.

Excluding the preaching and teaching professions, the North has a larger actual number of Negroes engaged in professional service than the South, and proportionately there is a larger number even of teachers and clergymen in the North. The profession earliest developed was that of the minister. Ministers of color were always the chief preachers to their people. The minister goes back to Africa and is the connecting link between heathenism and Christianity. A hundred years ago Richard Allen and Absalom Jones were ordained ministers in the Methodist and Episcopal Churches respectively in Philadelphia.

Some of the most intelligent men of the Negro race are to be found among its ministers, who in this State include men who were trained at the University of Pennsylvania, Oberlin College, the University of Chicago, Princeton University, Newton Theological Seminary. Boston University, Lincoln University, and other well equipped institutions. There are among them men who have studied abroad at the Universities of Berlin, Liepzig, Bonn, Paris, Cambridge and Rome. The Theological department in one of the largest

Negro institutions, Howard University, Washington, D. C., was practically founded by a Presbyterian minister, the Rev. J. B. Reeve, now for nearly fifty years a pastor in Philadelphia. On the other hand the average intelligence of the ministers is somewhat lower than the average of any other of the so-called learned professions.   This is due to several things. In the first place there is no State supervision of the granting of ministerial licenses as there is in other professions.   The State thus permits religious congregations to call ignorant ministers, while it prevents to some extent people from employing ignorant persons who would teach or practice law or medicine. Thus it is difficult to raise the ministry more rapidly than the laity.   In the second place, outside of a few large churches, the salaries are smaller than the necessities of life demand. Other opportunities, offering larger pecuniary returns and as much social prestige, are being gradually opened and many men of that best class that first entered the ministry are finding places in these new fields.   On the whole, however, the ministry is gaining in intelligence and is said to be considerably superior to the ministry of a generation ago.

The Negro physicians in the State now number about seventy and on the whole are an intelligent body, representing the best elements of Negro life.   As early as 1838, a Negro physician and dentist were reported in the Register of Trades in Philadelphia.   In 1841 several physicians were reported by the author of the "Sketches of Colored Society."   James Durham, a Pennsylvania Negro, was taken South to New Orleans, where he became very proficient in medicine in the eighteenth century.   In Philadelphia there are thirty-two graduated Negro physicians, three of whom are women.   Among them are graduates of the Medical Department of Howard University, the University of Pennsylvania, Harvard University, Jefferson Medical College, Hahnemann Medical College, the Medico-

Chirurgical College, Shaw University. Several have taken post-graduate courses, one of whom did so in the University of London. In 1896 the highest general average ever made before the Pennsylvania State Board of Medical Examiners, was made by a Negro, Robert Jones Abele, a native of Philadelphia, and a graduate of Hahnemann Medical College, Philadelphia. In Pittsburg there are sixteen physicians, six dentists and two pharmacists, graduated as follows: 5 from the Western University of Pennsylvania, 5 from Howard University, 2 from Shaw University, 1 from the Medico-Chirurgical College, Philadelphia, 1 from the University of Pennsylvania, and 1 from Harvard University. Harrisburg has 5 physicians, West Chester 1, Coatesville 1, Steelton 1, Chester 2, Washington 1, and West Grove 2. About one-third of the Negro physicians are college graduates holding the degree of A.B. or B.S. Among the institutions from which they graduated are Harvard, Lincoln, Wilberforce, Howard and Shaw Universities. The oldest physician practicing in Pittsburg is a native of that city and has been practicing more than thirty years; another has practiced twenty years, and another eighteen years; three from ten to fifteen years, six from five to ten years, nine under five years, three of whom have practiced less than two years. Negro physicians have not had free access to all hospitals, though there have been Negroes assisting in Hahnemann, Polyclinic and Jefferson Hospitals, in Philadelphia. In 1895 the Frederick Douglass Hospital, of Philadelphia, was established. Nathan F. Mossell, M.D., a native of Canada, and a graduate of Lincoln University and the University of Pennsylvania, was the chief spirit in the founding of that institution, and is still the Medical Director. During the last twelve years the Negro population has nearly doubled, and the demands for increased hospital room led to the opening in April, 1906, of the Mercy

Hospital and School for Nurses, in Philadelphia. A hospital is to be opened in the near future in Pittsburg.

The Negro lawyer does not have the opportunity to succeed that the Negro clergymen and physicians have had. These latter practically have the practice of their people, but not so the Negro lawyer. He is still a pioneer and at a disadvantage, in that his practice is not private, or among his own people, but he must plead before a white judge often against a white lawyer and generally, with a white jury. Yet, there is but little complaint on the part of the Negro lawyers. The average Negro coming from the South and knowing how great a handicap the lawyer of his race suffers in that section, hesitates long before employing a Negro lawyer. There are not more than a third as many Negro lawyers in Pennsylvania as physicians. In Philadelphia there are fourteen; in Pittsburg five; in Harrisburg, one.

Negro teachers are increasing rapidly each year. In 1840, there were 36 in the State; the census of 1900 reported 222. Negro teachers found employment as far back as the eighteenth century. In 1793, "The Committee for the Improveing the Condition of Free Blacks," suggested the opening of a new school for Negro children and stated that they had found a black woman well qualified for a mistress of such a school. In 1838, there were ten private schools in Philadelphia, conducted by Negro teachers. From its beginning in 1837, the teachers for The Institute for Colored Youths, have been principally Negroes. As long as the State recognized separate Negro public schools, many of the teachers of them were Negroes, and after the legal abolition of separate schools in 1881 many Negro teachers were retained. During the past decade Negro teachers have been rapidly increasing in public schools. This is due largely to the immigration of Negroes from the South. Though Negro schools have no legal exist-

ence, Negro teachers, as a rule, teach only Negro children.
There are more than sixty Negro public school teachers in
Philadelphia.

There are more than a score of journalists in the State.
These, with one or two exceptions are on Negro periodicals.
The first Negro newspaper in Pennsylvania of which there is
any record, was published in 1838, by William Whipper and
others. The next attempt was in Philadelphia in 1841, when
Robert Purvis and others started the "Demosthenian Shield,"
The oldest Negro publication now in existence in America is
published in this State—"The Christian Recorder," the organ
of the African Methodist Episcopal Church, which was started in Philadelphia in 1852. There were in 1908 three mag-
azines and about twelve weekly papers, published by Negroes in the State, chiefly in Philadelphia. Since the first
attempt, seventy years ago, there have been probably fifty attempts at newspapers and periodicals, the most of which have
failed for the lack of patronage. In Pittsburg, the first attempt was in 1848 when the Christian Herald was published
and of a dozen ventures since then, none have been able to survive as long as five years. Pittsburg now has an interesting
weekly paper—the Courier. The attempts at daily papers have
been all short-lived. The latest was in 1907 when the Philadelphia Tribune attempted to issue a daily. It was soon
discontinued as a daily, but is still running as a weekly as
it has for twenty-five years. Though the illiteracy of the
Negroes of the State is very small and though there are at
least 200,000 Negroes in the State, the combined circulation of
all the Negro newspapers in the State would hardly reach 25,-
000 copies per week. The Negro newspapers have not as yet
devoted much attention to the economic life of the people to
whom they are supposed to cater. They give but slight attention to business, to trade, to industrial life and industrial

6

opportunities. In this, they are not leaders of thought, but rather followers. They are devoted chiefly to church news, secret society news and personals. Now and then, they discuss politics and "The Negro Question." Their chief handicap is lack of capital. Negroes are not employed largely in the mercantile life of the State outside of menial positions. This is due chiefly to their race, for as a general rule they do not have the opportunity. Where civil service is operated, however, Negroes always have better opportunity. In the Post Office for instance, the Negroes have been able to secure employment. In Philadelphia there were in 1907, 175 Negroes in the Post Office:—126 clerks, 31 letter carriers, 16 special delivery messengers and 2 laborers; in Pittsburg, 65 were in the Post Office; in Harrisburg, there were 5 Negroes; in Wilkes-Barre, 2; in Oxford and Coatesville, 1 each. In the employ of the city of Philadelphia there were 126 Negroes in November 1907; in the city of Pittsburg, 5 messengers at $900 per year; 26 policemen; 1 chemical engine company, of six members; 1 city detective; and janitors and laborers. Most of the larger cities have one or more Negroes holding places under the civil service.

BUSINESS ENTERPRISES AMONG NEGROES.

The Negro entrepreneur existed as far back as there is any reliable information. In the registry of trades of Philadelphia in 1838, 344 Negroes—133 women and 211 men—were reported as being in business for themselves. Most of these were in the humblest kinds of business, such as vending, dressmaking, boot and shoe repairing, hair-dressing, barbering, and jobbing in various building trades. In 1849, another account revealed 166 shopkeepers and traders among Negro men of 21 years of age and over.

A complete enumeration of the business ventures in the principal cities of the State has been attempted and though only approximately correct, the results are not without value. In Philadelphia, the Colored Directory for 1908, gave more than a thousand Negroes conducting nearly a hundred different kinds of business. In Pittsburg, an enumeration disclosed more than 125 Negroes in more than fifty different kinds of business. In Harrisburg, an incomplete enumeration showed about fifty Negroes in business, the principal businesses being barber, etc. The Colored Directory of Philadelphia for 1908, by R. R. Wright, Jr., Ernest Smith, gives a complete list of the businesses conducted by Negroes in that city.

There are probably 2,500 persons in the State who belong to the entrepreneur class, most of them being engaged in small businesses. Doubtless many of them are not able to receive from their business any larger amount than they would if they were regular wage-earners. The only difference between them and the wage-earner is, that they have more control over their time. The largest number of persons is in the barbering business. In Philadelphia alone, there are 116 barbering establishments. In nearly every city or town in the State where there are as many as a hundred Negroes, there is such an establishment especially for the patronage of Negroes. The barbers and caterers have already been mentioned. While a few Negroes run restaurants and cafes for whites exclusively, the great mass serve their own race principally. The majority of these establishments are small and many of the restaurants are ill-kept. But as in the case of barbers, so with the restaurant and cafe, the standard of cleanliness in exclusively colored establishments has had rapid development in the past decade. There are ten small hotels in Philadelphia and ten in Pittsburg. In both West Chester and Johnstown, one of the largest hotels is conducted by a Negro. In the large cities the Negro hotel has grown up chiefly for the patronage of Negroes, whom the ordinary hotel conducted by whites serve with reluctance. These hotels compare favorably with hotels of the same size and grade of patronage conducted by whites.

The Negro barber, caterer, the cleaner and hotel keeper, are the developments from the Negro domestic servant, and are connected directly with the slave regime. There are other and newer lines of business in which Negroes had but little previous training and into which they have been forced largely by necessity. Real estate is one of these. There as 37 real estate dealers and 11 building and loan associations in Philadelphia and Pittsburg. These are chiefly the growth of the past two decades since the influx of Negro immigrants from the South. The loan and investment company and the insurance company are still later developments requiring larger capital and a different kind of ability.

With the evolution in the kind of business has gone a gradual complexity of organization. Most of the first enterprises were private concerns requiring chiefly skill, such as the knowledge of shaving, cooking, painting, etc., and but small capital. Thus an individual conducted a business alone. When the business grew larger and there was a necessity for combination, this necessity was met by taking in the wife or son or brother. This was the first development of the partnership and is to-day the most prevalent. But with the growth of the businesses requiring more skill and capital, than one individual possessed, the company was formed, several persons coming together with their small capital. The fraternal and beneficial societies are the earlier developments along this line. With the need for still larger capital and more thorough organization came the incorporated business, the oldest of which was the building and loan association. The first of these in Pennsylvania the Century Building and Loan Association, was incorporated in 1886. According to the report of the Banking and Insurance Commissioners of Pennsylvania for 1906, ten of these associations were reported as follows:

Name of Association	Year Organized	Total Members	Total Shares	Homes Bought in 1906	Receipts
Afro-American, Pitts.	1896	56	128	1	$ 1,690.06
Baker, Pitts.	1894	20	49	1	1,995.76
Banneker, Philadelphia	1905	39	121	0	1,771.78
Berean, Philadelphia	1888	426	2,351¾	14	59,077.78
Century, Philadelphia	1886	19	66	1	4,659.05
Cherry, Philadelphia ..	1904	103	431	2	6,842.02
Colored of North Philadel.	1906	32	106	0	616.72
8th Ward S'tlment, Philadel.	1906	73	294	0	2,091.48
Pioneer, Philadelphia	1888	140	705	4	17,725.18
William Still, Philadelphia	1905	62	129	2	1,873.34
Total		970	4,380¾	25	$97,742.91

There were 970 persons members of these societies of whom 382 were females, owning 4,380¾ shares. During the year 1906, 25 homes were bought, and $97,742.91 received as dues, interest, fines, etc. The assets of these associations were reported as $198,587.27.

The largest of these associations, the Berean Building and Loan Association, has purchased since its inception, more than 169 homes for its members, at an average cost of $3,000. During the year 1906, the association received $37,009.06, as dues, $18,667.70, on mortgages and loans unpaid, $1,450, from the sale of real estate, with other miscellaneous items, making a total of $59,077.52. The assets of the association were reported at $126,326.80, the undivided profits reported at $21,410.40.

Related to the Building and Loan Association is the incorporated real estate company, of which there are six in Philadelphia and three in Pittsburg, all of which have been incorporated during the past ten years. These associations, owing to a wider scope of operation are able to do an even larger business than the building and loan associations. They sell houses on the small payment plan, arranging the payments to suit the purchasers. One of the most successful of these in Philadelphia has been able to sell houses to parties who make about the same monthly payments, they would make if they were renting. Next to the incorporated real estate company comes the incorporated insurance company which grew out of the sick benefit society. According to the report of the Northern Aid Society, incorporated December, 1902, during the first three years of its existence, $266,478 of insurance was written up; $6,199 of sick claims; and $1,202.36 of death claims paid and $10,421.53, paid out to employes. Another, the Keystone Aid Society, also incorporated in 1902, employs 47 persons, has branch offices in Coatesville, Chester, Bristol and Pittsburg, and has insured 15,700 persons. Among other incorporated businesses are, six cemetery companies, four publishing companies, two loan companies, two grocery companies, one steam laundry, one excavating company, one department store, and one bank.

During 1906, there were 18 new business companies incorporated in Philadelphia. In Pittsburg, a syndicate has established four drug stores during the past four years.

The test of the business ability is not the launching of an enterprise so much as continuing it over a period of years. A study therefore of the number of years which Negro businesses have endured is highly important. It has not been possible to obtain information concerning every establishment, but a tabulation of 283 enterprises in Philadelphia and Pittsburg is here given:

Number of years established.	Phila.	Pitts.	Total
Under 1 year	29	13	42
1 year	23	10	33
2 years	12	6	18
3 years	22	7	29
4 years	15	5	20
5 to 7 years	35	10	45
8 to 10 years	14	6	20
11 to 15 years	14	7	21
16 to 20 years	19	2	21
21 to 25 years	6	1	7
26 to 30 years	10	2	12
31 to 40 years	5	1	6
40 years and over	8	1	9
Total	212	71	283

Of 283 establishments, 42 had been established less than one year, and seventy-two less than two years; 18 had been established two years and 29 for three years, being a total of 122 establishments of three years' standing or less. These may be said to represent the businesses in the experimental stage. They comprise about two-fifths of the total number of businesses among Negroes in the State. The 85 establishments which have continued from four to ten years, comprise about thirty per cent. of the total, and may be said to have passed the experimental stage, and to be in the second stage of the competition for permanency. Of those over ten years old, 76 or thirty per cent., which may be said to be firmly established. Forty-two of these have been established between ten and twenty years, while thirty-four had been established over twenty years. Nine establishments had an existence of over forty years; eight of them in Philadelphia and one in Pittsburg. They included, three caterers, three undertakers, one shoemaker, one furniture dealer and one hair dresser. In Allegheny, there was also a fish dealer whose business had been in operation for more than forty years. The oldest continuous business in the State is the catering business of Augustine and Baptiste on South Fifteenth Street in Philadelphia. In the early part of the last century, Robert Bogle, opened a catering establishment at the corner of Eighth and Sansom streets, Philadelphia, which he conducted very successfully until 1818, when the place was taken by Peter Augustin, a West Indian immigrant. Augustin conducted the establishment on an enlarged scale and he soon had one of the most famous catering establishments in America. Upon his death in 1892, the business was conducted by his wife, Marie C. Augustin. A partnership was formed with another West Indian Negro family and the firm in recent years has been known as Augustin and Baptiste. They own a handsome property at 255-257 South Fifteenth Street, the value of which is more than $60,000, and are among the largest Philadelphia caterers. Almost a hundred years ago one Allmond, a cabinet maker, established quite a reputation in the city for the quality of his work. Among other things, he made coffins. His son followed him in the trade and his grandson did the same. During the day of the latter the undertaking business took definite shape, became differentiated from that of the cabinet maker and included funeral directing, embalming and other things having no connection with the trade of the cabinet maker. This latter Negro, opened an undertaking establishment and two of his sons took up the business after him. To-day, there are in Philadelphia, three undertaking establishments conducted under their name. In Pittsburg, the oldest Negro business is that of hair-dressing and wig-making. In 1837, John Peck, a colored minister, who earned his living chiefly as a hairdresser, opened an establishment in the down-town district.

He was attentive to business and had much of a monopoly of what was then a kind of personal service. After he died, in 1875, his wife conducted the business for twelve years until her death in 1887. The business had been located in one place during these fifty years of operation. In 1887, however, it was removed and the son of Mr. and Mrs. Peck, took charge and has conducted it for more than twenty years. The establishment is located in the business district of Pittsburg, within a block of the place where the founder started it in 1837, just across the street from Joseph Horne's department store and within a hundred yards of four other of Pittsburg's largest hairdressing and wig-making establishments. It is interesting to note, that all of the businesses are to-day larger and more prosperous than they were at any time during the life-time of their founders. The establishment of Augustin and Baptiste is larger than that of the famous Peter Augustin in his most successful days. The property is valued at more; the equipment is larger; the number of Negroes to whom employment is given is greater; moreover, the present manager of the business, is a business man who plans and conducts the business side of the establishment against severe competition. He neither cooks the meals nor waits on the tables, but the famous Peter was both cook and waiter. Still the present establishment has not the reputation which the earlier one had a half century ago; no one can say that it is the establishment that makes "Philadelphia catering famous all over the country." This is because the standard in catering has been raised and the competition increased, so that the first-class Negro establishment of to-day does not attract the attention which smaller establishments commanded sixty years ago.

The solidarity of the Negroes as an employed group is gradually being broken up and many of them are becoming employers of labor. Many of the best class of Negro families employ domestic help. Negro business men are each year employing more of their race. In 1909 in Philadelphia, 199 Negro firms employed 888 Negroes; and in Pittsburg 67 firms employed 412 Negroes. A fair estimate is that between 9,000 and 10,000 persons, including proprietors, secure their living from Negro businesses. The barbering business gives employment to the largest number. Forty-seven Negro barbershops in Philadelphia employed 173 persons. Next come the caterers and general contractors, some of whom on occasions employ a hundred persons. The insurance business, real estate companies give employment to stenographers, bookkeepers, solicitors, collectors, etc. Fully ninety-five per cent. of the bookkeepers, clerks and accountants are in the employ of Negro firms. Of the members of the Philadelphia colored women's clerks' association only two were employed by whites, and these received less wages than some Negro firms paid. In some respects, there are greater difficulties in gaining superior proficiency in mechanical trades than in the professions. For the professional man in many instances has the competition only of his group (as for example the minister), and has a natural constituency in his race. The Negro teacher, preacher and physician, succeed wherever the Negroes congregate in large numbers. Then, too, there is every facility in the State for the professional education of the Negroes, while there are but few opportunities for acquiring a high degree of skill on the part of the Negro artisan. There are few industrial or trade schools for them in this State, and they are generally not admitted as apprentices to the large shops where skilled, mechanical trades are taught. Most of the Negroes who follow skilled trades are immigrants from the South or the West Indies, and learned their trades outside of Pennsylvania. Those who control the skilled trades have jealously guarded their possession and have not given Negroes much opportunity.

In nearly every study made of the Negro population in the State, the difficulty of pursuing skilled mechanical trades has been noted. In 1838 the reporter on the occupations of Negroes in Philadelphia, observed: "We are aware that the greater part of them are engaged in the most menial services and the severest labor, they are met (in the higher branches of labor) with prejudices with which they have to contend, which renders it difficult for them to find places for their sons as apprentices, to learn mechanical trades." In Edward Needles' report in 1856 the same sentiment was found still to exist in Philadelphia; and a generation later Prof W. E. B. Du Bois described "the practical exclusion of the race from the trades and industries of the great city of Philadelphia."

The Centennial Souvenir of the city of West Chester speaks of the "first colored high school graduate;" of that city as follows: "after his graduation, he tried at several places to apprentice himself to learn a trade; though skilled in the use of tool and willing to work, he found no employment."

The chief cause of the exclusion is the fact that the great majority of the white workmen refuse to work with Negroes. It is not necessary to offer evidences of this here, as Dr. Du Bois in his "Philadelphia Negro" has so fully presented the case.

Most of the Negroes who work at the mechanical trades are either jobbers or work exclusively with Negroes. Some who worked at trades in the South, on coming to Philadelphia and hearing of the difficulty which Negroes experience in attempting to follow trades in the State give up the attempt without serious effort. In fact, the prevalent opinion among Negroes as to the impossibility of pursuing a trade in the North, in a very large measure accounts for the scarcity of Negroes now in the trades. This is almost as important a cause as the attitude of the white workmen, for it keeps the Negroes from attempting to embrace the opportunities which really exist.

Still, there are many Negroes in all parts of the State following mechanical trades with varying success. According to the census of 1900, 10,427 Negroes were engaged in manufacturing and mechanical pursuits. The principal mechanical trades for males having 100 or more Negroes were as follows:

Trades.	Number of males in trade.
Blacksmiths	150
Boot and Shoemakers	105
Brick and Tile Makers	495
Carpenters and Joiners	192
Charcoal, coke and lime burners	525
Engineers and firemen	436
Iron and steel workers	1,582
Brick and Stone Masons	989
Miners and Quarrymen	1,616
Painters, Glaziers and Varnishers	137
Plasterers	106
Printers, Pressmen, etc.	104
Tobacco and Cigar Factory Operators	157

Other important occupations reported for Males are: bakers, 38; book-binders, 12; bottlers, 8; butchers, 55; glass-workers, 63; machinists, 74; paperhangers, 88; tin plate and tin ware workers, 72; wire workers, 49. In the list, there are 92 manufacturing and mechanical pursuits of males given by the census of 1900. Of these there are 13 pursuits, in which Negroes do not appear. These as given are, box-makers (wood), button makers, clock and watch makers and repairers, electro-platers, lace and embroidery makers, print-work operators, shirt, collar and cuff makers, silk mill operators, trunk and leather case makers, umbrella and parasol makers and well borers. All of these classes of labor are small, none having as many as a thousand persons, except watch and clock makers and repairers and silk mill operatives. It is a fact, however, that many of the classes of labor reported as having no Negroes in them, in 1900, did have Negroes in 1907. There were in this latter year Negro boxmakers, clock and watch makers and re-pairers, embroidery makers, piano and organ tuners, shirt, collar and cuff makers, umbrella makers and well borers.

In Philadelphia there is one Negro brick-laying contractor, who has put up more than fifty houses for himself in the last ten years; another, who has erected some residences in the suburbs of Holmesburg and another who works under a yearly contract to keep several stores and apartment houses in re-pair; a firm of plasterers which has plastered over seven hundred houses within the past four years. The buildings of the Downingtown Industrial School, and several Negro churches were erected entirely by Negroes; the contractor, on the new Congregational Church in Pittsburg was a Negro; and much of the work on Rockefeller Hall, Bryn Mawr College, was done by Negro mechanics. In the steel works there are large numbers of Negro workmen; all of the puddlers in the Black Diamond Steel and Iron Company in Pittsburg are Negroes: in the rolling mills at Reading, Steelton, West Chester, Coatesville, Columbia and other places there are skilled Negro workmen. In Clark's Mills, Pittsburg, there are three Negro foremen, having under them as high as twenty men, white, as well as black. Concerning the Negro workmen in the Steel industry, Mr. Chas. J. Harrah, president of the Midvale Steel Company, a successful competitor of the United Steel Corporation for the government's armor-plate contracts, testified before the Industrial Commission in 1900, as follows: "We have fully 800 or 1,000 colored men. The balance are American, Irish and Germans. The colored labor we have is excellent. They are lusty fellows; we have some with shoulders twice as broad as mine. The men come up here ignorant, totally un-tutored and we teach them the benefits of discipline; we teach the colored men the benefit of thrift, and coax them to open a bank account, and he generally does it and in a short time has money in it, and nothing can stop him from adding money to that bank account. We have no colored men who drink." As to friction, Mr. Harrah said, "Not a bit of it. They work cheek by jowl with Irish, and when the Irishman has a festivity at home, he has the colored men invited. We did it by trepidation. We introduced one man at first to sweep up the yard and we noticed the Irish, Germans, and Americans looking at him askance. Then we put in another. Then we put them in the boiler-room and then we got them in the open hearth and in the forge and gradually we got them everywhere. They are intelligent, docile and when they come in as laborers unskilled, they gradually become skilled and in the course of time, we will make excellent foremen out of them." And he added, "there is absolutely no difference between the wages of the blacks and the whites."

The great mass of Negro laborers are unorganized, and come in contact but little with the labor union. There are a few Negroes in Philadelphia who are members of some of the unions; viz., the carpenters, stone masons, bricklayers, painters, cement layers, asphalt pavers, etc. On the other hand, there are some unions which do not admit or have not admitted Negroes, such as the machinist, locomotive engineers, etc. In the more skilled trades, the Negro union laborers number less than 200 in Philadelphia, and less than 300 in Pennsylvania. Of unskilled labor, the most thoroughly organized group is that of the hod-carriers. Throughout the State there are Negro hod-carriers. In Philadelphia there is a local union composed chiefly of Negroes, with a Negro president. This union, the Light Star Lodge, owns a four story brick hall, valued at about $20,000. In Pittsburg also the hod-carriers' union is composed predominately of Negroes, but is not as large as the Philadelphia lodge. Next to the hod-carriers, come the miners. All of the Negro miners in the State are union men, and members of the United Mine Workers of America. These are located chiefly in the western part of the State, having their district headquarters at Pittsburg. The United Mine Workers is one of the few unions in which the Negroes agree that they receive fair treatment. In some of these miners' unions, there are Negro officers, and Negroes are always in attendance at the annual meetings.

Negroes have made some attempts at independent organizations. The most successful of these is that among the hoisting engineers, steam and gas engineers, started in Pittsburg in 1900 and incorporated in 1903 under "The National Association of Afro-American Steam and Gas Engineers and Skilled laborers in America. While the intention is to organize Negro labor on a racial basis, there is no antagonism to the general labor movement. It is merely believed by the promoters to be better for Negro workmen. This union has been of slow growth however. There are only three locals in the State; two at Pittsburg, having 50 members, and one at Reading, In Philadelphia there is an organization of hoisting engineers, which as yet is not connected with the Pittsburg union. There are numerous societies and clubs among Negroes which are organized along labor lines; but which are more social and beneficial clubs than labor unions. The largest of these is the Hotel Brotherhood, established at Philadelphia in 1881, and including present or former hotel employes. It pays sick and death benefits, and acts as a kind of clearing house for hotel labor. In 1906, the Brotherhood purchased a club house at the cost of $15,000. The bell-men, the Pullman car porters, the janitors, the private waiters, the caterers, the coach men and others in domestic and personal service, have similar but smaller organizations. These organizations serve largely as aids in securing work, but have made but little attempt to regulate wages and apprentices.

In and about Pittsburg, are many whose connection with
the labor unions in the steel industry is interesting and in-
structive, as it illustrates one aspect of the labor union's attitude
toward the Negroes.   In the early days of the steel industry,
the Sons of Vulcan, which included puddlers in its membership,
was organized but limited its membership to whites.   About
1875 there was a strike in one of the Pittsburg mills; Negro
non-union puddlers were brought from Richmond, Virginia,
to break the strike.   The next year, in 1876, the Amalgamated
Association of Iron and Steel Workers was formed.   In the
preamble to its Constitution it declared: "In union there is
strength, and in the formation of a National Amalgamated Association, embracing every iron and steel worker in the country, a union founded upon a basis broad as the land in which
we live, lies our only hope."   Still no Negroes were organized.
A few years later, however, the Negroes were organized both
in Pittsburg and in the South.   Their connection with the
union, which was at one time, the strongest in the country, has
not, however, been very satisfactory.

The general opinion of the Negro workers in the Pittsburg steel mills who were interviewed by the writer, is that the
unions are a hindrance rather than a help to the Negro.   Several have been members and one had been president of a Southern union and a delegate to the National Convention of Steel
Workers; some had gone out on strikes for the union.   Their
testimony is summarized as follows:

1.   The organizations out of which the Amalgamated Association of Steel and Iron Workers was formed did not admit
Negroes.

2.   After the Amalgamated Association was formed,
white union men refused to work with Negro union men or
to help protect Negro workmen, thus making union membership of no industrial value to the Negro workers.

3. All the new opportunities secured by Negroes have been gotten in spite of the union, not with its aid.

4. Membership was offered to Negroes only *after* they had successfully won their places against unions, and the pledges of membership generally broken by the white members.

In support of the first point, they say no Negro is known ever to have been a member of the Sons of Vulcan, the Associated Brotherhood of Iron and Steel Heaters, or the Iron and Steel Roll Hands' Union; and that one of these unions had a clause in its constitution which prohibited Negroes from membership. Amalgamating these bodies did not lesson prejudice. Although the constitution of the amalgamated association, did not put in the "for whites only" clause, but declared that the union ought to embrace every iron and steel worker in the country, it in spirit ignored the Negro. The most intelligent leaders may have meant to include Negro workers in this, but it was not so understood by the masses. In support of the second, several instances are given in which union men refused to work with their Negro brethren. One of the principal instances of this was the case at Beaver Falls. Some Negro workmen, who at their union's request had struck in Pittsburg, heard of the need of puddlers, at Beaver Falls, and were taken by the white secretary of the union, who tried to get work for them there, but the white workmen would not work with Negroes despite the pleadings of the secretary, and the need of workmen.

In support of the third statement it is asserted that Negroes now work only in non-union mills; that they secured their opportunity in the Black Diamond mills after they had been ignored by the union at Beaver Falls, by taking the places of strikers; that they secured their place in Clark's Mills in 1888, and in Homestead in 1892, and in most other places by going to work after white union men had quit. And they say that

7

only after they had gotten in the Park Bros.' Mill, were they offered membership in the union. The Negroes in Pittsburg were organized to insure against them acting as strike breakers, i. e., to protect the white unionists, but not particularly to advance the cause of the Negroes. The last attempt to organize the Negroes was in 1901, when many of them struck at Clark's Mill, in order to help maintain the union. The strike failed and since then the union has been very weak. Overtures, however, are being made to the Negroes to join again.

The whole history of the labor union situation among iron and steel workers has been an attempt of white workmen to use Negroes to their advantage without giving corresponding advantages. As late as 1905, at a general meeting of the Amalgamated Association of Iron and Steel Workers in Cleveland, Ohio, it was resolved that Negroes not be organized, or encouraged to learn the trade, as it might inspire Negroes from the South to come North and compete with white men. At the meeting in Youngstown, Ohio, in 1907, however, there seemed to be a change of sentiment, and it was resolved to organize Negroes wherever possible. But in 1908 no advance along this line had been made in Pennsylvania.

The hostile or indifferent treatment of Negroes by the unions, though quite opposite to that of the United Mine Workers, is to a large extent, the basis of opinion among Negroes that the unions are opposed to them. And of late years this opinion has grown to a very considerable extent. When Professor Du Bois wrote his "Philadelphia Negro," he was able to give a large number of instances of Negroes who had been refused by unions. But when the present investigation was made, ten years later, very few Negroes could be found who had recently applied to the unions for admission. As Professor Du Bois found, however, the present investigator also found a very pronounced opinion prevalent among the Negroes that they were not welcome in the unions. Now, instead of applying for admission to the unions,' the Negroes take for granted that the unions are hostile and they do not seek to join.

This attitude has the effect of preventing many Negroes from attempting to follow their trade. The newcomer who has probably worked at the trade of a carpenter in the South is informed as soon as he reaches the State, that he cannot work at his trade because of the hostility of the labor unions. Having probably heard this also before he left the South, after a desultory search, he gives up under the impression that the union is the cause of his inability to get work at his trade. The fact, however, is that it is not always the union as much as the increased competition and higher standard of efficiency of the more complex community into which he has come.

The leaders of the labor movement both in Pittsburg and in Philadelphia are agreed that there is in theory no hostility on the part of the union against the Negro. Most of them see clearly what a disadvantage to the labor movement it would be to have Negroes hostile to the movement or the movement hostile to the Negroes. They complain that the Negroes have been used in many instances to injure their cause and they know that, with increasing intelligence and skill, Negroes will be more capable of retarding the movement for the uplift of labor. Most labor leaders have to contend very largely with mediocre intelligence, and often gross ignorance among white men; with greed and selfishness, with human nature as it is. They claim that as the ordinary white man who joins the Christian church is not revolutionized in his idea about the Negro, so the one who joins the union probably has undergone but little change in regard to the Negro. They point out also that non-union white men are as averse to working with Negroes as union white men. At any rate, as the situation now

is, the majority of Negroes are non-union, and will probably
so remain until they develop enough strength independently
so that they can be of more definite help or hindrance to the
union cause. By keeping Negroes out of the trades, competition is lessened for the men in the union. As long as Negroes wait to be invited in by the unions they will remain outside. Only by succeeding in spite of the indifference of the
union and even its occasional hostility, can Negroes hope to
be recognized.

The Negroes who immigrated to the State before the Civil
War, came principally from the rural districts of the South,
and settled largely in the rural districts of Pennsylvania.
Friends of the race in the South who sent manumitted Negroes
North, rightly believed that these Negroes could better succeed as laborers on the farm, to which they were accustomed,
than as workers in the city. Many escaped slaves settled also
in the rural districts and some conducted successful farms until frightened away by slave hunters and the passage of the
Fugitive Slave law.

In the Southern and Eastern counties of the State, particularly Delaware, Chester, Lancaster, York, Cumberland, Franklin, Fayette and Washington, there were some well conducted
farms. But the era of the great industrial expansion occasioned by improved means of transportation and communication and improved machinery, has almost depleted the country
districts, so far as the Negro is concerned. The same motives
which caused the white boy and girl to leave the farm to go
to the city, also impelled the Negro boy: higher wages, more
excitement, greater opportunity for self-expression and ad-
venture. Good farms which were cultivated for years by the
fathers were deserted by the sons and daughters. And now
the Negro farmer in the State forms but a small proportion
of Negro workers.

In 1900, according to the Census, there were 3,696 Negroes in agricultural pursuits, about 4.6% of the total number of Negro workers; 3,037 of these persons, about five-sixths of the total were agricultural laborers, 518 were farmers, planters, and overseers. There are three dairymen; 89 gardeners, florists and nurserymen; 21 lumbermen and raftsmen; 11 stock raisers, herders and drovers and 16 wood choppers.

, There were in 1900, 585 farms operated by owners, 26 by part owners, 1 by owner and tenants; 145 by cash tenants, and 72 by share tenants. As to the size, 21 of these farms were less than three acres; 149 from three to ten acres; 91 from ten to twenty acres; 130 from twenty to fifty acres; 109 from fifty-one to one hundred acres; 62 from one hundred to one hundred and seventy-five acres; 2 from two hundred and sixty acres to five hundred; and none over five hundred acres. The principal sources of income on the farms were as follows: For 78 farms, hay and grain; for 3, tobacco; for 145, live stock; while 256 had various other crops. On the 585 farms, 562 reported the value of domestic animals at $154,118. On 386 farms, there were 2,514 head of neat cattle; on 362 farms, there were 1,571 dairy cows; and on 43 other farms, 900 head of other neat cattle. On 507 farms there were 1,220 horses, and on 37, there were 85 mules. There were reported 172 lambs, and 993 sheep, one year and over; 1,781 head of swine; 2 goats; $9,476 worth of poultry and $200 worth of bees. 25 farms reported bees and 458 reported chickens. 490 farms of 2,938 acres produced 108,258 bushels of corn and 262 farms of 1,988 acres produced 25,742 bushels of wheat; 237 farms of 1,484 acres, produced 45,007 bushels of oats. One farm used four acres, producing 100 bushels of barley; 60 farms employed 244 acres, producing 3,120 bushels of rye; 65 farms produced 3,557 bushels of buckwheat on 277 acres.

There are more than 75,000 Negroes living within this

State, who were born outside of its borders and who immigrated here between the ages of fifteen and fifty years. They are, therefore, principally able-bodied workers. Although the State expended nothing for their care during infancy and little for their education, it reaps the benefit of their toil. Unlike most foreigners who come to the State, the Negroes do not have to learn the language, or become used to the national customs; but they are able to adapt themselves quickly to our environment. Moreover, as a rule, they are a class of contented laborers and seldom disturb the industrial equilibrium. There are no Negro anarchists in Pennsylvania and as far as our knowledge goes, there never have been any. There are no violent antagonists to the social order. The Negroes are essentially a race of peace and patience. Their long suffering during the days of slavery, their religious temperament, childlike faithfulness and their wonderful adaptability, are calculated to make them a valuable asset to any community in which they may be settled, if they are given reasonably fair treatment. They are cheap workers because of circumstances. Much that they ought to receive in wages goes to society as a part of its surplus. They have laid most of the asphalt pavements in the State, helped to construct many of the principal sewers, the Philadelphia subway and the filter plant. If they have been underpaid in these matters it has benefited the taxpayers. At any rate many of the public improvements in the State have been made by these Negro laborers whom the State did not train, but who as able-bodied workmen immigrated from the South. Again, the Negro immigrants unlike much of the foreign labor, come to make this State their permanent home. Their savings are invested in the property and banks of the State, and what they spend is spent within the State. But a very small proportion of the money they earn is sent out of the State and practically none is sent out of the country. Negroes have shown despite their meagre opportunity, capacity for improvement in labor and the management of business. The best of them are able to rise above mediocrity and the majority of them are useful workers. Economically considered, from the point of view of the State, the Negro worker has been a very profitable acquisition.

OWNERSHIP OF PROPERTY.

The acquisition of property presupposes industry, thrift and self-sacrifice. The study of the wealth which Negroes have been able to amass is a study of the race's industry and self-sacrifice, and shows something of its higher strivings. For, as has been shown, the men of the group are largely engaged in unskilled labor, which barely yields enough to maintain even the lowest standard of decent living. To save, out of their meagre earnings, sufficient money with which to secure real property is, therefore, a sacrifice which only the best and most thoughtful undergo.

The first mention of a Negro in connection with property-owning in Pennsylvania is in the will which William Penn made in 1701 in which he gave to one of his Negro slaves, "Old Sam," "and to his children's children forever," one hundred acres of land. Whether this property was turned over to "Old Sam" or not, is uncertain, for this will was invalidated by a later one, in which no mention is made of "Old Sam" or any slaves, or of any property to be transferred to Negroes. When the first property was actually acquired by Negroes is, therefore, unknown. Ac-

cording to the report of the Pennsylvania Abolition Society, in 1796 there were 89 Negroes who were proprietors
of houses, the average value of which was about $200. In
1821, the amount of real estate owned by Negroes in Philadelphia was $281,162, assessed at $112,464. In 1832, the
Negroes sent a memorial to the Legislature in which they
claimed to pay $2,500 taxes on property, the market value
of which was about $300,000. In 1838, it was estimated
that the value of real estate owned by Negroes was $322,-
532, on which $3,252.83 taxes were paid and the personal
property $667,859. In 1849, Edward Needles reported 315
Negro property owners, having real estate in Philadelphia
with personal property valued at $630,886. In 1856, the
real and personal property of Negroes was valued at $2,-
685,693, on which they paid $9,766.42 taxes.

Dr. DuBois estimated the value of real estate and personal property owned by the Negroes of Philadelphia as
$5,000,000, in 1898. According to the census of 1900, there
were in the state 3,978 homes owned by their Negro occu-
pants, while 25,221 were hired and the ownership of 1,850
was unknown. The large majority of the houses which are
owned by Negroes are located in the smaller towns where
the cost of property is not as high as in the large cities.

The difficulty of estimating the value of property owned by Negroes is due to the fact that on the tax books no
account is taken of the color of the taxpayer, and one has
to rely on the recollection of the tax assessors and is dependent on the word of various individuals. The personal
registration law for cities of the first class provided for
registration of all voters by color, age, occupation and
whether they are lodgers, lessees or owners of the houses
in which they live. This is however, unsatisfactory, as it
gives nothing of those men who do not register or of the

women who own homes or of men owning property elsewhere. Nor does it give anything as to the amount of
property owned. One is left almost entirely to private
sources of information which may be inaccurate.

The following is based upon estimates made by old
citizens, reports of tax assessors, records of personal registration, lists of taxpayers given by clergymen, newspaper
editors, doctors, lawyers, charity workers and others and
verified by the tax assessor's books.

In every case, the estimate is possibly lower than the
actual amount of property. In 1907 there were 712 Negro
taxpayers having 802 pieces of property in Philadelphia,
paying taxes on $2,438,675. Eighteen of these properties
were assessed at less than $500 each, a total valuation of
$4,725; 52 between $500 and $1,000, a total of $412,500;
529 between $1,000 and $3,000, a total of $948,200; 116
pieces assessed between $3,000 and $5,000, a total of $426,-
150; 64 pieces assessed between $5,000 and $7,500, a total
of $388,100; 11 pieces assessed between $7,500 and $10,000,
a total of $89,500; 12 pieces assessed between $10,000 and
over, a total value of $169,500. This represents an invest-
ment of about $5,000,000. In Harrisburg, the first ward,
8 persons are reported as owning 11 pieces of property assessed at $12,200; in the tenth ward, the assessor writes
me, "We are glad to say that so far as we know, not one
foot of real estate in our ward is owned by Negroes;" in
the fifth ward, 9 persons are given, owning 9 pieces of
property assessed at $9,660; a total of twenty-five persons
owning $27,900. In Chester, 102 property holders, 76 males
and 26 females, were reported having property valued at
$160,000. Valuation of property of Negroes in various other
cities is estimated by reliable correspondents to be $50,000
for York; $150,000 for Coatesville; $100,000 for Wilkes-

Barre; $9,000 for Doylestown; $75,000 for Altoona; $2,000,-
ooo for Pittsburg and Allegheny; $150,000 for Washington;
$50,000 for Media; and $400,000 for West Chester.   In
Philadelphia there are several estates of Negroes said to
be worth a quarter of a million dollars.   The estate of the
late John McKee was said to be worth upwards of a
million dollars; that of Mrs. Henry Jones, widow of caterer Henry Jones, came very near a quarter of a million
dollars.   Near Altoona, three families owned more than
$10,000 worth of property.   Three Negroes in Johnstown
own property which is valued at $10,000; several in West
Chester and Carlisle have property valued at $10,000 or
more.   In the smaller places where there are but few Negroes, they often pay taxes on $3,000 to $25,000 worth of
property.

It is difficult to estimate the total value of the property
owned by Negroes in the state.   The average assessed value
of 802 pieces of property in Philadelphia was $3,041.   In
1900, Philadelphia County had about one-tenth of the
property owned by Negroes in the state.   To-day, Philadelphia property is assessed at $2,438,675.   If the same
proportion holds, the assessed value of the property of
Negroes in the State is between $20,000,000 and $25,000,000.
From the registration books in Philadelphia, it is possible
to secure the occupations of the men who are voters and
property holders.   The following table shows the occupations of the 485 men who registered as owning homes:

Occupation of home owners.	Number.
Laborers	68
Caterers	38
Teamsters and drivers	34
Waiters	32

Porters (in stores and on R. R.)..........27
Clerks 27
Dealers and merchants.................25
Janitors 17
Butlers 17
Clergyman 15
Barbers 14
Coachmen 13
Gardeners and farmers 10
Physicians and dentists................. 9
Messengers 7
Policemen 6
Stewards 6
Retired persons 6
Upholsterers 5
Insurance agents 4
Contractors 4
Teachers 4
Watchmen 4
Packers 4
Cooks 4
Firemen 4

Foremen, lawyers, shoemakers, musicians and livery-
men, 3 each; 15 hotelkeepers, undertakers, butchers, super-
intendents, cigarmakers, tailors, bricklayers, plasterers, bartenders, stonecutters, carpenters, engineers, lettercarriers,
artists, hucksters, bookkeepers, stable bosses, stockkeepers,
2 each; 36 expressmen, restaurant keepers, menders, wire
insulator, pilot, salesman, dyer, masseur, florist, operator,
bellman, journalist, elevator man, jeweler, blacksmith, pho-
tographer, manufacturer, longshoreman, agent, laundryman,
1 each. 21.

These tables show that the large majority of Negro

home-owners are in domestic and personal service. In Philadelphia alone, laborers, caterers, teamsters, porters, janitors, butlers, coachmen, messengers, stewards, watchmen, bellmen, cooks, firemen, elevator operators, barbers, comprise nearly three hundred of the four hundred and eighty-five home owners returned. In Chester, a large proportion of the home owners are laborers.

The same record shows that the 485 Negroes in Philadelphia, above referred to, were natives of the different states in about the same proportion as the general majority of Negroes. The largest number of Negro property holders were born in Pennsylvania, while Virginia, Maryland and North Carolina follow in the order given.

Ages and length of residence of property holders: The following tables are compiled from the registration books and show the age periods of property-holding voters, and the period of years that they have lived in the state:

Age Periods.	No. of Holders.	Percentage.
From 21 to 30 years,	32	6.6
From 31 to 40 years,	126	25.9
From 41 to 50 years,	177	36.7
From 51 to 60 years,	87	17.9
From 61 to 70 years,	42	8.7
From 71 to 80 years,	13	2.7
Eighty years or over,	2	.5
Age unknown or not given,	5	1.0
Total,	485	100.00

Length of residence in Pennsylvania:

	Immigrant (Negroes) born outside Pa.	Native (Negroes) born in Pa.	Total
From 1 to 5 years,	8		8
From 6 to 10 years,	38 (a)		38
From 11 to 15 years,	65 (b)		65
From 16 to 20 years,	56 (c)		56

	Born outside Pa.	Born in Pa.	Total
From 21 to 25 years,	39	3	42
From 26 to 30 years,	42	12	54
From 31 to 35 years,	26	14	40
From 36 to 40 years,	30	18	48
From 41 to 45 years,	14	22	36
Total up to 45 years,	318	69	387
From 46 to 50 years,	7	20	27
From 51 to 55 years,	1	14	15
From 56 to 60 years,	1	18	19
From 61 to 70 years,	2	14	16
From 71 years and over,	1	3	4
Residence not given,	13	4	17
Total,	343 (d)	142 (d)	485

The largest number of owners is between the ages of 41 and 50 years; the second largest between 31 and 40 years of age ; 336 owners are fifty years of age or younger, that is, practically seventy per cent. of those who own property were born since the beginning of the Civil War, and therefore belong to the generation of the free men.

These facts are deserving of more than passing notice, in view of the frequent assertion, that the younger generation of Negroes, born since Abraham Lincoln's Proclamation of Emancipation and especially those who have migrated North, are not equal to their fathers in the matter of acquiring property. These facts seem to point to an opposite conclusion.

It is impossible to get any accurate statistics of the savings of Negroes. Some idea may be given by reports received from two of Philadelphia's Savings Fund Societies. The result of a record kept of the colored depositors in the Western Savings Fund is summarized as follows: (From October, 1906, to March, 1907) "In 2,785 open accounts, 72 accounts were opened by colored persons. The books would show, approximately, 1,333 accounts with Negroes.

The percentage of money deposited is .1162. If this applies to $20,072,417, our total deposit in line to date, would show $268,101 to be the aggregate amount of deposits by Negroes. The Philadelphia Savings Fund, which is the oldest in the state, reported that 2,021 Negroes opened new accounts in 1905, and 2,000 in the year 1906, which were 4.2 per cent. of the total deposits for these two years. This bank had a total deposit on January 1st, 1907, of $95,966,-863.34. If the per cent. of depositors holds good for the percentage of deposits, the share of the Negroes would be 4.2 per cent. or $3,610,608.26. In the Starr Savings Bank, of the 15,142 open accounts in 1906, about thirty per cent. were of Negroes. In these banks, the majority of Negro depositors are women and 99 per cent. can read and write. The majority are domestic and unskilled workers. There are other banks in Philadelphia and all over the state which have savings of Negroes and it is impossible to estimate the total.

An increasing number of Negroes are investing their savings in stocks and bonds, in business enterprises, etc. Several Negroes own Pennsylvania Railroad stock and some own stock in the United States Steel Corporation. Many own real estate in the South and in other Northern states.

THE CHURCH AND SECRET SOCIETIES

Because of the place occupied by religion in the life of the African Negro and of the American slaves, it is not surprising that the church should be the first independent organization developed among them. The first separate

Negro church, with a Negro pastor, was established in Philadelphia in the latter part of the eighteenth century. The first organization of several distinct Negro churches into an independent denomination of Negro Christians was also formed in Philadelphia in 1816.

The census of 1890 was incomplete regarding the statistics of Negro churches from the fact that many Negro churches were under the supervision of bodies which made in their returns no distinction as to color. Thus for Pennsylvania, no colored Baptist Churches were reported as such and no separation is made of the Negroes who are members of the Episcopal, Presbyterian and Catholic churches. The whole number of colored church organizations given in Pennsylvania was 282. These had 234 church edifices, with seating capacity of 77,865, also 25 halls with a seating capacity of 3,025. The membership was 26,753 persons and their church property was valued at $1,156,408. The census gave the membership of Methodist bodies in Pennsylvania as 22,166, the number of church organizations among them as 179, having 189 church edifices and 20 halls with a combined seating capacity of 66,200 persons. The Baptists of Pennsylvania were, however, as large as the Methodists in 1890, if not larger. But allowing that the Baptists were in 1890 equal to the Methodists, there were in all probability then in the state at least 400 churches, having about 40,000 colored communicants, with 450 church edifices and halls valued at not less than $2,000,000. The census of churches now being taken ought to correct this error, and properly separate the Negro churches.

In the whole state of Pennsylvania there were in 1890, 1,726,640 communicants out of a population of 5,258,113 or 32.8 per cent.; while by the evidently incorrect count, 23.9 per cent. of the Negro population were members of some religious organization. By the corrected estimate of Negro church members, at least 37.2 per cent. of the race in the state are members of the church.

The principal denominations represented in the state are: Regular Baptist (colored); African Methodist Episcopal; African Methodist Episcopal Zion; American Union Protestant Methodist; Colored Methodist Episcopal (North); Protestant Episcopal; Presbyterian; Congregational; Roman Catholic, and the Church of God. The first five are entirely under Negro supervision, and represent the largest percentage of the membership.

The Baptist denomination has the largest number of members. The first church of this denomination was established in 1809 at Philadelphia. For three-quarters of a century the Baptists as a rule had the less influential and intelligent class of Negroes in its membership and held rather an insignificant place among the churches of the state. During the present generation, however, the Baptist denomination has taken the front rank among Pennsylvania's Negro churches, both as to number of churches and influence. The increase of the influence of the Baptist church has been due chiefly to the influx of Negroes from Virginia, where the Baptist denomination was probably the first established among Negroes and where it is to-day stronger than any other denomination. Many of the ministers of this church are Virginians. The Baptist church may truly be called the church of the people. There are in the state at least six Baptist churches with a thousand or more members, and two with more than two thousand members.

In 1813, there were six Negro churches in Philadelphia; one Episcopal church, the largest, with 560 members; three Methodist Churches, with 1,426 members; one Presbyterian Church, 300 members; and one Baptist Church with 80 members. In 1838, there were 16 churches in Philadelphia, of which eight were Methodist, having 2,860 members; four were Baptist, with 700 members; two were Presbyterian, with 325 members; one was a Lutheran Church with 10 members, and an Episcopal Church with 100 members. The total value of the property in 1838 was $114,000, of which the Methodists owned $50,000 worth; the Episcopalians, $36,000 worth; the Presbyterians, $20,000 worth; the Baptists, $4,200 and the Lutherans, $3,000 worth.

In 1907, there were in Philadelphia 31 Baptist Churches, a third of which were established during the past ten years; in Pittsburg there are about 20 Baptist Churches, the majority of which were established during the past decade.

The Methodists are the oldest distinctively Negro denomination in the state and country. The African Methodist Episcopal Church was established in Philadelphia in 1816, being constituted by 16 delegates representing churches at Philadelphia, Baltimore, Salem and Attleboro, New Jersey. Richard Allen, of Bethel Church, Philadelphia, was chosen Bishop and Philadelphia was selected as the headquarters of the church. Since that time the A. M. E. Church has grown to about 600,000 members, with organizations in nearly every State in the United States, Canada and the West Indies and West and South Africa. It had in 1908 seventeen living Bishops, all of whom are Negroes. This church has been very intimately connected with the development of Negroes of Pennsylvania. During the early years of its existence, it planted preaching stations in nearly every community where there were any considerable number of Negroes. During the period prior to the Civil War it was the chief church to minister to the fugitive slaves and manumitted slaves from the South. It started the first Negro college in the North, even before slavery was

8

abolished and it founded in 1852 what is now the oldest
Negro newspaper in the country, and in 1884 the A. M. E.
Church Review, now the oldest and largest Negro magazine. During the period before the war, its ministers were
among the most aggressive and influential Negroes in the
state, interested in most movements for the uplift of   the
race and consulted frequently by the whites who were interested in the people of color. Since the Civil War, and
the incoming of large numbers of immigrants from the
South, the A. M. E. Church, though increasing in actual
numbers, has gradually surrendered its leadership to the
Baptist Church. There are at present organizations of the
A. M. E. Church in more than a hundred cities and towns
with an aggregate membership of approximately 15,000
persons.

The A. M. E. Zion Church began a distinctive denomination in New York, New Haven, Connecticut and Philadelphia.
The Philadélphia church, which helped to form this denomination, was established in 1813. In Philadelphia and Harrisburg, where two of its oldest churches are, this denomination, like the A. M. E. Church, exercised considerable influence upon the Negroes in the early days. The denomination now had in 1908 eight living Bishops, all Negroes, and
about 500,000 members in the United States. The headquarters of its Financial, Missionary and Church Extension Departments, are located in Philadelphia. There are churches
in about fifty cities and towns in Pennsylvania, and the
membership in the State is about 5000.

The Colored Methodist Episcopal Church is the third
independent organization. This denomination was founded
in Georgia in 1870, by the Methodist Episcopal Church
South, which set apart its Negro members into a separate
independent organization. This church has a very small

representation in Pennsylvania. In 1890 there were six organizations having 247 members, 2 worshipping in church
edifices and 4 in halls. The church at large is located in
the South and has 7 Bishops and about 300,000 members.
The Church of God has a strong organization in Philadelphia, having possibly a thousand members. The Bishop
of this church is a Negro. It is popularly known as the
foot washers, because the practice of washing feet. A system of church stores has been organized, and receives liberal patronage from the members, who hold some things
in common and are supposed to give one-tenth of their income. Besides these there are other churches, which are
under the general góvernment of whites. These are the
Episcopal, Congregational, Presbyterian and Roman Catholic Churches. They have separate church organizations for
Negroes but no separate general organizations. The history of these churches extends far back, the first Episcopal
Church being established in 1794 and the first Presbyterian
in 1806. These denominations, like the Methodists, played
a very large part in the early history of the Negroes.
They appealed especially to the more intelligent class of Negroes. But with the exception of the Catholics, they are
of proportionately less influence than formerly, for they
have not been able to hold a large portion of the immigrant
Negroes who, as has been said, have gone largely to the
Baptist Church. There are 18 Negro clergymen, who were
in 1908, members of the Presbyteries in Pennsylvania, 14
of whom have charges and 4 have not. In 1908 there were
14 Presbyterian Churches in the State, 4 of which were in
Philadelphia, and 1 each in Harrisburg, Pittsburg, Reading, Carlisle, Chester, West Chester, Oxford, York, Chambersburg and Welsh Mountains. The total membership of the
Negro Presbyterian Churches was 1843 in 1908, more than

half of which was in Philadelphia. The total valuation of
property is $190,000, $112,000 of which is   in Philadelphia,
The Protestant Episcopal Church has in the State eight
churches, six being in Philadelphia, one in Allegheny and
one in Chester. The total membership at the last meeting
of Episcopalians was 1104.

The church is an important economic organization
among Negroes. It owns in Pennsylvania more than three
million dollars worth of property, and its income is not less
than a quarter of a million dollars a year. In Philadelphia
alone, within a year, there have been two purchases of
church buildings, at from $20,000 to $75,000, and a new Negro church erected at a cost of $90,000. The Negro minis-
ter in Pennsylvania, though to a less degree than formerly,
is still an important personage in the upward economic
movement of Negroes in the State. The largest building
and loan association among Negroes was organized by a
Presbyterian minister, and a minister is on the board of
nearly every incorporated business in the State. The first
industrial school in the State was organized by a minister,
and the two that are now operated by Negroes are supported largely by the Church. Most of the other private schools
in the State are the direct outgrowth of activity in the
churches. Most of the benevolent societies have connection with the Church; and all of the insurance societies save
perhaps one or two, grew out of church activity. There is
hardly an activity which is uplifting in its purpose, which
does not originate in or later find some connection with the
Church. Still most of the churches are in debt and find it
difficult to engage in many social activities which do not increase their income. Thus a large field of effective social
work is quite neglected chiefly because of lack of money.

On the social side, the Church is still the chief institution. Here strangers come and are introduced and find ready welcome. In a large city like Philadelphia or Pittsburg, where men are busy and time is valuable, the incoming immigrant from the South would be at a great loss had he not the church to which to go, at first, at least. These institutions have sociables nearly every night in the week, either in the church house or in the homes of the members. Concerts, tableaux and light operas are given in Negro churches, which introduces all kinds of talent to the Negro public. Negro lecturers, elocutionists and other entertainers find the easiest way to reach the people is through the Church. The Church is used for public meetings of various kinds. If the Business Men's League, or the Mechanics' Association want to reach the people they go to the church. Nor is politics barred. Some of the largest political meetings are held in churches—though the practice is growing less prevalent—and clergymen are among the most influential Negro political leaders. The only Negro member of the State Republican Committee is a Baptist clergyman, who has one of the largest churches in Philadelphia. In all social movements it is the Church which is expected to take a leading part, and it generally does. Any movement concerning the interests of humanity and the interests of the Negro in particular, finds audience in the Negro church.

Some churches are attempting special systematic social work. One of the most successful of these, is the Berean Presbyterian Church in Philadelphia, of which Rev. Matthew Anderson, a graduate of Oberlin and Princeton, is pastor. The church was founded in 1880, and located in a part of the city where but few Negroes lived. In 1884 the Berean Kindergarten was started. It has enrolled over 800 pupils since its beginning. In 1888 the Berean Building and Loan Association, whose work has already been mentioned, was formed. In 1894, the Berean Seaside Home was opened at Point Pleasant, New Jersey, providing a quiet resort, where Negroes of refinement will not come in contact with the unpleasant prejudices which prevail at many seaside places. The Home accommodates about fifty persons. In 1897, the Berean Bureau of Mutual Help was started, and in ten years has given employment to over seven hundred persons.

In 1899 the Berean Manual Training and Industrial School was started. In 1900 the Berean Educational Conference was established, under whose auspices such leaders as ex-President Cleveland, Hon. W. N. Ashman, J. William Martin, Robert E. Pattison have spoken. In 1904 the pastor of the church started the Berean Seaside Conference, and in 1906, the Berean Trades Association, and in 1908, the Berean Social and Economical Conference. Many other churches are doing similar work, but in a less extensive way. In Philadelphia, Calvary M. E. Church, Bethel A. M. E. Church, Zion Baptist, First Baptist, Central Baptist, and the Protestant Episcopal Church of the Crucifixion have institutional features more or less developed. The last named church has gone farther than most Negro churches in its dealing with the amusement question. It has gone against the general view of Negro Christians in establishing a poolroom and evenings for dancing. The First Baptist, has through its Minute Men's Association, purchased a building especially for work among men, and through its Charity Aid Society, purchased property for a home for aged persons.

The purely religious work of the church consists chiefly of preaching and prayer meeting and an annual or semi-annual "revival." In both preaching and prayer, emphasis is put upon the emotional, though to much less extent than formerly; the average Christian thinks that he fulfills his religious duty by **"feeling good."** The Negroes' religion is largely personal; they seek chiefly for communion with God; they like to "talk with God," "to feel His spirit;" their prayers consist largely of confessions of sin in general and expressions of humility, emphasizing God's judgment and His wrath and begging His forgiveness. They nearly always end with fervent expressions anticipatory of the glories of heaven and the joys of the after-life. When the religion of the Negro leaves the subjective and personal, and takes on the objective and social, it expresses itself chiefly in giving to the church and to the poor and unfortunate, and visiting the sick, and helping to bury the dead. It is quite difficult for anyone who has not kept in very close touch with the Negro church to realize the amount of casual charity done by Negro church members. Many times they give a part of their last dollar to the church and to the poor. "Give till you feel it," is an expression often heard from the Negro pulpit, and not seldom obeyed by the faithful Negro Christian. Nor is it an uncommon thing for the hard worked Negro cook, or washer woman, or housewife, after doing service from ten to fourteen hours a day, to visit the sick and sit up nearly all night with the distressed. With organized charity, however, the average Negro Christian, not unlike the average white Christian, has not yet harmonized his religion. That spontaneous and indiscriminate giving is the only real charity, is the belief of the majority. Yet the beneficial society is a very frequent attachment to the large Negro church and tends more or less to systematize its benevolence, while also a few churches have old age pensioners who are given regular allowances per week.

As to moral character, the church is still the institution of respectability, as well as piety. Generally speaking, the average of morality in the Negro church is much higher than the average outside of the church. Though the church cannot rigidly enforce all of its laws, yet its restraining influence in the grosser evils, and among the greater portion of its members is daily evident. Time was when the churches protested chiefly against dancing, theatregoing and card playing. Most of the churches still protest against these things, but have also increased their protest against greater evils. In the character of Negro ministers, there has been a notable improvement both in education and morality, although there is still a great deal lacking. The standards of piety known to the ignorant Negro, those of loud and long prayers, frequent shouting and constant church attendance, while still prevalent, are becoming less generally accepted than formerly. When it is remembered that the church takes all who come to it on their own word, on "profession of faith," that is on good intention and not on a certificate of past good character, but on their "conversion," it is easy to see how its progress in morality must of necessity be slow. Nor could it be expected that the Negro's religion would develop out of proportion to his intelligence, or his economic condition. Progress in religion and in morals, like progress in education and industry, is slow, notwithstanding the highly supernatural element in the religion.

But with those churches which have not been able to hold the masses, but have appealed to the more cultured classes of Negroes, there has been, as is to be expected, a more rapid progress, especially in the conduct of religious service. Regarding one of this group of churches Mr. Arthur Shadwell, an Englishman, visiting Philadelphia, writes in his book, "Industrial Efficiency": "I have no information on the subject but it appears to me that Philadelphia is the home of the colored aristocracy. There are eighteen African Methodist Episcopal Churches. I attended service at one of them on a Sunday, and found a striking contrast with others I had attended in the South. The service was practically indistinguishable from a high church (not ritualistic), Anglican, one in England, except the surpliced choir was formed by women. The sermon, the tone and manner of the whole service and the demeanor of the congregation reminded me of St. Mary Abbotts, or any church of that moderately high order which is now so general in England. The signs of refinement, taste and culture were striking. Every Sunday I spent in the States, I made it a point of going to as many churches of different kinds as I could get in, and my experience ranges from a pure specimen of Negro fervor in Columbia, S. C., to St. Patrick's Cathedral in New York, and Trinity Church, Boston, which corresponds (say) with St. Margaret's, Westminster, and is the resort of the intellectual aristocracy. The African service in Philadelphia was no whit less refined."

The secret orders come next to the church in social importance, and they, too, have an African foundation. But their chief hold on the people is not so much their secrecy as their sick benefit and life insurance features. The principal orders represented are the Odd Fellows, Masons, True Reformers, Knights of Pythias, Elks, Knights of Tabor and Gallilean Fishermen.

The Grand United Order of Odd Fellows is the largest secret organization in the State. It was introduced into this country from England in March, 1843, when the Philomathean Lodge, No. 646, was established in New York City. The first lodge in Pennsylvania and the third in the

United States, was Unity Lodge, No. 711, established in Philadelphia, May 14, 1844. According to the Journal of Proceedings of the biennial session of the Grand United Order of Odd Fellows, which met in October, 1906, there were 4643 lodges of Odd Fellows in the country, with a membership of 186,108. The complete statistics of the order were as follows, in 1906:

Name.	Lodges.	Members.
Active Lodges	4,643	186,108
Active Households	21,636	79,343
P. G. M. Councils	274	5,210
Juvenile Societies	395	12,245
Patriarchies	142	142
D. G. Lodges	39	
District Households	26	
Total number of lodges	8,155	285,931
Increase since 1904	1,641	66,190

The headquarters of the Odd Fellows are in Philadelphia, where they have erected a six-story building, at a cost of $125,000. The Odd Fellows' "Journal," the national organ of the order, is published here. In the State in 1906, there were 105 lodges.

The Grand United Order of True Reformers was established in 1882, in Richmond, Virginia, by a Methodist preacher. It is not merely a secret order, but it has as its chief object the economic elevation of the Negro race in America. To that end it has established an insurance department, a bank, hotels, mercantile establishments, a newspaper, an old folks' home, and other institutions of uplift. According to the yearly report in 1903, the receipts of the financial department of the order were $173,440.70; of the record department, $47,851.26; of the supply department,

$21,403.75; from rents of real estate, $27,219.86; from sales of regalia, $25,269.55. The receipts of the bank for this year were $853,591.53. The value of the real estate owned by the society was given at $367,050. The growth of the True Reformers in Pennsylvania is due chiefly to the heavy migration of Negroes from Virginia. The headquarters for the State are in Philadelphia. In 1903 there were reported 161 lodges in the State, in fifteen counties. Since then, however, the True Reformers have more than doubled their membership in this State.

The Most Worshipful Grand Lodge of Free and Accepted Masons of the State of Pennsylvania, according to the ninety-second annual communication in 1906, comprised 68 lodges, having 239 members, and were represented in thirty-seven places in the State. Their headquarters are in Philadelphia, where they own a four-story hall.

EDUCATION.

In most of the colonies but little effort was made to train the Negroes. As late as the middle of the eighteenth century, when they numbered at least a quarter of a million, more than half of whom were free, there is no record of a school for Negroes. As in other efforts for the elevation of the Negro, so in education, Pennsylvania was the leader. The Quakers were among the first to give attention to them. In 1750 Anthony Benezet, a French Quaker, opened the first school for Negroes, in Philadelphia, and for more than thirty years, was the ardent supporter of the cause of Negro education. When he died in 1784 he left possibly the first bequest for the education of the Negroes. The next step was taken by the Friends' Monthly Meeting of Philadelphia, in January, 1770, when it was decided to establish a school for "giving to the children of free Negroes and mulattoes the preference and the opportunity of being taught clear of expense to their parents." Accordingly the school was opened June, 1770, with twenty-three colored children and became the foundation of the system of private "charity schools" conducted by the Quakers. With the bequests from Benezet and others, the original school was enabled to accommodate more pupils and to offer night courses. In 1784 the Raspberry Alley School, which continues its existence to this day, was established and became one of the most useful of these Quaker schools. In 1827 the Infant School was established at Clifton and South Streets, and was in existence in 1836. In 1837 the Institute for Colored Youths was established; in 1838 the Adelphia School was established on Wager Street; in 1848 the School for the Destitute on Lombard, above Seventh Street, and in 1850, the Sheppard School, on Randolph, above Parrish Street. Besides the schools directly under the Quakers, there were semi-public schools and schools connected with the benevolent and reformatory institutions. Among these the earliest was the Orphans' Shelter, established in 1822, on Thirteenth Street, above Callowhill. In 1850 the school at the House of Refuge was started, and in 1855 the Home for Colored Children on Girard, above Ridge Avenue. Among the early institutions, there were also private schools, which were taught by Negroes. These were among the very earliest schools and show a healthy interest of the better class of Negroes in their own education. Absalom Jones taught a school in Philadelphia before 1800. Most of the Negro churches were used also for school purposes; indeed, the Negro church-school was the forerunner of the public school. In 1838, there were reported thirteen private pay schools, of which ten were taught by Negro teachers. In 1856 thirteen of them were reported as still in existence. These schools averaged about twenty-five pupils each. The oldest of them was that of Sarah M. Douglass, which was established in 1833, and had thirty pupils. The next was established in 1836 and was conducted by Diana Smith, in Prosperous Alley. The other eight Negro private schools which existed in 1838 had disappeared in 1856.

The public schools for Negroes were started fully seventy years after the first private schools. In 1822, the first public school was started at Sixth, above Lombard Street. This school still exists and is known as the James Forten School. To-day, however, it is chiefly attended by Jews. In 1830, the Roberts Vaux Public School was started on what was then called Coates Street, near Fifth; in 1839 an ungraded public school was organized in Frankford; in 1841, the Bannaker Public School was started in Paschallville. The same year a primary school at Sixth and Lombard Streets; in 1849, the Corn Street Ungraded School. In these public schools there were doubtless many colored teachers. In 1856 it was reported that the public schools were improving though they were not as efficient as the private charity schools.

With the abolition of slavery in the United States and the large immigration of Negroes to the State, the facilities furnished by private sources became less and less adequate, and the necessity for greater public interest in the education of Negroes more apparent. Education became less a matter of charity than of recognized public necessity. In the last forty years the private schools have gradually taken a less prominent place, having all dissappeared except the higher and special schools. The only efforts at their own education now in existence by Negroes, is that undertaken by churches. The unendowed charity institutions conducted by Quakers, which did such a great service in primary education before the Civil War, have also passed away. Those which have endowment have found that the public schools have been much better prepared than they to do the work. Several of them have changed their courses and those which have not done so, are inefficient as compared with the public schools.

The public schools existed from the beginning as distinctively Negro schools supported by public funds. There is no evidence to show that any great interest was taken in these schools as long as they were separate. They did not have the best teachers nor did the better class of Negroes always send their children to them. In 1881, however, an act was passed abolishing the Negro public schools as such, and giving the Negro children the right to attend any public school to which they were eligible without regard to their color. This act opened newer opportunities to Negro children all over the State and stimulated an improvement of the schools which Negroes attended. It did not, however, break up the already existing Negro schools, nor was it intended to do so. It merely made it illegal to exclude a Negro child from a public school because of its color.

In 1900 there were 43,349 Negroes of school age in Pennsylvania, of whom 20,408 were males and 22,988 were females. During the census year 1900, 19,235 of these persons, or 44.7 per cent. attended school. The total school attendance for the year 1909 was 19,573—9307 males and 10,-265 females, distributed as to age as follows: Ninety-seven

under 5 years of age, 6898 from 5 to 9 years, 9227 from 10
to 14 years, 2610 from 15 to 20 years, and 241, 21 years and
over. Less than half of those of school age go to school because of the large number of boys and girls who stop to go to work
after they reach the age of 14 years. Of the 19,573 Negroes
attending school in 1900, 18,185, or 92.7 per cent. attended
school six months or more; 118 (58 boys and 60 girls), one
month or less; 254 boys and 250 girls from two to three
months; 816 (318 boys and 418 girls) from four to five
months.

Our statistics of illiteracy must not be taken for the
population at large, as showing anything as to capacity for
reading and writing. They show rather, the relative opportunity for learning. When, for instance, it is said that
the Negroes of Pennsylvania have an illiteracy less than
that of the Negroes of Mississippi, it does not mean that
they are any better or brighter than the Negroes of the
Southern States but merely that Pennsylvania gives educational advantages which Mississippi does not give.

With the improving of school opportunities the illiteracy of Negroes is steadily being cut down. In 1856 nearly
half of the adults of Philadelphia could not read or write;
in 1890 the percentage was reduced to 18 per cent., and in
1900 was about 11.8 per cent. The illiteracy of Pennsylvania is affected by the migration of adult Negroes from the
South. The illiteracy of the younger persons is quite
small; that of those from 10 to 16 years of age being only
2.5 per cent., and from 15 to 20 years of age, about 6.5 per
cent. Moreover the illiteracy of the Negroes compares
more than favorably with that of our foreign population.
The illiteracy of the foreign population of Pennsylvania is
increasing; that of the Negro is decreasing. In 1880 the
illiteracy of Pennsylvania's foreign population was 15.1 per

cent.; of Pennsylvania's Negroes, 27.1 per cent.; in 1890, the illiteracy of the foreign-born was 17.8 per cent.; and that of the Negro 17.8 per cent.; in 1900, the illiteracy of Pennsylvania's foreign-born population was 19.9 per cent., while that of the Negroes of the State was 15.1 per cent. The Negro and foreign population are compared as to illiteracy in the following table taken from the United States Census of 1900:

ILLITERACY OF NEGROES AND FOREIGN WHITES IN PENNSYLVANIA BY AGE PERIODS. 1900

Age Periods	Negroes			Foreign Whites		
	Population	Illiterates	Percent	Population	Illiterates	Percent
10 to 14 years.............	12,037	299	2.5	31,393	2,643	8.4
15 to 24 years.............	35,619	2,648	7.4	157,410	30,969	19.6
25 to 34 years.............	35,262	4,074	11.8	242,982	56,740	23.3
35 to 44 years.............	22,787	4,290	18.8	207,148	42,997	20.8
10 to 44 years and over	105,787	11,111	10.7	638,933	133,349	20.9
Unknown	786	269	34.2	2,538	801	31.6
45 years and over.......	22,444	7,952	35.4	321,118	57,556	17.9
Total over 10 years.....	128,945	19,532	15.1	962,589	191,706	19.9

The illiteracy of the foreign immigrants is higher than that of the Negroes at every age period. Negro children from 10 to 14 years of age, have among them only 2.5 per cent. of illiterates, while foreign children of the same age have more than three times as large a percentage of illiterates, 8.4 per cent. From 15 to 24 years of age the illiteracy of the foreigner is more than twice as great as that of the Negro, being 19.9 per cent., as against 7.4 per cent. From 25 to 34, the per cent. of the illiteracy of the foreigner is 23.3 per cent., just twice the percentage of the Negro at that age period, 11.8 per cent.; from 35 to 44 years of age, the illiteracy of the Negroes is 18.8 per cent., and that of the foreign-born is 20.8 per cent. The younger generation of Negroes who were born since the close of the Civil War, varying in age from 10 to 44 years, inclusive, have among them about one-half the percentage of the illiterates as have the foreign immigrants of the same age. But among the older generation of Negroes, born prior to the Civil War, there are proportionately more illiterates than among the foreigners of the same age. In the State there were in 1900 191,706 foreigners and 19,532 Negroes who could not read and write their names; there were 133,349 illiterate foreigners and 11,311 illiterate Negroes under 45 years of age. In all there were ten illiterate foreigners to one illiterate Negro; and twelve illiterate foreigners between the ages of 10 and 45, to one illiterate Negro of that age. The rapid decrease of the illiteracy of the Negroes is due to the superior educational advantages which they have in the State of Pennsylvania as compared with the South. A very important factor also is the compulsory educational law, which, though not rigidly enough enforced in the large cities, is a great advantage to the child whose parents are indifferent as to education.

Inquiry was instituted among forty-four colleges in the State to find out just to what extent they had been of influence upon the life of the Pennsylvania Negroes. One of these, Lincoln University was established especially for Negroes. Of the remaining forty-three, Negroes had attended but few, mainly the University of Pennsylvania, the Western University of Pennsylvania, Temple College, Allegheny College at Meadville, Dickinson College at Carisle, Washington and Jefferson College at Washington. Sixteen of the colleges which answered inquiries said that they had never had any Negro students whatever. Two religious institutions replied that they would not receive Negro students, one saying: "The Moravian Seminary is exclusively for **white** young ladies;" the other, St. Vincent's College, Beatty, Pennsylvania: "We would not take any Negro students now." The secretary of the Westminster College, New Wilmington, after stating that no Negro had

9

ever entered, adds: "It has been the policy of our church to make Knoxville (Tennessee) College our denominational center for Negro education." Of those which had had Negro students, the following replies were received: From Beaver College, "We have never had any Negroes in our college with the exception of a very few in the music department, who were always good students; none ever graduated here." From the Moravian College and Theological Seminary, Bethlehem, "We once had a mulatto, J. C. Moore, son of a missionary from Demarara, South America, who came to us from the college at Georgetown, Demarara; he spent four years here (1896-1900), taking a two years' theological course, and showing fair ability." Susquehanna University, Selinsgrove, had one Negro from Africa about twenty-two years ago. Nothing more is said of him. Juniata College, Huntingdon, has enrolled only two Negroes—"a young man in the preparatory work, about ten years ago; and a young lady in the preparatory work, about three years ago." Nothing more is said of them. The secretary of Washington and Jefferson College, Washington, writes: "John C. Asbury, through Freshman year, the best of all our colored students, studied law and practiced in Norfolk, Virginia, elected District Attorney; of Class of 1885." (Mr. Asbury is now editor of the Odd Fellows' Journal, with headquarters at Philadelphia.) Graduates: (1) F. J. LeMoyne Johnson, '94; M. D. University of Pennsylvania '97; died about 1900. (2) Frederick Douglass Johnson, 1901, M.D. (3) Welcome T. Jones, M.D., now practicing at Newport News, Va. A few others have been in college for a while."

Only one Negro has ever been a student of Lehigh, and he died about a year after entering. One student attended Lebanon Valley College, at Annville, graduating in 1902. He is Charles Alfred Tennyson Sumner, now a teacher in the Albert Academy, Freetown, West Africa, a mission school under the United Brethren in Christ. One Negro has graduated from Allegheny College, Meadville, in 1880. He is William Charles Jason, now president of the Delaware State College; he has since had the degrees of A.M. and D. D. conferred upon him. From Dickinson College, the following comes: "I know of but one Negro graduate, namely, Mr. J. R. P. Brock, 1901, who was of the Phi Beta Kappa rank, and a very excellent man; now teaching in Baltimore, Md." The dean of the College Department of Temple College, writes: "There have been Negro students in the school ever since it has been opened. We had one very bright student graduate from the Medical School last year. He passed successfully his State Board examination, and is now practicing in this city. His name is Joseph Paul Hudgins. G. Edward Dickerson, this city, graduated in 1901 from the Law School, and is, I believe, very successful. Miss Elaine Triggs will graduate from the Domestic Art Course in June, 1907; and Mr. J. T. Winder will complete the College Preparatory course, expecting to enter Harvard next fall. We have had a number of Negro students in our Theological School, but they have all, or nearly all, dropped by the wayside. There is a very exceptional student, a West Indian, taking the course at the present time. These that I have mentioned have all held their own with the very best white students." Geneva College, Beaver Falls, reports Negro students, stating, "We have Negro women every year. When in school we find that they do as well as whites." The Pennsylvania State College reported two students, but no graduates. No Negro women have ever applied for admission at Bryn Mawr. A graduate of the Central High School—Alain LeRoy Locke, of Philadelphia, won the Cecil Rhodes Scholarship to Ox-

ford University, England, in 1907. Mr. Locke graduated
from Harvard in the Class of 1907, winning the Bowdoin
prize. From the College and Engineering School of the
Western University of Pennsylvania, of Pittsburg, there
have been eight graduates. Two with the degree of A.B.,
B.S.; three with C.E.; and two with E.E. All of these students were beneficiaries of the Avery Scholarship Fund, established by Charles Avery. These scholarships were
twelve in number and provided for the payment of $100
upon the term bill of the beneficiaries (who must be colored males) in the College, or Engineering School. Of the
above graduates the Registrar writes: "Of the A.B.'s, one
is studying law, the other is editor of a newspaper, Charleston, W. Va. Of the engineers, I have no extended personal
knowledge. I believe, however, that they are all in positions of a character corresponding to the special nature of
their preparation. One of them has, I understand, done
some original work in the lines of perfecting railway sig-
nals. This is Mr. W. H. Damond, C.E., 1893, who at last
accounts was with the Michigan Central Railroad." At
present ten of the Avery scholarships are taken. Besides
these, there is one young woman in the College Department. From the professional schools, especially Medicine,
there have been a dozen or more graduates. The enrollment November, 1907, was 26, 11 in the College and Engineering School, 9 in the Medical School, 4 in the Pharma-
ceutical, and 2 in the Law School.

In 1907 Negroes were enrolled only in the following
Colleges: Allegheny College, Meadeville, which has two
Negro students; Geneva College, Beaver Falls; Pennsyl-
vania State College, Temple College, the University of
Pennsyvania, and the Western University of Pennsyl-
vania. The colleges of the State evidently have had but

small influence upon the Pennsylvania Negroes. Indeed, quite as many Negroes have attended and graduated from colleges outside of Pennsylvania, as from the colleges of their native State. Harvard University has had several Negro students from Pennsylvania, and three graduates; so had Oberlin College, and several smaller colleges.

More Negroes have graduated from the professional schools than from the colleges. Twenty-six have graduated from the Medical Department of the University of Pennsylvania. As a rule, these men have been successful. One Dr. S. P. Lloyd, of Savannah, Georgia, was appointed city physician of his native town, and was the first Negro in the South to hold such a position. Another, Dr. N. F. Mossell, established the Frederick Douglass Hospital in Philadelphia. There are at present five medical students, two from Pennsylvania; the others from the South. There have been five Negroes to graduate from the Legal Department, who are practicing in Philadelphia. Five Negroes are members of the Department of Veterinary Medicine, from which one Negro graduated in 1897. Two Negroes have been granted the degree of Doctor of Philosophy; one of whom is L. B. Moore, Dean of the Teachers' College of Howard University, of Washington, D. C., and the other, Rev. Pezavia O'Connell, District Superintendent of the M. E. Church in Maryland. Negroes have also graduated from the Jefferson Medical College, Hahnemann, and the Medico-Chirurgical College, Drexel Institute, the Pennsylvania School of Industrial Art, and have studied at the Academy of the Fine Arts. Henry O. Tanner, the Negro Artist, of Paris, France, studied at both the last named institutions, and is one of the most distinguished of the former students. Another of the former art students is Miss Vaux Warrick, the creator of a set of models of 150 characters representing the history of the Negro race in America, for which she was awarded a gold medal at the Jamestown Exposition.

Although the private primary schools have generally disappeared because of the public schools, there exists a half dozen private institutions for technical and secondary education, such as is given by the State only to a limited degree. The oldest and most prominent of these are: The Institute for Colored Youths, Cheyney; Lincoln University, Chester County; the Avery Institute, Pittsburg; the Berean Manual Training and Industrial School, Philadelphia; Downingtown Industrial School, and the Paoli School, Paoli.

The Institute for Colored Youths has held a unique place in the history of Pennsylvania Negroes, and especially those of Philadelphia. Richard Humphreys, who made his wealth from slaves, made the following provision in his will, dated February 18, 1829: "I give and bequeath unto my friends * * * the sum of ten thousand dollars * * * having for its object the benevolent design of instructing the descendants of the African race in school learning, in the various branches of the mechanic arts and trades, and in agriculture, in order to prepare, fit and qualify them to act as teachers." He died in 1832. This $10,000 was the nucleus for the Institute for Colored Youths. In 1837, the institute was founded and located in Philadelphia; in 1842 it was chartered by the State. In 1844, Jonothan Zane gave another large sum to the institute. From 1846 to 1851 not much was done except the conducting of a night school. In 1851 buildings were erected on Lombard Street, and from that time the influence of the institute began to be felt all over the city. Mr. Charles L. Reason, of New York, one of the best educated Negroes of his day, was made principal in 1852, but only remained till 1854, when he was succeeded by Professor Ebenezer Don Carlos Bassett, another Negro and a graduate of the New Britain, Connecticut, State Normal School. In 1868, Professor Bassett was succeeded by Miss Fanny M. Jackson, a graduate of the Rhode Island State Normal School, and also a Bachelor of Arts and Master of Arts of Oberlin College, Ohio. Miss Jackson, who became Mrs. L. J. Coppin in 1882, was the principal until 1902, a term of thirty-four years. During this period the chief work of the institution was literary and it attained a very creditable reputation throughout the North. All of the teachers were Negroes and included graduates from Oberlin College, Harvard College, Lincoln University, Wilberforce University, Yale College and other institutions. From 1856 to 1902, there were 412 graduates, of whom 71 are known to be deceased. Many cannot be located. The occupation of 156 of them are as follows: Teachers, 104; physicians, 11; dentists, 3; lawyers, 7; clergymen, 5; Government clerks (Washington), 6; Post Office clerks, (Philadelphia), 8; other clerical service, 5; real estate, 2; editors, 2; bookkeepers, 2; electrician, 1; architect 1; tailor, 1; undertaker, 1. The institute furnished a large number of Negro teachers to the South after the Civil War, and to-day many of the most prominent positions in New Jersey and Eastern Pennsylvania are held by its graduates and former students. It has furnished seven principals of Philadelphia public schools; three of whom are now serving, one of whom has taught more than forty years in the city. It has furnished eight principals in New Jersey, six of whom are now serving; one in Delaware, one in Washington, D. C., and several in smaller cities of Pennsylvania. Twenty-five of its graduates have taken higher courses at Lincoln University, Howard University, Univer-

in the country. It was very possibly inspired by the efforts of several Negroes, who desired to have higher training to fit themselves for the ministry. The actual organizer of the school, however, was the Rev. John W. Dickey, a Presbyterian clergyman, who had been giving a Mr. James R. Amos private lessons. In 1853, the New Castle Presbytery took steps to establish a school for the Christian education of the Negroes; and in 1854, Ashmun Institute secured its charter from the State of Pennsylvania. The school opened formally January 1, 1857. In 1866, the name of the Institution was changed from Ashmun Institute, to Lincoln University, Chester County, Pennsylvania. The departments are the College and the Theological Seminary, the latter alone being under the control of the Presbyterian Church of America. The property consists of one hundred and thirty-two acres of land in lower Oxford Township, Chester County; 12 buildings, endowments and apparatus. The heating plant alone cost about $30,000. There are eleven "officers of instruction and government," all of whom are white. There are three additional instructors in the college department, who are also students. These are Negroes. During the year 1907-8 there were 94 students coming from twenty-three different States. The largest number from a single State was thirty-four, from Pennsylvania. The aims of the institution are thus set forth in the catalogue and announcement:

"The design of Lincoln University, as embodied in its character, is to provide intelligent Christian helpers for our Negro population, for Africans in their ancestral continent or scattered throughout the world. Every thousand laborers and mechanics and farmers need a pious, well educated devoted minister. Of the 10,000 educated ministers of the Gospel required to meet this necessity, not as many as 2,000 have been thus qualified by all the Churches to fulfill in part their duty toward the Negroes. Every fifty children need a com-

sity of Pennsylvania, Wilberforce University, Yale University and Hahnemann Medical College. One of its students studied very acceptably in Edinburgh University, Scotland. With a more liberal attitude toward the Negroes and better opportunities in the public schools the special work of the Institute in the city was thought by the Board of Management to have been complete and in 1903 the school was reorganized and removed to Cheyney, about twenty miles from Philadelphia. Here on a tract of 117 acres, several buildings were erected and instruction is given in normal school work, domestic science, mechanical arts, including cooking, sewing, dressmaking, millinery, raffia work, carpentry and woodwork, forging and blacksmithing, together with mechanical drawing necessary to these operations.

Rev. Charles Avery, a merchant minister, of New York and Pittsburg, was one of the most practical friends of the Negroes before the war. Besides contributing generously to the poor, he left large endowments to their churches, and for their churches, and for their uplift, both in Africa and America. He gave $25,000 as an endowment for a school for Negroes, which was established in 1849, and known as Avery College. Its charter gives the right to confer degrees. The school held a prominent place in the early history of Allegheny County but with the development of the free public school system of later years, it has been of less influence in purely literary work and devoted its attention more to industrial work. The course includes ordinary English branches, dressmaking, millinery, cooking, laundering, table waiting, bookkeeping for girls and tailoring for boys. Carpentering, bricklaying and other mechanical trades were taught but have been suspended. The enrollment rarely reaches 100 pupils. The principal is a Negro, and the teachers are of both races.

Lincoln University is one of the largest Negro colleges

petent, conscientious teacher. The highest skill in trades and other manual industries will not alone qualify and one to be a preacher to a congregation of sinners, or to be the pastor of a flock of believers, or to be a teacher of a community of youth in the moralities of life. Lincoln University is pledged by its charter and by the trusts which it has accepted, to apply all its resources hitherto received to promote this higher education of the man in the mechanic, of the family in the community and of the immortal in this present life."

"The higher Christian education of the Negro is one of his highest necessities. He must have the higher education because he is a man having the high dignity of being made in the image of God. His higher wants and their supply cannot be deferred to his physical needs without peril to his spiritual nature. Manual industry is not in itself a prelude to religion. Skilled workmen are not thereby Christians. Industry is God's law; but it must be sanctified to be a blessing. We are reconciled to work because it is God's ordinance, and He makes it a blessing to all who keep His law of six days' work, and Sabbath change from manual labor to religious work. The only way to make education Christian is to teach the Christian religion to the student. This is the natural duty of the parents. But when the parents are incompetent through ignorance, or are prevented by the necessity of protracted and exhausting toil, it is the province and duty of the Church to lend a helping and guiding hand."

Lincoln University has sent its students into nearly every State in the Union where they have done and are doing effective service largely as ministers, teachers and physicians. In Philadelphia more than a score of professional men were graduates from this institution.

The Berean Manual Training and Industrial School, Philadelphia, grew out of the work of the Rev. Matthew Anderson, as pastor of the Berean Presbyterian Church. It was organized in 1899, opened in February, 1900, and has been operated principally as a night school. It was incorporated in 1904, and since then has been a distinct institution from the church. Beginning with less than fifty pupils, its enrollment was more than two hundred during the past year. The branches taught are English, mathematics, penmanship, shorthand and typewriting, bookkeeping, dressmaking, cooking, millinery, housekeeping, carpentry, bricklaying, architectural and mechanical drawing, practical work in electricity and printing. The teachers are mainly Negroes. The pupils are generally young men and women, who during the day earn their own living at manual work. The last legislature made an appropriation to this school. Its chief support is from voluntary contributions.

The Downingtown Industrial School, Downingtown, is a new institution, started in 1905, and grew out of the work of the Rev. Dr. William A. Creditt, pastor of the First African (Cherry Memorial) Baptist Church, and its purpose is to meet the increasing need of Negro youth for industrial as well as literary training. It also acts as a preparatory school for Lincoln University. The enrollment for the year 1906-7 was 65. Its largest building, Pennsylvania Hall, was erected entirely by Negro mechanics. A full industrial course is to be offered. The teachers are all Negroes. The chief source of income is voluntary contributions. There is no endowment. The state legislature has made appropriations to aid this institution.

CRIME AMONG NEGROES.

It is important that a careful and somewhat detailed study of the subject of crime among Negroes be made. A consideration of some of the fundamental facts of criminalogy may serve for a proper introduction to the subject; for the same principles which enter into crime in general, must be active in crimes of Negroes.

A crime is an infraction of any legal enactment whose purpose is to preserve peace, common order and decency, as interpreted by the social group. There is no absolute uniformity as to what constitutes a crime in all countries, or all parts of the country. It is a crime in Georgia punishable by a heavy fine and imprisonment, for Negroes and whites to marry; but it is no crime in Pennsylvania and New York. It is a crime in Pennsylvania to employ a child under the age of fourteen years but it is not in Mississippi. Furthermore, as it is true what constitutes a crime is not uniform, it is also apparent that the mere number of crimes committed, does not represent with any accuracy the moral status, or even the criminality of a people. For in a complex community it is harder to escape crime, than in a simple community. In judging criminality, the environment must be considered as to complexity. The criminality of one community, other things being equal, is to the criminality of another about as the proportion between the possible crimes and actual crimes.

In popular writings, concerning the crimes of Negroes, the number of arrests has often been taken as the measure of crime. But arrests do not give an accurate picture of crime and especially for comparing one group with another. Hundreds of persons are annualy arrested who have not committed any crime whatsoever, and hundreds escape who have committed crimes. It is better to compare convictions, although absolute accuracy cannot be obtained even by this method; for since a large number of criminals are never arrested, they cannot be convicted; also some guilty ·persons, who are arrested, escape conviction. Even here, another serious error is possible. For it is conceivable that one place may be much more criminal than another though the latter has proportionately more convictions. In the first place, each arrest and conviction lessens the criminality. For example, when Philadelphia's "Tenderloin" was "wide open," it was conceded that there was much crime; liquor was sold freely on Sunday, and without license, bawdy houses flourished and prostitutes openly plied their trade in the streets; pick-pockets, sneak thieves, hold-up men and petty gamblers were practically undisturbed, and policy shops did a large business among the ignorant poor. There were fewer arrests and fewer convictions than at a later time when the laws were more rigidly enforced. But there may have been more, rather than less crime. When the city tried in the popular phrase to "close up" the resorts the actual amount of crime in the community was diminished, but the arrests and convictions for awhile increased. The real change was in the enforcing of the law against crime and not in the increase of crime; crime was really on the decrease. Only, therefore, when there is uniformity in the administration of executive and judicial machinery, both as to arrests and convictions, can either of these be taken as guides for comparison with any degree of accuracy.

But when there is uniform enforcement, the *mere* number of convictions would not mean much. An analysis of the offenses must be made. For general convenience, the division into petty offenses or misdemeanors and gross offenses or felonies, is used. It may be that a dozen petty offenses may not be as far reaching as one gross offense. If forty men are taken in a crap game, and sentenced to five days confinement in the county prison, there are forty arrested and forty convictions; but the amount of criminality represented is comparatively small. Crap shooting is not a very great crime. It affects few, if any more people than those engaged in it. Few fortunes are lost at it; few families suffer because of it and society is but little affected. On the other hand, a bank official may misuse the funds of his institution and be arrested and convicted. But he counts for only one. It is therefore clear that mere statistics of arrests and convictions, will here be misleading; for this last named criminal many have operated systematically for years, ruining many people, debauching society, as well as corrupting finance, causing public confidence to be shaken, with harm to himself, his own family and many other families. The actual bad moral influence of the forty crap shooters is not to be compared with that of the bank defalcator, but in statistics, it appears forty times as great, which of course is absurd. And of course if the banker is never arrested or escapes on a technicality, the absurdity is increased.

When it comes to comparison of crime among the Negroes with that of the larger community, there are even greater difficulties. First, there is the historical difficulty. Historically, Negroes have had to prove their innocence and not their prosecutors prove their guilt. Under the Laws of Slavery, T. R. R. Cobb, an eminent Southern jurist, wrote:

"Reasons of policy and necessity, so long as two races of men live together, the one as masters and the other as dependents and slaves, demand that to a certain extent, *all of the superior race shall exercise a controlling power over the inferior*. Hence, have arisen in the states, the various police and patrol regulations, giving to white persons other than the master, under certain circumstances, the right of controlling, and in some cases, correcting slaves."

Thus, in most of the Southern states, the police system was primarily for Negroes and not for whites. Another historical factor relates to the crimes for which Negroes can be arrested. Historically, any word of protest against a white man by a Negro was insolence or disorderly conduct; and it was a serious crime for a Negro to strike or "presume to strike" a white person; but a white man was simply exercising his right as a member of the "superior" caste in abusing the Negro, and could strike him with impunity, only some laws prohibited maiming and killing. A box of the ears was no crime when given by a white to a black, but the reverse was punishable by flogging. This was true by law or custom of every Southern state, and by law in many Northern States.

A further and most important historical factor is the credibility of witnesses. By law in most Southern States, and some Northern States, a Negro could not testify against a white man even for himself. In some cases several Negroes would not, to the contrary, be strong enough according to the law, to outweigh the testimony of one white person. It cannot be doubted that these historical factors have a very decided influence in the cases of Negroes in our courts to-day, even in the North, while the best observers agree that there is but little possibility of obtaining justice for a lone Negro against a white man in the South, except in rare cases. Then there is the condition of poverty. The crimes of the poor are generally their vices, which affect them more than the community; but the vices of the well-to-do are seldom termed criminal, unless they become of great social concern. A fashionable set may give a euchre or a bridge party and hundreds of dollars may change hands and women earn their "pin" money thereby; but no one disturbs them, unless they become too bold. The "drunks" of a fashionable club, or a student "lark" are sent home in cabs, undisturbed, while the poor man, who has to walk home, is often arrested. The shop-lifter of means, is too often merely a "kleptomaniac," while the poor woman is a thief. These facts should be considered when it is remembered that "drunks" and "disorderlies" and petty larcenies are chief causes for running up the statistics of arrests and convictions among the poor. Negroes of the cities, being largely among the poor, must be affected by the differences which poverty makes in these matters. *Then there is the matter of the trial after arrests. Even before justice, poverty suffers.*

Coming to the subject of criminality of Negroes in Pennsylvania, it is clear that nothing more than mere tendencies can be pointed out. For the available data are too meagre for anything else. There are no separate statistics of arrests, or convictions for Negroes in the state as a whole. The only statistics published for the state are those of prisoners in jails and penitentiaries. The city of Philadelphia published the number of Negroes arrested, but this is of little value, as no hint is given of the causes for the arrests. The city of Pittsburg publishes no statistics, not even the number of arrests of Negroes. With the data available it is impossible to reach any but tentative conclusions. The increase of arrests in Philadelphia may, however, be compared with the ratio of the increase in population, and if it is found that the arrests have increased more rapidly than the population, this may represent an increased tendency to criminality. On the other hand, if arrests have not increased as rapidly as the population, the opposite tendency may be noted. For this comparison, the number of arrests in Philadelphia from 1864 to 1907 is available from the report of the police department, and the increase of population is shown by the census. The following table exhibits the comparison:

TABLE SHOWING THE ARRESTS OF NEGROES, FROM 1860, AND THE NEGRO POPULATION, AND PER-CENTAGE OF INCREASE OF EACH.

Year.	Population.	Number of Arrests.	Per Cent. of Population	P.C. of Inc. Arrests.
1860	22,185	....	....	....
1864	......	3,422	....	....
1865	......	2,722	....	....
1869	......	3,907	....	....
1870	22,147	2,070	1.7*	39.5*
1873	......	1,380	....	....
1874	......	1,257	....	....
1875	......	1,539	....	....
1877	......	2,524	....	....
1879	......	2,360	....	....
1880	31,699	2,204	43.1	6.6
1881	......	2,327	....	....
1882	......	2,183	....	....
1883	......	2,022	....	....
1884	......	2,134	....	....
1885	......	2,622	....	....
1887	......	3,256	....	....
1888	......	2,910	....	....
1890	39,371	3,167	24.2	43.7
1891	......	3,544	....	....
1892	......	3,431	....	....
1893	......	4,078	....	....
1894	......	4,905	....	....
1895	......	5,137	....	....
1896	......	5,302	....	....
1897	......	5,893	....	....
1898	......	5,806	....	....
1899	......	6,052	....	....
1900	62,613	6,531	59.0	106.2
1901	......	6,519	....	....
1902	......	6,711	....	....
1903	......	8,140	....	....
1904	......	7,811	....	....

(* Decrease.)

These figures do not show any regular increase from year to year. For instance, the arrests for 1864 were more than those for 1865, or any one of the years from 1870 to 1890. In 41 years from 1864 to 1904 inclusive, the increase in arrests

10

was 128.2 per cent.; from 1879 to 1904 inclusive, 277.3 per cent.; from 1880 to 1904, 254.4 per cent. In other words, the percentage of increase is more or less, according to the years taken. From 1864 to 1870, both arrests and population decreased; but arrests decreased 40 per cent. and population 1.7 per cent. From 1870 to 1880, the arrests increased 6.5 per cent.; but in the same time the Negro population increased 43.7 per cent. and the total population 24.2 per cent., while from 1890 to 1900 the arrests increased 106.2 per cent. and the population 59.0 per cent. These percentages, so far as arrests are concerned, are entirely due to accident. If the figures of one year are taken they are more; if another, less; from 1864 to 1869, arrests increased 14 per cent. but if we take the next year, it decreased 40 per cent.; or from 1900 to 1903, there was an increase of 23.1 per cent., while if we take the increase from 1900 to 1904, close scrutiny of these figures leads to the conclusion as far as there can be any conclusion, that the increase of crime among Negroes has not been as great as compared with the increase of the Negro population. Only when crime increases more rapidly than population, can it be said that the group or community is increasing in criminality.

In 1849, Edward Needles, reporting on the condition of Negroes as to crime in Philadelphia, published the following table showing the Negro prisoners received in the Eastern Penitentiary from 1829 to 1849, in periods of five years:

Years	Total received	Average per year
1829-1835	124	24.8
1835-1840	321	64.2
1840-1845	209	41.8
1845-1849	116	31.5
1849-1849x	115	26.75

The total number of Negroes received in the Eastern Penitentiary during 21 years reported by Mr. Needles, was 780, an average of 37.1 prisoners per year. For the past twenty-eight years from 1880 to 1907, the number of Negro prisoners admitted to the Eastern Penitentiary has been as follows:

Negro prisoners admitted to Eastern Penitentiary, 1880 to 1907:

Year	Total admitted	Year	Total admitted
1880	70	1895	109
1881	55	1896	126
1882	32	1897	69
1883	76	1898	80
1884	75	1899	103
1885	78	1900	84
1886	72	1901	83
1887	71	1902	128
1888	71	1903	99
1889	85	1904	134
1891	161	1905	87
1891	68	1906	120
1893	117		
1894	127		

Total admitted 2,517

The above figures of prisoners admitted to the Eastern Penitentiary, like the figures of arrests, cannot show conclusively the amount of criminality yet they do reflect a tendency. But as in the case of the statistics of arrests, so those of prisoners show no regular increase from year to year, but considerable fluctuation. There were fewer prisoners admitted to the Eastern Penitentiary during the year 1907, just closed, than the year 1897, ten years previous. There were fewer in 1906 than in 1896; fewer in 1905 than in 1895. There are twice as many in 1904 as in 1897, yet the very

next year, 1905, the number admitted falls off nearly 40 per
cent., only to rise again in 1906, and fall again in 1907, thus
showing how difficult it is to make a comparison. We may,
however, make a fair comparison by contrasting periods of
greater or less length. For this purpose, these figures of the
Eastern Penitentiary given above, may be compared with
those of the earlier period, given by Mr. Needles, on the
preceding page. During the period from 1829 to 1849, inclusive, according to Mr. Needles' report, 780 Negro prisoner-
ers were admitted to the Eastern Penitentiary, an average
of 37.1 per year. During the latter period, from 1880 to
1907 inclusive, 2,517 were admitted, an average of 89.9 per
year. The increase, therefore, of Negro prisoners admitted
to the Eastern Penitentiary during the latter period was
141.8 per cent., as compared with the earlier period. The
average population of Negroes of the state during the earlier
period was 46,626 (i. e., the population in 1830 was 38,333;
in 1840, 47,918; in 1850, 53,626) and during the latter period
was 116,659, (i. e., in 1880, 85,535; in 1890, 107,596; and in
1900, 156,845). The increase of the average Negro population in the later over the earlier period was 150.2 per cent.
By this test it appears that the number of prisoners increased
less rapidly than the population of Negroes.

The above comparison of arrests and prisoners admitted
to the penitentiary may justify the conclusion that the actual amount of crime among Negroes has increased more
rapidly than the Negro population. A fair and conservative
conclusion from the data present would be that crime among
Negroes as compared with the growth of the Negro population has relatively decreased.

Since no official statistics of the nature of crimes committed by Negroes are published in this state, a detailed study
of the police records of one section of Philadelphia is here

presented. The section chosen was the Nineteenth Police District of Philadelphia. This includes the Seventh Ward, which is the largest ward in the city so far as Negro population is concerned. It also includes more of the poorest and least efficient Negroes than any other ward in the city. Although only one-sixth of the Negroes live in this ward, nearly a third of the arrests are made within its bounds. The district, therefore, is not the most favorable to the Negro and will in no sense exaggerate the better side. During the year 1906, there were 2237 Negroes arrested in the Ninteenth District.

More than half of these arrests were on the five charges of disorderly conduct, breach of the peace, drunkenness, drunk and disorderly conduct, and shooting crap, for which arrests were as follows: Disorderly conduct, 428; breach of the peace, 275; drunk, 204; drunk and disorderly, 157; shooting crap, 86; making a total of 1150. Other arrests for offenses of a trivial nature were: 10 for acting suspiciously; 53 for corner lounging, and 8 for blocking cars, trespassing, and impersonating officers. Seventeen were arrested to be held as witnesses; nineteen for malicious mischief; while eighty-eight were arrested on suspicions of various kinds and one hundred and eight were arrested for being inmates of disorderly houses. The more serious causes of arrests were: 140 for larceny and 1 for murder; 1 for accessory to murder; 5 for burglary; 13 for highway robbery; 154 for assault and battery; 46 for aggravated assault and battery; 5 for rape; 1 for robbery; 1 for shooting man; 1 for immorality and neglect of children; 6 for fornication and bastardy; 40 for nonsupport; 58 were held for violating the liquor license law and 84 for keeping disorderly houses. About one-third of those arrested were held on serious charges.

A method of arrest practiced commonly among the poorer

districts known as the raid, is employed very effectively in the
19th District, for the suppression of liquor selling on Sunday, or without license, gambling and bawdy houses. The
parties who are caught in the house are generally taken to
the police station and entered, the paraphernalia seized, the
owner bound over to the grand jury and the inmates either
discharged or given light sentences. The first thing is for
the place suspected of violating the law, to be watched and
if possible, entered in order to get evidence. This is done
chiefly by the detectives of the Law and Order Society.
Having evidence, a warrant is sworn out for the owner or
operator. Not only is the operator taken, but all who are
found in the place. The number of arrests ranges from two
to more than thirty. This, of course, runs up the criminal
statistics of Negroes. For example, July 14, 1906, in the territory of the 19th District, eight raids were made, one result-
ing in the arrest of 46 persons. On the next Sunday in one
raid 34 persons were taken. The following is the record in
the police station:

1. July, 14, 1906, house at No. —— S. Camac Street,
raided; 5 men and two women taken; charge, selling liquor
on Sunday, and without license; the four "inmates" discharged, the keeper bound over to grand jury.

2. Same date, same charge, No. —— Jessup Street, 5
arrested, all women; sentence, 10 days imprisonment for
each.

3. Same date, same charge, No. —— S. Eleventh Street,
6 arrested, 4 women; sentence, all discharged except proprietor, who was held under bond.

4. Same date, same charge, No. —— Lombard Street,
15 arrested; all men, given 10 days in county prison.

5. Same date, same charge, No. —— Panama Street, 3
arrested, all women, all discharged except proprietor.

6. Same date, same charge, No. —— Pine Street, 3 arrested, all women, all discharged except proprietor.

7. Same date, charge, keeping bawdy house, No. —— Panama Street, 4 arrested; 3 women, all discharged except the proprietor.

8. Same date, charge, keeping house, No. —— S. Eleventh Street; 5 persons arrested, 3 women; all discharged except proprietor.

9. July 22, 1906, 1.45 A. M., No. —— Lombard Street, charge, shooting crap; 34 arrested, all men; given 10 days in county prison.

Of the 2237 Negroes arrested during 1906, in the 19th District, at least 779, or 34.82 per cent., received no punishment whatever but were discharged after a preliminary hearing as shown in the table given. In the main, the cases were heard by the magistrate of the distirict and a large majority settled by him. Persons who were drunk were kept until they were sobered up, usually over night, and then discharged. Of the 204 drunks, 169 were discharged and only 35 were held. Some were sent for a few days to the county prison and others to the hospital rather than to jail. Next to drunkenness comes disorderly conduct in the matter of light punishment; of the 428 who were arrested on this charge, 249 were discharged; most of the remaining 179 who were not discharged at the magistrates' hearing were sentenced to 5, 10, 15 or 30 days in the county prison; 3 months, 6 months and as high as 1 year in the house of correction. For disorderly conduct, women as a rule were more harshly dealt with than men. Of the 275 arrested for "breach of peace," 131 were discharged. Some were bound over under $500 bond to keep the peace, and others were incarcerated for from 10 days to 1 year. Many of the cases of breach of peace were husbands and wives, who presumably had some trouble among themselves. They were sometimes discharged, sometimes one sentenced and the other discharged, often both sentenced. "Idle and disorderly characters" and vagrants, the first chiefly women, and the second men, received sentences from 10 days to 2 years in the county prison or house of correction. The keepers of gambling houses, bawdy houses and houses of ill fame, were bound over under bond of from $600 to $800. Of the 117 inmates of these places, 36 were discharged and most of the others were given from 5 to 30 days or 3 months in the county prison or house of correction. Street loungers received generally from 10 to 20 days imprisonment; crap shooters, 10 days and other minor offences about the same.

More than three-fourths of the cases were settled by the magistrate in the district. Most of the serious crimes which were not settled by the magistrate went to the grand jury. It has been impracticable to follow them through the higher courts. But many of those arrested on serious charges were released on preliminary hearing; 12 out of 140 arrests for larceny were discharged; 3 out of 13 for highway robbery; 29 out of 154 for assault and battery; 2 out of 46 for aggravated assault and battery; 1 out of 20 for receiving stolen goods. What proportion of the remainder were convicted it is impossible to ascertain. It is certain, however, that only a small proportion of them were sent to the penitentiary; for only 33 colored persons were received at the Eastern Penitentiary from the whole of Philadelphia County during the year 1906 and only 36 during the year 1907.

The table given above shows that in the Nineteenth District of Philadelphia of a total of 2237 persons arrested, 691 or 30.8 per cent. were females. Of the eighty-five charges, on which there were arrests, females were arrested on seventy-five charges. The chief charges on which women were arrested were as follows: Disorderly conduct, 152 arrests; breach of peace, 102; idle and disorderly characters, 70; drunk, 49; inmates of disorderly house, 45; drunk and disorderly, 41. On these six charges, 459, or about 66.4 per cent. of the arrests of females were made. Upon preliminary hearing, the major portion of these were dismissed or given a light sentence of thirty days or less. The more serious charges were: Selling liquor on Sundays without license, 35 arrests; assault and battery, 34 arrests; larceny, 31 arrests; keeping disorderly houses, 26 arrests; aggravated assault and battery, 8 arrests; 1 arrest for murder; 22 on suspicion of larceny; 8 for threatening; 10 for witnesses; 6 for street walking.

During the year 1907, no Negro females were admitted to the Eastern Penitentiary, but 9 were discharged, leaving 8 Negro females in the institution January 1, 1908. The number of Negro females admitted from 1880 to 1889 inclusive, was 55; from 1890 to 1899 inclusive, 60; from 1900 to 1907, inclusive, 35, a total of 150 Negro females in 28 years, an average of less than half a dozen per year.

In the reformatories of the state there were in September, 1904, 1,372 juvenile delinquents, of whom 1,137 were boys and 237 girls. During the year from September, 1903, to September 10th, 1904, 699 were admitted, of whom 428 were in the House of Refuge, at Glen Mills and Philadelphia, and 271 were at the Pennsylvania Reform School at Morganza, Washington County. In the latter institution were 42 colored children, 31 boys and 11 girls. In the former there were 12 colored girls and the number of colored boys is not given. The average for the year was 58 girls in both institutions and 78 boys in the Reform School.

Of the 136 Negro children reported during 1904, 26 had been in the reformatories before. About one-fifth of those re-admitted were absent less than three months; 29, from three to six months; 27, from six to twelve months; 1 from one to two years; 15, from two to three years and 5 from three to four years and over.

Of the 568 children committed, five were nine years of age; 23 between nine and eleven years; 81 between eleven and twelve; 221 between thirteen and fifteen years; 235 between fifteen and twenty years and three over twenty years of age. Of the eight Negro girls committed to the House of Refuge, only one had both parents living; of thirteen boys committed to the Reform School, the parents of four were living, while of seven girls three had both parents living; while of the 48 white girls in the same House of Refuge, 24 had parents living and of the 37 to the Reform School, 30 had parents living and of the 109 boys in the latter institution, 55 had both parents living. Hence, it appears that the lack of parental oversight must be a great factor since it is not the children with the homes as much as those without homes who fall into crime.

The percentage of illiterates is much larger for the Negro children who go to the reformatories than for the white children. Sixty out of 540, 11.1 per cent. of the white boys and girls were illiterate; while six out of 28, or 21.4 per cent. of the colored were wholly illiterate.

The offenses for which Negro children are committed are simple as compared with those of the white children. Incorrigibility is the chief charge against the Negro children, and larceny the second. Other charges against Negro children were: assault and battery, delinquency and vagrancy. Half of the Negro girls entered in the House of Refuge were entered for larceny, while only about one-fourth of the white girls were entered on this charge. Forty per cent. of the Negro children entered in the Reform School were entered for larceny, while less than 34 per cent. of the whites were entered on this charge; all of which reflects not a racial but the low economic position of the Negro family and the neglected condition of many Negro children.

The lack of parental oversight over Negro children is a most potent cause of juvenile delinquency and crime and is but faintly reflected in the cases which come before the juvenile courts. Many children are left with friends and relatives, many do not have any care-taker whatever. In the slums of Philadelphia one may daily meet children who do not know their parents. Next to having no parents comes the work of women, as a cause of juvenile delinquency. It cannot be denied that the presence of the mother in the home when the child comes home from school, is a deterrent from temptation. Yet as has been shown, a large porportion of the women must work. And when they have a family, they must still keep at it. Thus it often happens that children are left in idleness and temptation. In one of the schools of the Seventh Ward, 41 out of 210 children in the first and second grades averaging in age between seven and eight years, or 19.5 per cent. of the total were reported as having mothers but no fathers; 24 children, or 11.4 per cent., as having fathers but no mothers. Only 133 children or less than two-thirds of the whole number had both parents living. Of the 174 children who had mothers, 114 or 65 per cent, were left by their mothers early in the morning, and on their return home found them away, as they were working out. In other words, in this school, 150 children out of 210 had no motherly care during the day, and all these children are under nine years, of age. Of the children in the higher grades, 3rd and 4th, a still larger proportion had neither fathers or mothers and were without parental care after school hours. In a Germantown school a count was made of 108 pupils in all grades. Nineteen had no mother; 22 had no father. Of the 89 who had mothers, 46 of the mothers were working out, having to leave home before school hours and return after school dismissed to find their children in the streets; that is, in this school 64 out of 108 children, or 59 per cent., had no maternal oversight during the day.

It is extremely difficult to compare the crime of Negroes with that of whites, because of the considerations previously given. If the statistics of arrests alone were taken, it appears that the Negroes furnish twice as large a number of arrests as they ought in proportion to the population. The Negroes are about 5 per cent. of the population and furnished during the past eight years, 1900-1907, 10.4 per cent. of the arrests. But it has been seen that arrests alone mean very little in comparing criminality of different groups. The following table shows arrests in the city of Philadelphia from 1860 to 1907 inclusive:

TOTAL ARRESTS, AND ARRESTS OF NEGROES COMPARED WITH GROWTH OF POPULATION.

Year.	Population.		Arrests		Negro Population.	Per cent, Arrests.
	Total.	Negro.	Total.	Negro.		
1860	525,329	22,185	......	.....	3.9	...
1864	......	.....	34,221	3,114	...	9.1
1865	......	.....	43,226	2,722	...	6.3
1870	674,022	22,147	31,717	2,070	3.3	6.5
1875	......	.....	34,553	1,539	...	4.5
1880	847,170	31,699	44,097	2,204	3.7	5.0
1885	......	.....	51,418	2,662	...	5.1
1890	1,046,964	39,371	49,148	3,167	3.8	6.4
1895	......	.....	60,347	5,137	...	8.5
1896	......	.....	50,072	5,302	...	9.1
1897	......	.....	62,628	5,893	...	...
1898	......	.....	62,907	5,806	...	...

Year.	Population. Total.	Negro.	Arrests. Total.	Negro.	Negro. Population.	Percent. Arrests.
1899	......	......	62,075	6,052	...	...
1900	1,293,697	62,613	65,360	6,531	4.8	9.9
1901	......	......	61,189	6,519	...	...
1902	......	......	65,468	6,711	..	...
1903	......	......	75,699	8,140	..	...
1904	......	......	73,061	7,811	..	...
1905	......	......	80,875	8,404	...	...
1906	......	......	83,325	8,733	...	...
1907	......	......	85,863	8,904	...	...

While the number of arrests of Negroes is far greater in proportion to the population than the arrests of whites, it is no greater than it was forty years ago. Immediately after the Civil War there was a comparative decrease in Negro arrests, but during the past three decades, there has been an increase so that now, the proportion between Negro arrests and white arrests as compared with the population is about the same as it was at the beginning of the Civil War.

In the foregoing discussion it has been pointed out that, in proportion to the growth of population, crime is not greatly increasing among Negroes, if increasing at all. In comparison with the white population so far as the proportion between the increase of crime and the increase of the population is concerned, the blacks hardly show any greater tendency to crime than they have always shown. But although there is no greater increase than is evident among the white portion of our population, there is about twice as large a proportion of Negro arrests and imprisonments as of whites. But this condition is not new; it has existed for a century, not only in Pennsylvania, but in the country generally, the Negroes appear to have a larger proportion of arrests and prisoners than whites. The question therefore naturally arises, "Why is there a larger proportion of the Negroes than whites arrested and imprisoned?" Some light may be thrown upon this by the comparison of arrests in the Nineteenth District. Here there was but little difference between the number of arrests of Negroes and whites, who lived in close touch with one another and under somewhat similar circumstances. There does not seem to be anything of a special racial characteristic which makes for excessive criminality among Negroes. The excess of criminality merely indicates what the excess of illiteracy indicates, namely, a lower social efficiency. Compared with the whites of their economic group, there is but little difference.

The Negroes of the higher economic group very rarely are among the criminals or have to appear in court because of criminal prosecution directed against them. They are not the college and high school graduates, the professional and business men who are among the Negroes arrested. These are, with very rare exceptions, peaceable, law-abiding citizens. The criminal Negroes come from a very different group altogether.

The most numerous and serious crimes committed by Negroes are stealing, fighting and disorderly conduct, which are characteristic of those of low intelligence and of low economic status. Those who steal, do so largely because they want things and have not the ability or the opportunity to satisfy these wants by honest labor. Many are honest, but being shut out by the lack of opportunity or efficiency, they acquire habits of dishonesty and disinclination to work. Those who keep "speak easies" do so for the money they get, which in many cases they are unable to earn. They frequently have the protection and active aid of the political boss, who is generally a white man. Fighting is everywhere the unintelligent man's way of settling a dispute and is resorted to quite frequently by the Negro who has not yet learned the lesson of self-control or the value of arbitration.

The sudden congregating of many Negroes in the large cities like Pittsburg and Philadelphia, where they cannot be easily detected and where they can frequently secure protection from the police, tends also to the increase of crime among them. In the large cities opportunities for crime are often many times greater than in the small towns and rural districts from which most of the Negroes come, while lack of home, church and other social restraints, doubtless cause some to fall into crime who might have lived normal, self-respecting lives had they remained in the smaller, simpler environments.

POVERTY AMONG NEGROES.

There are but few property holders among Negroes and the amount of property owned is small in comparison with the total valuation of property in the state. Judged from the standard of luxury, 90 per cent. of the Negroes would be in a condition of poverty; but if the standard be lowered to the necessities for the maintenance of a normal standard of living—allowing just enough to prevent physical deterioration, because of the lack of good food and sufficient clothing and other things absolutely necessary for economic efficiency—fully forty per cent. of the Negroes would be classed as poor. According to Prof. DuBois' study of Philadelphia, 8.9 per cent. of the persons of the Seventh Ward were in the class of the "very poor;" 9.6 per cent. were "poor" and 47.8 per cent. were "fair."

Among the poor, women are the chief workers, because there is more steady demand, and a smaller supply of house-

hold workers, washer-women, cleaners, etc., than there is
of the kind of unskilled labor generally done by the men.
Moreover, women who are employed chiefly within doors,
work in bad weather as well as in good, while men work
largely out of doors and must be "laid off" in unfavorable
weather. As has been seen the Negro men are concentrated
in the occupations which pay the least. They are almost entirely shut out of the skilled trades and the higher branches
of labor. A cessation of labor for two weeks or a month
often means that outside charity must help or that crime must
be resorted to, in order to make up the deficit, or the family
sinks into almost hopeless poverty.

Then there is the other economic handicap; poverty
causes its own perpetuation. The Negroes were slaves and
as such, owned but little, and had no large experience in self-
direction or in independent initiative. When they were freed,
they were left poor. Like the poor everywhere, they have
to pay higher prices than the well-to-do pay for what they
get. It is no common thing for Negroes to pay $2 and
$2.50 per week for an unclean, poorly lighted, poorly ven-
tilated and otherwise unsanitary room and $3 to $3.50 per
week for two rooms of this same description. In such cases
the annual rental is from 20 to 40 per cent. of the assessed
value of the property. In Philadelphia, for instance, among
the many examples of the excessive rents paid by the poor,
is a house in a narrow twelve foot alley in which the better
circumstanced people put their garbage, which is assessed
at $1,000. It is a dilapidated brick building, with no modern
conveniences and has six rooms. This house is rented to
from three to six families and brings as high as $32 per
month, a yearly rental of $384. It is occupied by poor
Negroes who seek out a living by unskilled labor and domestic

service. Every three years, they pay more than the assessed value of the house. The rent which the poor pay seldom decreases. As their number increases, their rent goes up. As these old buildings are torn down for newer ones for business purposes, the demand for the remaining shacks is greater and the rent is raised—and rent must be paid.

Next to rent, comes the price of food and fuel. In proportion to what they get, the poor pay enormously high prices for these necessities, and are thus kept poor. They buy their coal in most cases by the bucket, and they pay one hundred per cent. more than the better circumstanced person who buys by the ton. They buy five cents worth of flour or meat; three cents worth of sugar; they take their lamps to the shop and have them filled for a few pennies at the time, but paying an exorbitant price for the same. Not only do they pay proportionately high prices for what they purchase, but they are ignorant of how to use to the best advantage what they get. When they are temporarily prosperous, they are apt to be unduly extravagant, to waste their money on unnecessary and often unwholesome luxuries, only thenceforth to plunge themselves into deeper poverty. This often happens to those who buy furniture, clothes or pictures on the installment plan, always paying very high rates for what they receive. Thus with the Negro poor, as with the poor in general, poverty tends to perpetuate itself.

Sickness is another fruitful cause of poverty. But it is also often a result as well as a cause of poverty. Twenty-four and five-tenths per cent. of the applicants to the charity organization above referred to, gave sickness as the immediate cause of their having to ask for relief Professor Du-Bois' family budgets show that the poorest people pay the highest doctor's bill in proportion to their income. He gives

11

a family whose yearly expenditure was $121.50 and whose bill for sickness in proportion was $10 or 8 per cent. of the entire income; a family of two spent $206 for all purposes, $15 of which was for sickness; a family of four spent $338 and $40 for sickness; another family of four spent $520, but only $10 for sickness; a family of seven spent $683 of which $50 was for sickness and "one of the best families" consisting of five persons, spent only $5 for sickness. A conservative estimate places the number of Negroes who are sick during the year at 20,000 in Philadelphia, or about one-fourth of the entire population.

Not only does sickness mean the paying of doctor's bill, but also the loss of time from work and consequently of wages. An attempt has been made to estimate the Negroes' economic loss on account of sickness, using for the purpose the records of the University and the Frederick Douglass Hospital. From January to March 30, 1906, there were 85 Negro patients in the University Hospital who remained from 2 days, the shortest, to 64 the longest. The total length of confinement was 1,817 days, or about 21 days for each patient. There were thirty males and thirty-five females—persons whose average weekly wages was about $4.50 for women and about $9 for men, which means about $18.24 per person for the time lost.

In the Frederick Douglass Hospital (conducted by Negroes) the record for a longer time was taken and the average of confinement was longer.

Occupation, days confined and wages of patients in the Frederick Douglass Hospital, Philadelphia:

Females:

Occupation	No. patients	Days confined	Weekly wages	Total wages
Nurse	3	104	$4.50	$67.00
Domestic	41	1112	4.50	779.33
Maid	5	135	4.00	77.15
Housekeeper	11	315	3.00	135.00

Occupation	No. patients	Days confined	Weekly wages	Total wages
Chiropodist	1	39	7.00	39.00
Cook	3	142	5.00	101.45
Laborer	1	41	6.00	35.14
Laundress	2	46	5.00	32.85
Matron	1	14	5.00	10.00
Singer	1	18	7.00	18.00
Waitress	2	30	3.50	15.00
Atd. school	5	103		
Not given	2	56	3.00	24.00
Total	78	2255		$134.22

Males:

Occupation	No. patients	Days confined	Weekly wages	Total wages
Laborer	24	661	9.00	$850.50
Caterer	2	29	10.00	41.00
Waiter	6	129	10.00	184.30
Cook	2	36	10.00	51.40
Steward	2	99	12.00	169.68
Porter	6	192	10.00	174.30
Coachman	2	72	10.00	102.90
Elevator opr.	1	7	9.00	9.00
Newsboy	1	7	5.00	5.00
Marble dresser	1	7	12.00	12.00
Janitor	1	14	10.00	20.00
Barber	1	14	10.00	20.00
School	1	22		
Dentist	1	11	15.00	23.55
Not given	1	43	6.00	36.00
Total males	52	1343		$1800.13
Total patients	130	3598		$3144.35

According to this table, of the 130 persons confined in the hospital, 124 are workers. There were 78 females and 52 males. The total confinement of females was 2,255 days, of males 1,343 days. Calculating the wages according to current rates, the total loss in wages was $1,344.22 for females and $1,800.13 for males, a total of $3,144.35 and an average of $24.19 per person.

None of the cases reported in the hospitals was a consumptive who loses more time than the average sick person. On account of the prevalence of tuberculosis among the Negroes, it is safe to say that $500,000 is a low estimate of the loss of annual wages of Philadelphia Negroes on account of sickness and this tends to keep them poor.

The average age at death of whites of fifteen years or over was 53.4 years and of colored for the same time was 44.1, a difference of 9.3 years. This latter record is of much significance, as showing the length of possible economic activity of the races.

The census gave no complete record for Pennsylvania, the state as such not being in the registration area. But our calculations may not be far wrong if the average longevity of the Negro for the country is applied to the state. It is clear then, that if the average loss of the Negroes per person is 9.3 years and if the economic value of each year is, say $100, the average economic loss of each Negro is $930. If 2,000 Negroes die in a year in Pennsylvania, the annual economic loss is $1,860,000, which is equal to the annual interest at 5 per cent. on $37,200,000.

Notwithstanding the large amount of poverty among Negroes, they are by no means the chief contributors to the pauper class of the community. Long experience in stinting and in hereditary poverty, has taught the race "how

to get along" on a little, and though this is too often injurious both to themselves and to the society which makes it
necessary, it is the resort of the vast majority of the Negro
poor. Besides, there are also numerous benefit societies and
fraternal organizations, churches, clubs and friends who assist their needy fellows when necessity arises. Hence, as
compared with the foreign population, for instance, the Negroes show but a small amount of pauperism in the country
at large and in the state of Pennsylvania.

According to the report of the United States Census on
"Paupers in Almshouses" on December 31, 1903, there were
6.910 colored paupers, who comprised 12.1 per cent. of the
81,764 paupers of the entire country. In Pennsylvania there
were 361 colored paupers out of a total of 8,693 or 3.99 per
cent. There were 4,089 foreign born paupers, or 45.16 per
cent. There were 41.6 foreign white paupers in the Pennsylvania almshouses to every 10,000 white foreigners; while
there were 22.5 colored paupers to every 10,000 of the colored
population of the state. During 1904, there were 9,738
paupers admitted to almshouses in Pennsylvania of whom
583 were colored, 4,225 foreign whites; 4,877 native whites,
53 of unknown nativity.

During the same year, 8,550 paupers were discharged
from almshouses, of whom 515 were colored, and January 1, 1905, there were present in Pennsylvania almshouses, 9,513 white and 429 colored paupers, a total of 9942
paupers. As compared with conditions before the Civil War,
there is much evidence that the proportion of pauperism
among Negroes has decreased.

INTER-RACIAL CONTACT AND SOCIAL PROGRESS

The earliest relations of Negroes and whites in this state were as slaves and masters. Black servants were a distinct group from whites from the beginning, and public sentiment and law both tend to emphasize this separation. In 1700, laws were brought before the General Assembly looking toward separate criminal proceedings for the two races.

Negroes early awakened suspicion and were deprived of the privilege of carrying fire-arms, of congregating and of free movement on the Sabbath days. As early as 1714, a group of Quakers, who as a class, were always the best friends of the Negroes, passed a resolution to give the Negroes a burial place separate from the whites. Indeed, all through the period of their long and courageous activity on behalf of the Negroes, the Quakers always encouraged independent action among them, believing that such action, though separate from the whites, gave Negroes self-confidence and opportunity. Hence, they aided them in establishing separate places of worship, separate schools, separate beneficial societies, separate burying grounds, etc.

Negroes are almost entirely separate from whites in the church. They have been so for a century. The first separate Negro church was organized in Philadelphia in the eighteenth century, because the white Christians would not permit their black brethren to sit on the same floor with them, or to kneel at the same altar. Negroes had to sit in the gallery, or in some part of the church set apart for them, and were separated even at the communion altar. They naturally rebelled against this as being un-Christian and thus began separate Negro churches.

It is quite significant that perhaps there is no part of our social life where the races are so distinct as they are in the church, which in theory, at least, is the strongest advocate for fellowship and brotherhood. To-day the great mass of Negroes never enter a church where whites worship. Two-thirds of the Negro church members are Methodists and Baptists and have their own conferences and conventions, bishops and executive general officers, as well as their own pastors. They are therefore, outside of the influence of the whites. Only a few Episcopalians, Catholics, Presbyterians, and one group of Methodists have white supervision. The separation has done much to develop leadership among Negroes; it has also robbed both the Negro and the white church of a great deal of sympathy for one another, and consequent spiritual development.

Not only are the clergy of the common Christ in but little touch with one another but still less, the laity, so far as church affairs are concerned. The Episcopalian Church has an association which is supposed to bring together Negroes and whites, but so far as the local influence is concerned, it is but small. A few Negroes attend the churches of the whites, but the number is decreasing. Where they attend in large numbers, they are often advised to withdraw and form a separate church; where there are large numbers of children in the Sunday School, they are in separate classes or a separate school is formed. In Philadelphia several hundred Negroes are connected with one of the largest Episcopal Churches, as members of the church and pupils in the Sabbath School. In the church report of 1906, however, a separate Negro school building was recommended. Very few of the churches have white pastors. The Negroes prefer to have ministers of their own race and in no case does the white clergyman minister to a large Negro congregation.

Negro Methodist clergymen are further removed from the white clergy except in one branch. In the Methodist Episcopal Church, there is a separate conference, but the presiding bishop is white, and most of the general officers are also white. The annual conference is a part of the general conference which is composed of both whites and Negroes. The Baptists were, up to but a few years ago, members of the Baptist Association, which makes no distinction in color. But with the great increase of Negro Baptists, they have established separate bodies of their own. There is now a colored Baptist Association in Pennsylvania which is not associated with white Baptists. Both the Methodists and Baptists maintain in the larger places, Pittsburg and Philadelphia, separate ministers' meetings for the discussion of local topics.

The Episcopal churches are organized in the main, along racial lines, yet they are not supervised by Negroes. Some of the vestrymen in Episcopal churches are white and some Negro churches have White pastors. The church convocations include Negroes as well as whites. In the publication of the minutes of the General Assembly, the Negro ministers and churches are not named according to color. There is, however, among the Negro clergy of the state almost entirely unanimity with regard to the advisability of appointing separate Negro bishops for Negro dioceses in the South. In the Presbyterian Church, the Negroes as a rule, are separated from the whites in individual churches. The clergymen, however, are members of the same Presbyteries and Synods without distinction of color. Unlike the Episcopalians, the Presbyterian clergy opposed separate Presbyteries when the General Assembly several years ago sent the suggestion down

to the various Presbyteries to be voted upon.   In the Catholic
Churches there are no Negro clergymen in this state.   The
ministers of the Congregational Churches are all Negroes.

The contact of the races is closer in the schools than in
the churches. While a large percentage of the colored
children are segregated in the public schools, they are largely
taught by the white teachers and go to schools attended by
Negroes and whites alike. In many of the high schools and
colleges of the state, the races go side by side and there the
Negro boys and girls have the opportunity to compare themselves with their fairer schoolmates. In the schools, however, there have been two forces at work tending toward
separation. On the one hand, there is the positive desire of
a larger number of Negroes chiefly immigrants from the
South, for separate schools, such as they have been accustomed to in that section. More often this demand is
brought forth more forcibly because of the desire to have
Negro teachers. Of late years this spirit has had considerable
growth because of the increase of race prejudice in the
country causing many Negroes to doubt whether white
teachers can efficiently teach their children. On the other
hand there is the increasing unwillingness on the part of the
white parents to have their children go to the same school
with Negroes. This has increased almost in proportion to
the growth of population. It is also seen in the attitude of
the pupils. One very rarely sees Negro and white girls playing together at school, or coming together in the same group
from school. Though they may have the same recess, and
may be engaged in the same kind of play, they are generally
separated of their own accord. I am informed that there
are but few friendships between the Negro and the white

children in the schools as compared with former times. The awakening of the Negro's racial self-consciousness also keeps Negroes from forcing themselves upon whites, even among children, where there is the slightest hint that they are not wanted.

Equality in the privileges of common comforts and common carriers was at one time denied Negroes throughout the State. Indeed as late as 1865, Negroes were not permitted to ride in the street cars of Philadelphia and were often assaulted for attempting to board cars. A pamphlet entitled "Why Colored People are Excluded from Street Cars" published in 1866 gives a full account of these outrages. On one occasion a Negro was ejected by a policeman; the matter was complained of to the Mayor (Henry), who is reported to have said concerning the ejectment, "it was not by my order, but with my knowledge and approbation. I do not wish the ladies of my family to ride in cars with colored people." A bill to prevent this discrimination was passed by the State Senate, but never came to a vote in the House. Courts were importuned, but to no avail. A committee appointed to help obtain the privileges of the cars for Negroes in 1865, reported that it had "attempted to bring suits for assault in seven difrent cases of ejectment, all of which had been ignored by various grand juries." In one case, a white man, a highly respected physician, who interposed, by remonstrance only, to prevent the ejectment of a colored man, was himself ejected. He brought action for assault and his complaint was ignored. The last case of ejection, was that of a young woman, so light of color that she was mistaken for white and invited into a car of the Union Line by its conductor. When he found she was colored, he ejected her with violence and somewhat to her personal injury. This state of affairs did not last long. March 22, 1867, a bill was passed designed to give Negroes the same rights on railways as whites. Later. a bill to provide "Civil Rights for all People Regardless of Race or Color," was passed by the legislature to prevent any discrimination against Negroes in cars, hotels, restaurants, theatres and other public places of convenience and amusement. The law, however, did not cause discrimination to entirely disappear, for it still exists. In the street cars, on the railroads, and in some hotels and restaurants, Negroes have the same treatment as whites, but in most hotels and restaurants they do not. In the large cities, there are restaurants and hotels where it is known that Negroes will not be served. There are also theatres where Negroes have been refused seats in parts of the house in which they wished to sit. In this kind of discrimination, Pittsburg is worse than Philadelphia. As a rule, however, Negroes do not go to the places where they are not desired.

By common consent of both races, it appears that separate barber shops for Negroes and whites exist even in the smallest towns, no matter whether the proprietor is white or black. Negroes conduct barber shops for whites only, and in Pittsburg, a white man conducts a barber shop for Negroes only.

Under the law prohibiting discrimination on account of color, the numerous cases which have been brought, have usually turned out unsatisfactorily to the Negro complainant. There are two possible modes of procedure under the law for the offended Negro against the party discriminating. One is to sue for damages in the civil court and the other is to have the offender arrested for misdemeanor and tried before the criminal courts. The act provides for a fine of not less than $50, or more than $100. But neither of these have accomplished the purpose of the law. Where the proprietor is bent on violating the intent of the law, he is generally able to do so. For example, in some restaurants in Philadelphia, the Negro is merely ignored and when he complains the proprietor sim-

ply begs pardon and declares the matter an oversight. He
may then be served, but to save his own feelings he seldom
returns to that restaurant. In Pittsburg, however, the means
are often different. In the Pittsburg Dairy Lunch Room,
and other cheap restaurants and lunch places, where people
of moderate means go the waiters put a tablespoonful of salt
in the coffee, or a teaspoonful of pepper in the milk sold to a
Negro; or charge him 25c for a cup of coffee or a sandwich
which is usually sold for five cents. In some ice cream parlors
of the city, the same method is pursued. Still it has been very
difficult for Negroes to have the proprietors convicted. This
disposition to discriminate against Negroes has greatly increased within the last decade.

In lines of labor, as has been seen, with the exception of
the miners and hod-carriers, the great mass of Negroes are
without direct connection with the labor union movement and
most of them look upon the movement as antagonistic to their
best interests. But not only in labor union circles, is there
indifference toward Negro labor, but elsewhere. In very few
lines of work, do Negroes and whites work together, side by
side. In a department store all of the salesmen and sales-
women are white, while the elevator men and caretakers
may be colored. On a building, the bricklayers are generally
white, the hod-carriers may be Negroes. Even where there
is unskilled labor there is generally a separation, one gang
is composed of Italians, another of Negroes, as was the case
on the Philadelphia subway and other public works. Often,
to put a Negro, no matter how efficient he is, to work in a
group of whites, will mean violent protest or a strike. In asphalt laying and unskilled railroad work, however, it is common to see Negroes and whites working together, sometimes
under a Negro foreman.

Even in domestic service where there are two or more
employes, they are generally all white or all Negroes. In ho-

tels and resturants, waiters and bellmen are all white or all
black, except where there is a white head waiter, or white
head bellman or elevator starter, who has been placed as su-
pervisor over Negroes. In a few private establishments an
individual Negro here and there has worked himself up into
a place of responsibility and sometimes authority, where his
working associates are not of the race to which he belongs.
In one of the leading architectural establishments in Philadelphia, an exceptionally bright Negro is head draughtsman,
and in the office of the Vice President of a Steel Company in
Pittsburg, a Negro is private secretary, but cases like these
are rare. The great majority of Negroes work among men
of their own race or they are occupying menial positions.
They are, as a rule, shut out of competition by reasons of their
race. Just as the Christian Brotherhood does not seriously
include Negroes, so the labor fraternity does not include them.

As a rule, the business of Negroes is done by whites.
In this the Jews have a very large share. They live among
the Negroes, often until they can get a start, under worse
conditions than the Negroes, and sell to them. Negroes buy
groceries, shoes, clothing of all kinds chiefly from whites.
They rent chiefly from whites; they buy their land from
whites and have white men build their houses. But Negroes
are gradually getting control of a small proportion of the
business of their race and indications are that in some lines
a much larger proportion will be secured by them.

In philanthropic work for the Negro, many whites are
directly engaged. In Philadelphia, there are three social settlements: Starr Centre, on Lombard Street, founded in
1892; The Eighth Ward Settlement, on Locust Street, founded 1897; and the Spring Street Mission Settlement, on Spring
Street, founded in 1906; all of which are supported and
managed by white people and are doing valuable social work.
At the largest of these settlements, the Starr Centre, there

are many Jews and Italians, as well as Negroes, among the beneficiaries. In the Kindergarten at the Eighth Ward Social Settlement, there are Negro, Italian, Jewish, American white and Chinese children. Several other institutions for Negroes: day nurseries, Sunday Schools, missions, private schools, homes for children are supported entirely by whites. In Philadelphia, such helpful institutions as the House of the Holy Child, the Wissahickon Boys' Club, are conducted personally by whites. But all of these institutions have as their purpose the amelioration of conditions among Negroes and the contact is of benefactor and beneficiary and not of social equals.

Although the law against inter-marriage in Pennsylvania was repealed more than a century ago, there has been but little marriage between blacks and whites. According to the records of the city of Philadelphia, there were during the years, 1901, 1902, 1903, 1904 only 21 marriages of this kind. In 1900 there were six cases of inter-marriage out of 633 marriages. Three Negro men, aged 26, 35 and 40, respectively, married three white women, aged 26, 23 and 28, respectively; and three white men aged 26, 29 and 34 years, respectively, married three Negro women, aged 28, 33 years, and of unknown age, respectively. There were more inter-marriages when there were fewer Negroes than there are to-day. Of three white women above mentioned, one was born in the South (Virginia), one in Philadelphia, and one in Ireland; the white men were from Philadelphia, New Jersey and Wales. Professor Du Bois found 38 cases of inter-marriages in the Seventh Ward of Philadelphia and estimated 150 for the city. In Pittsburg the number is estimated at 50. In other places in the State where the Negro population is smaller, the actual counting is possible, there is an aggregate of less than sixty cases. The number of known cases is small. The so-called mixed marriages are not approved by either the white or Negro group. Negro women especially object. When, however, such marriages are consummated in spite of Negro public opinion, the couple is almost always ostracized by the Negroes. Perhaps there is no more pathetic injustice inflicted by Negroes than the cruel scorn and contempt which they show toward those who have chosen to marry "outside the race." In church, or society, there is very little opportunity for such persons and though no law prevents, there are very few persons who dare disregard this public opinion.

Though there is but little contact between the races at the top, there is but little to keep them apart in the lower world. In the lowest stratum, the blacks and whites meet in prostitution and vice. There are in the slums both of Pittsburg and Philadelphia, and to an extent, in the smaller cities, frequent cases of cohabitation chiefly of white women and Negro men, less frequently of white men and Negro women. It is impossible to give the number of cases. Now and then, they come up in the Police Court, such as the following cases copied from the records of the Nineteenth District Police Station:

1. August 6, 1906, for keeping disorderly house —— Rodman Street, John H. ——, James H——, both colored, aged 26 and 29 years, given 30 days in prison, and Mary ——, white, born in the United States, aged 39, married (not to either of the men above mentioned), six months in the House of Correction, and —— colored girl, aged 13, sent to House of Detention. One of the men was afterward tried for rape on the colored girl.

2. August 20, Mary W. ——, aged 27, colored, and Mary D. ——, aged 25, white, 12—— Pine Street; colored woman discharged, white woman given 15 months in House of Correction as "idle and disorderly character."

3. August 26, 3 A. M., at 15th and Pine Streets, Mary

B. ——, aged 25 years, colored, residence 16—— Lombard
Street, and L. P. T. ——, white, residence 8—— N. 42nd
Street, charged with disorderly conduct; discharged 7:30 A.
M.

4. September 13, Mary S. ——, colored, aged 36, re-
sisting officer, and selling liquor without license; Bessie W,
—— Mamie ——, Annie ——, colored, aged 21, 34, 34, all
single, inmates, 5 days in House of Correction, and Joseph
——, aged 21, white, inmate, sentenced 10 days in County
Prison.

One of the most interesting studies of the American
Race Problem is that of the Mulatto. This paragraph will
deal only with one phase of the mulatto question, which may
throw light on the economic aspects of the problem. There
are in both Pittsburg and Philadelphia a number of persons
with Negro blood in them, fair enough to pass as white persons. These are, as a rule, the sons and daughters of Southern white men and mulatto women, and in some cases of mulatto men and mulatto women. In their homes in another
part of the country they were known as Negroes. When they
migrated to the city, where they were entirely unknown and
where their racial identity would not be easily discovered,
they found themselves for the first time able to enter free
economic competition. In both of the large cities there are
Negroes of this class, who hold responsible positions, which
they would probably lose were it known that they were not
members of the white race. Every well informed Negro
knows of such cases, but there is but little disposition on the
part of any one to expose them, for nothing but harm can
come of it and most Negroes take the position that these persons are more white than colored anyway.

Now and then some one of these Negroes is discovered
and his race identity revealed. The result is, that he generally loses his position and is often therafter at an economic

disadvantage. Occasionally the conscience of these persons force them to reveal their race. It may be a dark colored mother, or wife or child, because of whom one fears to invite his white friends to visit his home, or it may be some other fear. But often the conscience of a Negro who is "passing for white" troubles him and he reveals his identity. Mr. Ray Stannard Baker mentions one such Philadelphia case, in his book, "Following the Color Line."

The Negro as a Negro is the victim of race prejudice. But we cannot take the time to add to the evidence of the existence of prejudice, but rather to point out some of the consequences. Race prejudice, wherever it manifests itself in any strong form, tends to lower the economic efficiency of the community. In Pennsylvania, as in Georgia, the Negroes being the weaker element in population, suffer more from it than the whites, although the whites suffer some, as does the body politic.

Pennsylvania has had her full quota of race riots. Frequent reference is made during the early colonial days to "tumultuous gatherings of Negroes." But there is no record during these times for any very serious outbreak among Negroes in the State, such for instance, as occurred in New York in 1712. The riotings in which Negroes have been involved, have been chiefly instigated by whites. These riots have had largely an economic basis. During the first half of the past century, while the free Negro population was increasing quite rapidly, it came into sharp competition with the foreign element. Both these groups competed for the unskilled work of the community and became natural enemies. The unrest among Negroes throughout the country and the organized attempt on the part of the American Colonization Society to discredit them, together with their poverty and the comparative paucity of their numbers, put them almost at the mercy of their assailants.

12

From 1829, until after the Civil War, these riots occurred at frequent intervals. The first of the more important of these, was during June and July, 1829, occasioned by a series of public addresses given in favor of the cause of abolition by a Scotch woman, Mrs. Fannie Wright Dartmont. During one of the last of these, in 1871, Octavius V. Catto, a very highly respected school teacher, was murdered by those who differed from him and the Negro politically.

Shut out from the society of whites, the Negroes are developing their own society, and without doubt the great mass of them prefer the society of their own group to the society of an outside group. In the cities, one can easily see the social divisions of Negroes. Their groupings are chiefly along the lines of culture and wealth. One finds a group of well educated men, largely in the professions and business, who are the recognized leaders of their people in social affairs. Then there is a group of skilled artisans, not so well educated but often as well off financially as the better schooled group; and next to them, the domestic servant group, the unskilled laborers and lowest of all, the casual worker and semicriminal. Between the lowest and highest of these groupings, there is but little social contact. Business and profession alone, carry the men of the highest to the men of the lowest; the women never meet except as benefactor and beneficiary in charity. And only of late years has it been possible to interest the best class of Negro women in active philanthropic work which took them among the lower element, because they feared they might be considered by the outside white world as members of the group they went to help. Still, these groups shade almost imperceptibly into one another.

Perhaps there is no better illustration of the differentiation which has taken place in Negro society, than the position of the coachman's ball, of Philadelphia. Thirty-five years ago, the chief function among Negroes was this ball.

To gain admission one had to be especially invited and to pay five dollars. To-day, the coachman's ball is public, and the admission fee is twenty-five cents, which indicates its decline in social importance.

The development of social organizations has gone on very rapidly during the past ten years. The chief organizations were formerly along the lines of vocations, Caterer's Social Club, Bellman's Social, Coachman's Social, etc. These still exist, but have less prominence than formerly. The larger clubs are along the line of higher thought. In Pittsburg, the Loendi Club is composed of men of different occupations. It is established as a center of friendly intercourse among men of some intellectual aspiration. The club owns a house costing $15,000. In Philadelphia, the Citizen's Club is a social political club which has recently bought property at $16,500. There are in Philadelphia more than fifty social clubs. Some of these are both social and beneficial. The chief ones of those and those having their own club rooms are the Citizen's Club, Hotel Brotherhood, Corinthian Club, Bellman's Club, Waiters' Club. There are also several literary and musical associations. Of these, the principal ones are the Philadelphia Concert Orchestra, consisting of forty-five pieces; the Mandolin Club; the Treble Clef Club; St. Peter Clavier's Orchestra; Hobb's Band and Wilmore's Band. The Philadelphia Concert Orchestra is the largest of these, and gives six concerts per season, always to large audiences. The chief literary association is the American Negro Historical Society, which has a large and valuable collection of books, pamphlets, papers, pictures, manuscripts and other records of the history of the Negro race. Other literary societies are the Aurora Reading Circle of Pittsburg, composed chiefly of ladies; the Phillis Wheatley Literary; the Paul Lawrence Dunbar and the J. C. Price Literary Societies of Philadelphia. There are several private circles for the study of literature and for the study of modern languages.

The Negroes have also developed something of a literature of their own.   As early as 1808, a Pennsylvania Negro
published a pamphlet.   Between that time and the Civil War
many pamphlets were published by men and women of the
race.   The most ambitious piece of work done before the
Emancipation, was that of Rector William Douglass, entitled,
"The Annals of St. Thomas' Episcopal Church," published in
1862.   There have been about fifty books and pamphlets published by Negroes of the State, the most important of which
have been poems by Mrs. F. E. W. Harper and James E. Mc-
Girt, the historical and theological works of Bishop B. T. Tanner and Bishop Levi J. Coppin.

The Negro race has been looked upon as objects of charity largely since the early settlement of Pennsylvania, but during this time the more fortunate have always assisted the less
fortunate.   In recent years there has been considerable development in charitable efforts.   The Home for the Aged and Infirm Colored People, which was founded in 1864 largely
through the beneficence of Stephen Smith, a Negro lumber
merchant and minister, now has property worth a quarter of
a million dollars.   More than a score of Negroes have contributed to this work.   The Board of Managers are both whites
and Negroes.   William Still, a Negro coal dealer, was once its
president.   The institution now accommodates one hundred
and forty inmates, and is one of the largest of its kind in the
country.   All of its officers and employees are Negroes.   In
Philadelphia is the Priscilla Home for Aged Colored Men and
Women, which was started in 1897 by women connected with
the Zion Baptist Church.   This institution is small yet and
without any endowment.   In Pittsburg is the Home for Aged
and Infirm Colored Women, which was started by Negro wom-
en in 1880; in 1890, a home was built which, with furnishings,
cost $52,900.   It has twenty-eight rooms, including six bath-
rooms and a large hospital room.   The Board of Managers, as

well as the salaried officials and employees are Negroes. In 1907, it received aid from the Pennsylvania Legislature. At Ruffsdale, an "Aged Minister's and Laymen's Home" was founded in 1902, principally through the efforts of Rev. R. C. Fox, a Baptist minister in Pittsburg. This is supported chiefly by the Baptists of Central and Western Pennsylvania. The Pennsylvania Grand Lodge of Masons have also purchased land for the erection of a home to be located near Harrisburg, for the aged of their race.

Next to the aged and infirm, come several institutions for young women, many of whom immigrate from the South to the State and are often without any family ties in the places to which they have come. The Young Women's Christian Association, a small institution, was established in 1902 in Philadelphia. The same year the Industrial School for Colored Girls was begun in Pittsburg. Like the Y. W. C. A., it still rents its house and is able to reach only a few, accommodating with room and board only eight or ten at the time but keeping in touch with a larger number who work at domestic service. The Association for the Protection of Colored Women was established in 1905, in Philadelphia. It furnishes a home for working women, having classes in domestic art, a working women's club, and an officer at the docks to meet the young women who come in from the South on the boats. This association is now buying its new home. There is a chain of these associations; one in Norfolk, one in Washington, one in New York, one in Boston, and one in Philadelphia, which is the national headquarters.

In Philadelphia, the Woman's Union Day Nursery, 707 South Nineteenth Street, is supported by colored women who are purchasing a house. The nursery has about thirty-five children a day. In Pittsburg a movement is now on foot among Negroes for a day nursery for Negro children, since no Negro children are admitted into the existing day nur-

series. The Federation of Colored Women's Clubs of the
State also is making an effort to establish an Orphan Home
for Negro Girls. The above institutions are the most important efforts of the Negroes to assist one another.

CONCLUSIONS.

It was not my intention at first to write any word of personal conclusion; but merely to describe the economic condition of Negroes in this State. But because the Negro has been
looked upon so long as a "problem," and is to-day largely
treated as such, it seems well to append a few practical conclusions. For after all, one who has taken special pains to
study a situation, ought to be able to present some conclusions
at least interesting, and not entirely without value.

A survey of the history of the Negro is a most fruitful
study, in that it shows the various changes in the problem of
the Negro and the difference in the attitudes of the various
people or groups of people approaching the problem at different times. Only after one has obtained knowledge of the history, is he fully competent to deal with present problems, and
then he is less certain than ever that any of the ordinary problems of life are particularly Negro problems.

There is always great difficulty in discussing any social
problem, and especially a race problem. The whole system of
education of every race is generally such as to inspire its children with belief in its superiority. The Greeks divided the
world into Greeks and barbarians; the Romans into Romans
and plebians; the Hebrews into Israelites—God's chosen people—and gentiles. Ask a German boy what is the greatest nation, and he says Germany, and the American boy, America.

Of course all cannot be absolutely correct. But each is correct from his own standpoint, for the superiority of his race has always been impressed upon him.

Trained to believe one thing, it is very difficult for men to be fair when they deal with racial and national differences. This is especially difficult in the case of the judgments of a stronger people with regard to a weaker.

In dealing with the Negro it is difficult for the community as a whole to do the race justice. The old instinct in all of us which prompts us to magnify the evil and minimize the good of a group, different from ours, affects the Negro in all walks of life. White men do not associate with the best Negroes; they rarely enter their homes; they are excluded from their social circles; they cannot become members of their secret societies; they do not become members of their churches; they are seldom business partners and they cannot know the inside life of the higher group of Negroes. On the other hand, they are often benefactors of the poorer Negroes; they meet the criminal Negro in the court, the pauper at the poorhouse; they have the servant in their kitchen, and they read the newspapers in which are sensational reports of Negro crimes, written by reporters, most of them who never saw the inside of the homes of the well-to-do Negro.

It is not an exaggeration to state that the community as a whole, is ignorant of the real life of Negroes. It is a very rare thing to find a white man who rightly interprets the facts which have come to him regarding Negro life. It is difficult for trained investigators to secure accurate information, especially, if these investigators be white. Time was when a Negro would, for the mere asking, or in order to secure sympathy, reveal his life to the Northern white man; but that time has passed in Pennsylvania at least, and they are few and fortunate indeed to whom the Negro, intelligent or ignorant, will reveal his soul.

Yet, in spite of this difficulty in securing reliable information, and the greater difficulty in interpreting the same, it is quite common to find men and women with decided views as to the Negro's capacity, his rights, his limitations, his suffrage and all questions bearing on the race. The basis of their conclusions is often some isolated incident. One man believes Negroes all ought to be chiefly domestics, because he has a good Negro domestic; another says Negro domestics are degenerating, because he has one or two incompetent servants. Another says Negroes are corrupting politics because he has bought some few Negro votes, or knows some white men who have done so. Another says the Negroes are mentally deficient, because he has happened to come across two or three feeble-minded Negro children. A very interesting case was brought to the writer's attention by a highly honored citizen of Philadelphia. A Negro boy who had been very backward in his studies, was brought to his attention. He had the boy examined by one of the leading psychological specialists in the country. This eminent gentleman said that the deficiency was entirely racial. Not being satisfied, my friend sent the boy to another special school presided over by another specialist. The latter said that the boy's mind was entirely normal; but that he was kept backward because of poor nutrition. Better food was given, and now the boy is all right. The case was not racial at all.

So common is this error among intelligent and honorable white persons, that it is the usual thing to hear one Negro say to another, who is going to work with some influential white person: "Be careful, for the whole race depends upon you. Whatever you do, if it be wrong, he (i. e., the white employer) will think we all do," or, "if you do well, you will make friends for the race." One of the most cultured Negro ministers of Philadelphia speaking to an intelligent congregation recently, with regard to the Negro servant class, made his plea as follows: "You all ought to be interested in them for every one of them is a missionary to the white people. The whites will not judge the race by you, or by me; they do not know our homes, our business, or our society; but they will judge by these servants." Continuing, he said: "You may look down upon them, but in a way, they have more weight in influencing the country than you and I have, and for that reason, if no other, we must help them. Our people are peculiar. We are judged by our lower class, while others are judged by their upper class."

Many confuse the problem of the Negro with problems of ignorance, or crime, inefficiency and other pathological conditions. This arises from a lack of careful analysis of every aspect of the so-called problem. The Negro problem in Pennsylvania certainly is not a problem of ignorance; for ignorance as indicated by illiteracy is neither peculiar to the Negroes or common to them, or characteristic of them. In Pennsylvania, there were in 1900, 191,706 illiterate persons over 10 years of age, of whom only 19,532 were Negroes, a small proportion of the whole. Thus illiteracy, representing ignorance, is not peculiar to the Negroes. Nor is illiteracy common to them, for there were 109,403 literate Negroes and only 19,532 illiterate Negroes, or nearly six times as many literate as illiterate over 10 years of age in the State. Nor is the Negro race more illiterate than other groups, for it has been shown that the illiteracy of the foreign group in Pennsylvania is much larger than that of the Negro group in this State.

The preceding discussion has shown also that the Negro problem is not one of crime. In Pennsylvania there were 2215 whites and 606 Negroes in the penitentiaries on December 31, 1908, and in Philadelphia the same year nine whites were arrested to one Negro. Although there is very much of a problem of crime among Negroes, there certainly is no reason to think that the "Negro Problem" is a problem of crime. Nor is it a problem of inefficiency. There are no accurate statistics of inefficiency, but the statistics of pauperism may be used to show certain tendencies as regards inefficiency; for pauperism represents the lowest industrial efficiency. In January, 1905 there were 85,290 paupers in the almshouse, of whom 77,855 were white and 7435 colored. In the State there were 9942 paupers in all almshouses, of whom 9513 were white and 429 were colored. In Pennsylvania there were twenty-two white paupers to one Negro pauper. If pauperism indicates any tendency toward inefficiency, then inefficiency is certainly not the "Negro Problem." For inefficiency is neither common to all Negroes, or peculiar to them.

The "Negro Problem"—that condition which is peculiar to Negroes, and common to them—is rather found in the attitude of the white race toward the Negro; an attitude of a majority which seeks to shut out a minority from the enjoyment of the whole social and economic life. It is an attitude which will not permit a Negro, no matter how efficient, to compete in certain lines of work, for example, to become a railway engineer, or a public high school teacher, or take even the less highly esteemed position of motorman or street car conductor. It is this attitude, which does not give Negroes a fair chance in labor unions and which causes Negroes to be unwelcome as members in some Christian churches. A Negro girl wins high honors in our High School, wins a scholarship to Cornell University, graduates with honors and returns to her native city, but finds the doors of our High School shut. This is the "Negro Problem." This attitude only complicates the general problems of crime, of ignorance, of poverty, etc., among Negroes, which some mistake for the "Negro Problem."

Not only is the "Negro Problem," not a problem of inefficiency but quite to the contrary, the conditions which make the problem are most keenly realized by the efficient Negroes of the community. The discriminations against Negroes increase with increasing intelligence, benefit and efficiency, on the part of the Negroes, and increased competition. In the economically and intellectually lowest stratum—that of the pauper and criminal—there is but little race problem. The white pauper and criminal and the Negro pauper and criminal are found in the same institutions and often in close association. In the lowest stratum of independent occupation, that of the unskilled laborer, Negroes and whites are frequently found working together. In the higher vocations of skilled service, they are rarely found together, notwithstanding the efficiency of the Negro.

But while the Negro problem is not a problem of inefficiency, poverty or crime, these conditions are exaggerated in the Negro race because of the exclusion of the race from the ordinary competition of men; and there therefore arise very serious problems of labor. Crime, poverty and so forth which are different from the ordinary problem of the same kind in that the element of racial antipathy enters to complicate them. The most serious of these problems is that of industrial improvement. This relates both to the opening of the new avenues of labor, and the improvement in those already opened. For a century, indeed, ever since the Negro became a free man, there has been complaint about his low efficiency. This complaint has been more at some times than at others. A careful study of the circumstances accompanying more or less complaints will convince one that the complaints as to the Negroes' low efficiency are contemporaneous with increased prejudice against the race.

The Negroes' industrial standard cannot be raised from without, but must be from within. In the first place there must be an open competition. The community must insist that all men have a fair chance in order that the best man might have greatest success and society thus secure all that is its dues. At present, no such open competition exists. Negroes who compete only with themselves, cannot but have a low standard. This was well illustrated by a Negro bricklayer, who in a meeting of members of his trade, was giving reasons why he thought that colored men could not do a certain piece of work. He said that he would be afraid to have to be responsible for a certain number of first-class bricklayers, for it would be hard to secure them. "Take myself, for example," he said, "when I came here from Virginia, I was a good bricklayer. I could not get work on large jobs or fine ones, I merely did small jobs and patchwork for people who could not pay for a good job." He concluded, "and gentlemen, I have degenerated, I would not take a large first-class job if you would give it to me." This may not be the true status of the case in all of its bearings but it is true with regard to efficiency in many instances. The efficiency of the Negro cannot be raised unless Negroes are permitted to enter competition on their merits. The theory of Negroes for Negroes only means low efficiency always, and society therefore loses in the end.

Another means by which Negroes will raise their industrial efficiency will be by the breaking up of their comparative solidarity as a serving class. As long as the race occupies menial or small paying positions, there is but little incentive to a standard of high efficiency; for all of them will be on the same social level and able to command about the same amount of the social products. So long as the Negroes of ability are not permitted to exercise their talents merely on account of their color or race, there is no opportunity for the superior ones to rise above the inferior, and therefore, no inducement to increased efficiency. There must be both social and economical rewards for efficiency, if high efficiency is ever to be obtained. And a community has but little right to complain of the low efficiency of a struggling group of Negroes, or others, when by its custom and its public opinion, it shuts the door to high efficiency against them.

On the other hand, it must not be forgotten by the Negro group, that the economic opportunities are seldom ever "given" by one group to another as a gratuitous favor. The struggle between groups is such that even in a country professing to be a democracy, a sharply differentiated minority group is generally at a disadvantage, both politically and economically, as for example, the Jews in Russia, the Japanese in California, and the Negroes in the Southern United States. And that group is able to rise economically to the extent that its rise becomes of economic advantage to the larger group. So the Negroes of this State have a large part to play in increasing their own industrial opportunities. They cannot expect those opportunities to be given them except they prepare and strive for them as best they can. They can expect but little from the larger group except as they can be of service to them. When the Negro uses superior skill, or gives the same skill for a smaller return, he becomes an advantage to those who engage him and makes an opportunity. This is already seen in domestic service and unskilled labor where Negroes are most generally employed because they give as good service at a lower rate than whites. Still, while this is apparently economic law, it is not moral law, or is it the ideal of the intelligent, social and political leader.

The problem of the Negro children presents several serious aspects. In the first place it has been pointed out that many Negro parents, because of certain industrial conditions, which make it necessary for both of them to be absent from their homes during the day, cannot give the attention to their children which they should give. This means that a large portion of the education of their children comes from the streets; that the discipline of the morning and early afternoon hours at school is largely counteracted by the lack of discipline in the later afternoon and early evening. In the second place, the training given in most of the schools is inadequate. The public school course, leads as a rule, to a commercial life; it also points to the ideal of brain work chiefly and manual work secondarily. The Negro boy or girl who goes through the eighth grade, can do nothing well. Very few of them go to the High School because by that time they find that they are circumscribed by race prejudice which keeps them from open competition, and they do not see that the four years' course in the High School would be of any special economic benefit to them. It is a well known fact that a Negro girl finishing the eighth grade at present, has about as much chance economically, as her sister from the High School. It is also a fact that the chief opening outside of teaching for the educated Negro girl is a clerkship in a Negro business establishment, and that the vast majority of these pay no more than the partially educated Negro cooks earn. With Negro young men who finish High School courses, there is often a larger amount of discouragement. The reason is, that the Negro boy is not permitted to enter competition for clerical or other positions with his white classmates, though they be no better intellectually or economically than he is. He is not even half prepared for any other work and he must turn to domestic service, where he is often held up by the Negroes as sufficient proof for other boys and their parents, that a High School course is useless for Negroes.

The Negro child needs much of inspiration but gets but little. The average Negro parent does not appreciate the economic value of higher education and is unwilling to make sacrifices for it. Those who have finished the ordinary High School course, because they are the only ones in their immediate group who have done so, frequently think that they should have greater recognition than they receive. When they see their white schoolmates going into positions of opportunity and responsibility, they are apt to become discouraged and pessimistic. They have not been led to understand some of the economic reasons why a father who himself is educated and who has business and social connections can possibly give his boy a start in life, whereas the Negro who has none of these, must make the start himself from the bottom. Therefore, instead of being inspired to create, the Negro too often becomes discouraged and embittered. Furthermore, the schools give the Negro children very little which is calculated to make them contented with being physically Negroes. Unfortunately, as a noted historian wrote to a Negro teacher, "Historians have not searched history with an eye to the deeds of Negroes." Much that the Negro child learns about his race is calculated to make him ashamed of it. He knows that they were slaves and he thinks they were the only race that had been enslaved. Instead of trying to develop what he has, he too often bewails his fate.

The Negro child needs to be taught something useful in school. At present the most useful things that Negro children are taught, are to be had in reformatory and special schools. The need of the Negro boy and girl to know some particular thing is also emphasized by the present low economic status of the race in the State. As has been seen, more than three-fifths of the Negro males are engaged in domestic, personal and unskilled service, in which they earn the lowest wages. This necessitates the working of women in order to make up the family income. On this account four times as large a percentage of married Negro women work as of married white women in Pennsylvania. Ninety per cent. of these women are in domestic service. The Negroes must be raised out of this condition. The men must' be elevated into higher grades of labor, into trades, into business and so forth. This can only be done by helping the Negro boy to some definite training which leads to some useful vocation.

I have not meant the above as a basis for separate schools in Pennsylvania. Such would be an unfortunate retrogression.

The law of 1881, which made it illegal to discriminate against Negroes was a step toward democracy. The schools ought to be the training places for democracy. No law should force one normal child to one school, and another to another either because of race, religion or politics. Whatever may be the justification for separate schools in other parts of the country, there is not justification here. In the first place, separate schools would be an economic burden, and the minority generally suffer by not having adequate equipment. In the second place, separate schools generally put the Negroes at a disadvantage in the matter of school supplies and equipment, and often inferior teachers. The problem of the colored child in the schools, is not a problem of legal separation. According to the school census of Philadelphia in 1904, there were Negro children between six and thirteen years in every ward in the city except the Eleventh and Thirty-first. But there were only four Negro children in the Sixth Ward; twelve in the Sixteenth; fifteen in the Seventeenth; three in the Eighteenth; twenty in the Nineteenth, and so on. Considering that these children may live miles apart, may be in different grades, it is impracticable in a large and busy city like Philadelphia to require Negro children to go to a special school. In the next place, all Negro children are not all alike and do not need the same training. It has been shown that Negroes are developing social and economic grades. And, although this discussion is for the average child and for those below it, it would not apply to all Negro children. The son of the Negro physician who has both economic opportunity and a good home life, does not need all that the son of the illiterate Negro laborer needs. The daughter of the Negro of three generations of culture does not need the same as the daughter of the recent immigrant from a Southern cotton field. The boy whose father has succeeded in his business and who will send his boy to college and turn over to his son his business, does not need the exact kind of training as

the boy whose father and mother together do not earn enough
to keep their son in school past the age of fourteen. The cases
are very different, and although they all happen to be Negroes,
they are not the same. For economic reasons, to say nothing
of constitutional and political reasons, there is no necessity to
force Negroes into separate schools. What is needed is the
adaptation of the schools to the needs of the community which
it serves. In doing this, one of the most important factors is
the teacher. Negro children suffer largely from the lack of
teachers, who are both competent and interested in them, and
who can point them to opportunities and inspire them. This
does not necessarily mean Negro teachers; yet, other things
being equal, a Negro teacher is to be preferred as the instruc-
tor of a Negro child. In fact this seems to be almost a necessity, if the Negro child is to be guided into a wholesome respect for himself and be inspired to aspire. But teachers
should not be selected merely because they are Negroes and
have finished a normal course, or at the expense of efficiency.
They should be experienced persons and should be carefully
selected and their methods and results should be closely watched. Moreover, the atmosphere of democracy should always be
around them. They should not be under the stigma of teaching in "Negro schools," but if possible they should be made to
feel as we make our "special school" teachers feel, that to them
is committed one of the most important problems of our educational life, and that success in this field will bring the recognition it deserves. But the whole matter of teachers is a subject for school administration, and not legislation.

The Negro has been the object of philanthropy in the
State of Pennsylvania since the very beginning. And although
much of this philanthropy has been of the most beneficial sort,
and contributed helpfully toward the advancement of the Negroes of the State, much of it has been of positive harm.
When it comes to philanthropy as expressed in schools, in re-

13

ligious instruction, in pleading for the freedom of the slave, Pennsylvania is possibly the foremost State of the Union. But as relates to the economic side of Negro life, which is most fundamental, Pennsylvania has not always done the best by the Negro.

In the colonial days, the slave system by its very nature encouraged laziness, as Benjamin Franklin was quick to note. When a Negro had served his probation of slavery and was given his freedom, Pennsylvania instead of putting him on his merit and compelling him to compete for his living, followed the example of other colonies in making the master who manumitted the Negro, forever responsible for him. This was, of course, not calculated to raise the economic standard or self-confidence of the Negro. In fact, it is doubtful, whether the purpose was primarily to help the Negro, or to relieve the Government. But possibly the greatest instance of misplaced philanthropy was that of the American Colonization Society, to which reference has been made in a previous chapter. This could hardly be called philanthropy as far as the Pennsylvania Negroes are concerned.

There are to-day, many philanthropies for Negroes in the State; but there are few which aim at creating an atmosphere of democracy for Negroes. There are practically none which aim at the Negroes' real economic problem—the man's chance among men. The greatest thing which the Negroes need to-day is to be allowed to enter as a full-fledged competitor, to insist that they be men, citizens, with the duties and responsibilities of the same. But many philanthropists proceed on the theory of an antiquated ethnology that the Negro is distinctly different from the white man and must not be treated as such.

"Social equality" is a bugbear which has deprived the Negroes of many economic opportunities. Within ten years, public opinion has changed greatly. Negroes are denied, in violation of the law, many of the common comforts, and public opinion has remained silent, largely because the white public does not believe in "social equality." But it is not social equality which Negroes seek; it is economic opportunity. Dr. Seligman, of Columbia University, in his treatise on the "Principles of Economics," says: "The real equality which is important for economic purposes, is threefold; first, legal equality, or the certainty that one man is as good as another before the law and that his economic rights will be equally protected; secondly, equality of opportunity, in the sense that no man is shut out by legislation or social prejudice from free access to any vocation or employment for which he deems himself fitted; thirdly, such a relative equality at least in the conditions of bargaining, as not to put one party to a contract at the virtual mercy of the other. Without such a threefold equality, freedom becomes illusory."

Illustrating the economic disadvantage of certain prejudices and local discriminations, a young Philadelphia Negro business man relates the following experiences: "I was in a Southern State on a business trip, but had planned to return to Philadelphia on a certain day. A few days before I returned, I wrote making three engagements. I looked at the schedule and found the train would arrive in Philadelphia about 10 A. M., so I set my first engagement for 12 o'clock noon; my other two for 2 and 4 o'clock respectively. All engagements were important and that at 2 o'clock could not be deferred. All engagements were with white men on whom for purely business reasons, I was anxious to make a good impression. The noon engagement was with a man with very wide and influential business connections. I purchased a ticket from a small town to Atlanta, Ga., thence I expected to secure a ticket to Philadelphia. I had two changes to make, one at Atlanta and one at Washington, D. C. I left the small town in which I was, early in the morning, reaching Atlanta before ten o'clock, expecting to leave on the 12 o'clock train. When I went to the ticket office in Atlanta to get a ticket for Philadelphia I was told that I could not ride on the train leaving Atlanta at noon, because it carried only Pullman coaches and that it was illegal for a Negro to ride in Pullman coaches in the State of Georgia. I explained and pleaded with the ticket agent but to no avail. He became angry and ordered me away under threat of arrest. 'You'll have to go on the 2.15 (a slow train), or not at all,' he said and that was final. I took the 2.15 train, the only one a Negro could take and got to Philadelphia too late for any one of my three engagements. Now, what was I to do? I do not care especially to sleep or ride with white people. All I want is a chance to compete for business. I lost these opportunities, not because of inefficiency but because of prejudice. Yet, I am told that I must not complain. Still, if the white man excels me, I am told that I am inefficient. 'That is my dilemma.' " Another incident is told by a young Negro, thus:

"I was called across the river from Philadelphia to Camden on business one day about 11 o'clock. After I had attended to my business I returned to Philadelphia by the Market Street Ferry. It was then 1 o'clock, and living about two miles away, I found I could not go home to lunch as my usual custom was. I decided, therefore, to stop at the first restaurant in my route. I saw one just opposite the ferry which I entered. I remained there ten or fifteen minutes; men on every side of me were served, but I was unnoticed. I appealed to the head waiter, who became so violent in his expressions against me that several of the men who were eating protested. After their protests he consented to serve me. I ordered roast beef. When the waiter who brought it to me received it, plainly within my sight, he poured cold water over the beef and gave me a glass of dish water to drink. When I protested, a policeman was called, I was threatened with arrest. I, of course, was excited and before I knew it, it was half past one. I hurried to my engagement hungry and excited and, I confess, angry. I got there late but not too late to talk business. The transaction involved about $300 cash and a large opportunity for further business, but I lost it. I attribute that fact almost entirely to my physical and mental condition at the time. I did not want to eat with white men, I only wanted to refresh myself so as to bring my best physical self to my business."

These incidents are but examples of hundreds that have been brought to the writer's notice. They lead one to ask, "How can the community ask the Negro to compete when it will not let him eat or sleep?" It is not social equality but it is economic privilege. A public restaurant ought not to discriminate against Negroes because such discriminations add to inefficiency. How can a hungry Negro compete with a well-fed white man in the downtown district? How can a half angry Negro, threatened with unjust arrest, because he wants to eat a meal in a decent place, compete with the man who has all his powers in complete composure? Shall we ask the Negro to spend ten cents and an hour and a half to go home and get his lunch, or to ride to a restaurant in the Negro district? If so, how can he compete with the white man who saves that time and money each day? Yet this is only a part of what the community does and still it complains of Negro inefficiency. There is another phase of the matter which the community ought to understand better. The Negroes who complain against this treatment are generally the best and most ambitious Negroes. They do not want favors and they despise conventional charity. Many whites because they have heard so much talk about "social equality" and do not understand these Negroes' economic strivings, think that the well-to-do Negroes desire to eat and drink with them and their kind without an invitation. This is far from being the case. The complaint which comes from Negroes is almost entirely for economic reasons and has but little to do with the purely social. It is not heard by the masses of Negroes, merely because the masses are not in as keen competition as the so-called upper classes. The more intelligent Negro wants the best and cleanest place he can get, for it helps him to compete in his business. He wants to get to his appointments as quickly and in as good condition as the white man. That is why he complains when he is discriminated against in a hotel, a sleeping car or other public convenience.

That Negroes are not desiring "social equality" may be seen by the fact that Negroes rarely invite whites to their tables. Indeed, it is probable that Negroes are invited more often than they invite, and they only invite their friends. When some very white Negroes "pass for white" they are immediately ostracised by the Negroes. But the most convincing argument against the Negroes being especially anxious for "social equality" with whites, in the sense of association with whites on terms of intimacy, is seen in the small proportion of mixed marriages and race mixture occurring in the State. Although the law against mixed marriages was repealed over one hundred and thirty-five years ago, there is less mixing to-day in the free State of Pennsylvania than in the State of Mississippi, where Negroes and whites are not permitted to marry.

Social classes among Negroes are a conspicuous development. Notwithstanding the general complaint among native-born Negroes concerning the immigration of Southern Negroes, it is this very immigration of large numbers of Negroes to the cities that has been the basis upon which social classes among Negroes are gradually being formed. Were it not for these Negroes, the Negro professional group, which is forcing its way upward to both social position and comparative wealth, could never have been developed; the Negro business man would have had no field; and the great mass of intelligent Negroes, with a few exceptions, would have been domestic servants, as the Negroes of the North have generally been. Immigration of Negroes is beginning to do for the development of Negroes what the immigration of foreigners did for the Germans, Irish, Italians and others. The older groups, with more experience, more money and more education, are rising upon the newer ones.

As long as there are very few Negroes in a community, there is generally but little prejudice and the Negroes enjoy a reasonable degree of security. But at the same time, only a few of them rise above the position of a menial. They may be respected by the community, but they are respected as good servants. Now and then, some exceptionally bright Negro or the protege of some philanthropic person is allowed to rise, but this is very seldom. When, however, heavy Southern Negro immigration sets in, the conditions of security and tranquility are often upset; the old inhabitants, both black and white, complain of the "incoming Negroes from the South" and the evils they have brought, and they deplore the changed conditions. Yet it is upon these incoming Negroes and these alone, that the Negroes begin to rise and to diversify their occupations. They increase the competition among the Negroes themselves and among whites and they therefore, raise themselves in efficiency. And although they increase prejudice on the part of their competitors, they lay a foundation on which other Negroes can rise in business and professions.

The two hundred thousand Negroes in the State make it possible for the Negroes to differentiate into classes based on wealth, culture and character. The differentiation of the Negro group will be slower than that of the immigrant white group, since the Negro's field of operation, because of public opinion, is limited. Public sentiment requires Negroes to work among their own, as it does not require the Irishman or Italian. If one of the latter succeeds he is looked upon as a citizen and not as an Irishman. But it is not so with the Negro. If a Negro girl graduates with honors in our High School, wins thereby a scholarship to a leading university, and graduates there with honor, she cannot come back to her native city and teach in her Alma Mater, as white girls who stood lower than she have done. She must be content to teach in the graded schools or go South to teach. If a bright young Negro wins a Cecil Rhodes' Scholarship, and represents his State at Oxford, England, his best friends are at a loss to find for him an opportunity in his native city and State, whereas there are large opportunities for white boys with such scholastic honors, in the service of the State in which they have striven and shown their superiority.

Crime among Negroes, to-day in proportion to fifty years ago, has decreased. That is, it has not increased as rapidly as the Negro population in the State. All the evidence at hand, however, although meager and hard to interpret, tends to show that the Negroes still commit twice as many crimes as whites do. But this is better than it was a half century ago. There are not facts to show that Negroes are naturally more criminal than whites. But facts do seem to show that there is close connection between the crimes of Negroes and the lack of economic opportunity. Negro criminals are rarely efficient or regular workers. It is only by giving Negroes the equal opportunity in all lines of industry that the crimes of Negroes will be diminished. Work, regular work, and the incentive which the hope of promotion inspires, will do for the decrease of crime what preaching, lecturing, and abusing and even punishment have not yet accomplished.

The aim of our nation is the common weal; is equal opportunity as far as possible. Race, nationality or religion should not interfere with American economic progress. The greatest need of the Negro is economic freedom, economic justice. This is all the best Negroes of this State ask. And it is indeed a high platform upon which to stand. It is not a bid for charity; it is not a bid for hostility. It is only to be permitted to enter American rivalry, to go down if incompetent, to die out if weak, to go up if capable. It is the request that the same rules by which whites, with all their generations of culture, are judged, be the rules applied to the Negro. It is for an opportunity to be a part of an industrial democracy that Negroes plead; an opportunity to make the best living possible. To give them this is most difficult indeed; it requires the most profound economic foresight and the highest religious devotion. It is the common ground of political economy and the teaching of Jesus. For indeed, it is easier to "give one's body to be burned;" to give alms to the poor, to speak wisdom and write learnedly, than to give simple Pauline charity, which is an attitude of mind and not particularly a material gift. What the Negroes want most and need most, and what ultimately is best for our State and nation, is economic charity, i. e., economic justice, a state of public opinion that will give a fair field to struggling individuals identified with a submerged minority.

╀ Certainly, Pennsylvania which could pass the Abolition Act, establish the Abolition Society, the Anti-Slavery Society, various associations for the promotion of religion and reform, the foremost of philanthropic States of the Union, so far as the Negro is concerned, can give the Negro that simplest of all things, the right to earn his bread, and as much of it as he is capable of earning for the support of his family and to maintain a respectable place in the community; and will not deny him what Professor Seligman says is absolutely necessary for the best economic development of the State itself—that "equality of opportunity in the sense that no man is shut out by legislation or *social prejudice* from free access to any vocation or employment for which he deems himself fitted."

Appendix

LAWS OF PENNA., 1810, CH. 870, P, 492-497.

"AN ACT FOR THE GRADUAL ABOLITION OF SLAVERY," passed March 1, 1780:

"When we contemplate our abhorence of that condition, to which the arms and tyranny of Great Britain were exerted to reduce us, when we look back on the variety of dangers to which we have been exposed, and how miraculously our wants in many instances have been supplied, when even hope and human fortitude have become unequal to the conflict we are unavoidably led to a serious and grateful sense of the manifold blessings, which we have undeservedly received from the hand of that Being, from whom every good and perfect gift cometh. Impressed with these ideas, we conceive that it is our duty and we rejoice that it is in our power to extend a portion of that freedom to others, which hath been extended to us, and release from that state of thraldom, to which we ourselves were tyrannically doomed, and from which we have now every prospect of being delivered. It is not for us to inquire why, in the creation of mankind, the inhabitants of the several parts of the earth were distinguished by a difference in feature or complexion. It is sufficient to know, that all are the work of an Almighty hand. We find, in the distribution of the human species, that the most fertile as well as the most barren parts of the earth are inhabited by men of complexions different from ours, and from each other; from whence we may reasonably, as well as religiously, infer, that He who placed them in their various situations, hath extended equally His care and protection to all, and that it becometh not us to counteract His mercies. We esteem it a peculiar blessing granted to us, that we are enabled this day to add one more step to universal civilization, by removing, as much as possible, the sorrows of those who have lived in undeserved bondage, and from which, by the assumed authority of the Kings of Great Britain, no effectual, legal relief could be obtained. Wearied, by a long course of experience, from those narrow prejudices and partialities we had imbibed, we find our hearts enlarged with kindness and benevolence towards men of all conditions and nations; and we conceive ourselves at this particular period extraordinarily called upon, by the blessings which we have received, to manifest the sincerity of our profession, and to give a substantial proof of our gratitude.

II. And whereas the condition of those persons, who have heretofore been denominated Negro and Mulatto slaves, has been attended with circumstances, which not only deprived them of the common blessings that they were by nature entitled to, but has cast them into the deepest affliction, by an unnatural separation and sale of husband and wife from each other and from their children, an injury, the greatness of which can only be conceived by supposing that we were in the same unhappy case. In justice, therefore, to persons so unhappily circumstanced, and who, having no prospect before them whereon they may rest their sorrows and their hopes, who have no reasonable inducement to render their service to society, which they otherwise might, and also in grateful commemoration of our own happy deliverance from that state of unconditional submission, to which we were doomed by the tyranny of Britain.

III. Be it enacted, and it is hereby enacted, That all persons as well Negroes and Mulattoes as others, who shall be born within this State from and after the passing of this act, shall not be deemed and considered as servants for life, or slaves; and that all servitude for life, or slavery of children, in consequence of the slavery of their mothers, in the case of all children born within this State from and after the passing of this act as aforesaid, shall be and hereby is, utterly taken away, extinguished, and forever abolished.

IV. Provided always, and be it further enacted, That every Negro and Mulatto child, born within this State after the passing of the act as aforesaid (who would, in case this act had not been made, have been born a servant for years, or life, or a slave) shall be deemed, and shall be, by virtue of this act, the servant of such person, or his or her assigns, who would in such case have been entitled to the service of such child, until such child shall attain unto the age of twenty-eight years, in the manner, and on the conditions, whereon servants bound by indenture for four years are or may be retained by his or her master or mistress, and to like freedom dues and other privileges, as servants bound by indenture for four years are or may be entitled, unless the person, to whom the service of any such child shall belong, shall abandon his or her claims to the same; in which case the Overseers of the poor of the city, township or district, respectively, where such child shall be so abandoned, as an apprentice, for a time not exceeding the age herein before limited for the service of such children.

V. And be it further enacted, That every person, who is or shall be the owner of any Negro or Mulatto slave or servant for life or till the age of thirty-one years, now within this State, or his lawful attorney, shall, on or before the said first day of November next, deliver or cause to be delivered, in writing, to the Clerk of the Peace of the county, or to the Clerk of the Court of Record in the City of Philadelphia, in which he or she shall respectively inhabit, the name and surname, and occupation or profession of such owner, and the name of the county and township, district or ward, wherein he or she resideth; and also the name and names of any such slave and slaves, and servant and servants for life, or till the age of thirty-one years, together with their ages and sexes severally and respectively set forth and annexed, by such person owned or statedly employed, and then being within this State, in order to ascertain and distinguish the slaves and servants for life, and till the age of thirty-one years, within this State, who shall be such on the said first day of November next, from all other persons; which particulars shall, by said Clerk of the Sessions and Clerk of the said City Court, be entered in books to be provided for that purpose by the said Clerks, and that no Negro or Mulatto, now within this State, shall, from and after the said first day of November, be deemed a slave or servant for life, or till the age of thirty-one years, unless his or her name shall be entered as aforesaid on such record, except such Negro and Mulatto slaves and servants as are hereinafter excepted; the said Clerk to be entitled to a fee of two dollars for each slave or servant so entered as aforesaid, from the Treasury of the county, to be allowed to him in his accounts.

VI. Provided always, That any person, in whom the ownership or rights to the service of any Negro or Mulatto shall be vested at the passing of this act, other than such as are herein before excepted, his or her heirs, executors, administrators and assigns, and all and every one of them, severally, shall be liable to the Overseers of the Poor of the city, township or district, to which any such Negro or Mulatto shall become chargeable, for such necessary expense, with costs of suit thereon, as such Overseers may be put to, through the neglect of the owner, master or mistress of such Negro or Mulatto, notwithstanding the name and other descriptions of such Negro or Mulatto shall not be entered and recorded as aforesaid, unless his or her master or owner shall, before such slave or servant attain his or her twenty-eighth year, execute and record in the proper county a deed or instrument, securing to such slave or servant his or her freedom.

VII. And be it further enacted, That the offenses and crimes of Negroes and Mulattoes, as well as slaves and servants as freemen, shall be inquired of, adjudged, corrected and punished, in like manner as the offenses and crimes of the other inhabitants of this State, are and shall be inquired of, adjudged, corrected and punished, and not otherwise, except that a slave shall not be admitted to bear witness against a freeman.

VIII. And be it further enacted, That in all cases, wherein sentence of death shall be pronounced against a slave, the jury, before whom he or she shall be tried, shall appraise and declare the value of such slave; and in case such sentence be executed, the Court shall make an order on the State Treasurer, payable to the owner, for the same, and for the costs of prosecution, but in case of remission or migration, for the costs only.

IX. And be it further enacted, That the reward for taking up runaway and absconding Negro and Mulatto slaves and servants, and the penalties for enticing away, dealing with or harboring, concealing or employing Negro and Mulatto slaves and servants, shall be the same, and shall be recovered in like manner, as in case of servants bound for four years.

X. And be it further enacted, That no man or woman of any nation or color, except the Negroes and Mulattoes who shall be registered as aforesaid, shall at any time hereafter be deemed, adjudged or holden, within the territories of this Commonwealth, as slaves or servants for life, but as free men and free women; except the domestic slaves attending upon Delegates in Congress from the other American States, foreign Ministers and Consuls, and persons passing through or sojourning in this State, and not becoming resident therein, and seamen employed in ships not belonging to any inhabitant of this State, nor employed in any ship owned by any such inhabitant; provided such domestic slaves be not alienated or sold to any inhabitant, nor (except in the case of Members of Congress, Foreign Ministers and Consuls) retained in this State longer than six months.

XI. Provided always, and be it further enacted, That this act, or anything in it contained, shall not give any relief or shelter to any absconding or runaway Negro or Mulatto slave or servant, who has absented himself, or shall absent himself, from his or her owner, master or mistress, residing in any other State or county, but such owner, master or mistress shall have like right to aid, to demand, claim and take away his slave or servant, as he might have had in case this act had not been made; and that all Negro and Mulatto slaves now owned and heretofore resident in this State, who have absented themselves, or been clandestinely carried away, or who may be employed abroad as seamen, and have not returned or been brought back to their owners, masters or mistresses, before the passing of this act, may, within five years, be registered, as effectually as is ordered by this act concerning those who are now within the State, on producing such slave before any two Justices of the Peace, and satisfying the said Justices, by proof of the former residence, absconding, taking away, or absence of such slaves, as aforesaid, who thereupon shall direct and order the said slave to be entered on the record as aforesaid.

XII. And whereas attempts may be made to evade this act, by introducing into this State Negroes and Mulattoes bound by covenant to serve for long and unreasonable terms of years, if the same be not prevented.

XIII. Be it therefore enacted, That no covenant of personal servitude or apprenticeship whatsoever shall be rated or binding upon a Negro or Mulatto for a longer time than seven years, unless such servant or apprentice were, at the commencement of such servitude or apprenticeship, under the age of twenty-one years; in which case such Negro or Mulatto may be holden as a servant or apprentice, respectively, according to the covenant as the case shall be, until he or she shall attain the age of twenty-eight years, but no longer.

XIV. And be it further enacted, That an act of Assembly of the Province of Pennsylvania, passed in the year one thousand seven hundred five, entitled, "An Act for the Trial of Negroes;" and another act of the Assembly of the said Province, passed in the year one thousand seven hundred twenty-five, entitled, "An Act for the Better Regulating of Negroes in this Province;" and another act of Assembly of the said Province, passed in the year one thousand seven hundred sixty-one, entitled, "An Act for Laying a Duty on Negro and Mulatto Slaves Imported into This Province;" and also another act of Assembly of said Province, passed in the year one thousand seven hundred seventy-three, entitled, "An Act for Making Perpetual an Act for Laying a Duty on Negro and Mulatto Slaves Imported into This Province," and for laying an additional duty on said slaves, shall be and are hereby repealed, annuled and made void."

Passed March 1, 1780. Recorded in Law Books, Volume No. 1, Page No. 339.

ADVERTISEMENT FOR RUNAWAY NEGRO SLAVE.

"American Weekly Mercury, Philadelphia. Printed and Sold by Andrew Bradford. Dec. 29, 1719. Second Issue. Advertisement: "Run away from his master, Phillip Ludwell, of Green Spring, in Virginia, on Saturday, the fourth of July, 1719, a mulatto man named Johnny, but of a very white complexion, aged about twenty-two years. He is tall and well limb'd, he has a little lump on the small of his left leg, and small holes punched in the upper part of each ear, short dark hair and broad teeth (he is my coach-man). Whoever shall take up such mulatto slave and bring him to his said master in Virginia, or to Henry Evans at Philadelphia, or give notice thereof so that he may be had again, shall have five pounds as reward, with all reasonable charges paid by Phillip or Henry Evans."

FIRST PROTEST AGAINST SLAVERY IN PENNSYLVANIA, GERMANTOWN, FEB. 18, 1688.

"This is to the Monthly Meeting held at Richard Worrell's. These are the reasons why we are against the traffic of men-body as followeth. Is there any that would be done or handled at this manner? Viz: To be sold or made a slave for all the time of his life? How fearful and faint-hearted are many on sea, when they see a strange vessel, being afraid it should be a Turk, and they should be taken and sold for slaves in Turkey. Now what is better done than Turks do? Yea, rather worse for them, which say they are Christians; for we hear that the most part of such Negroes are brought hither against their will and consent, and that many of them are stolen. Now, though they are black, we cannot conceive there is more liberty to have them slaves (than) it is to have other white ones. There is a saying that we shall do to all men like as we will be done ourselves, making no difference of which generation, descent, or color they are. And those who steal and rob men, and those who buy or purchase them, are not they all alike? Here is liberty of conscience, which is right and reasonable; here ought to be likewise liberty of the body, except of evildoers, which is another case. But to bring them hither, or to rob and sell them against their will, we stand against. In Europe there are many oppressed for conscience sake; and here are those oppressed who are of a black colour. And we know that men must not commit adultery, some do commit adultery in others, separating wives from their husbands and giving them to others; and some sell the children of these poor creatures to other men. Ah! do consider well this thing, you who do it; if you would be done at this manner? And if it is done according to Christianity? You surpass Holland or Germany in this thing. This makes an ill-report in all those countries in Europe when they hear of (it), that the Quakers do here handle men as they handle their cattle, and for that reason some have no mind or inclination to come hither. And who shall maintain this your cause, or plead for it? Truly we cannot do so, except you shall inform us better thereof, Viz: That Christians have liberty to practice these things. Pray, what thing in the world can be done worse towards us, than if men should rob or steal us away, and sell us for slaves to strange countries; separating husbands from their wives and children. Being now this is not done in the manner we should be done (by), therefore we contradict, and are against this traffic of men-body, and we who profess that it is not lawful to steal, must likewise, avoid to purchase such things as are stolen, but rather help to stop this robbing and stealing if possible. And such men ought to be delivered out of the hands of robbers, and set free as in Europe. Then in Pennsylvania to have a good report, it hath now a bad one for this sake in other countries. Especially whereas the Europeans are desirous to know in what manner the Quakers do rule in their province: and most of them do look upon us with an envious eye. But if this is done well, what shall we say is done evil?

"If once these slaves (which they say are so wicked and stubborn men) should join themselves, fight for their freedom and handle their masters and mistresses as they did handle them before, will these masters and mistresses take the sword at hand and war against these poor slaves, like, we are able to believe, some will not refuse to do? Or have these Negroes not much right to fight for their freedom, as you have to keep them slaves?

"Now consider well this thing, if it is good or bad? And in case you find it to be good to handle these blacks in that manner, we desire and require you hereby lovingly, that you may inform us herein what at this time never was done, Viz: That Christians have such a liberty to do so. To this end we shall (may) be satisfied in this point, and satisfy likewise our good friends, and acquaintances in our native country, to whom it is a terror or fearful thing, that men should be handled so in Pennsylvania.

"This is from our meeting at Germantown, held on ye 18 of the 2 month, 1688, to be delivered to the Monthly Meeting at Richard Worrell's.

> GARRET HENDERICH,
> DERICK UP DEGREFF,
> FRANCIS DANIELL PASTORIUS,
> ABRAHAM j'r DEN GRAEF."

"At our Monthly Meeting at Dublin, ye 30-2 mo., 1688, we, having inspected ye matter above mentioned and considered of it, we find it so weighty that we think it not expedient for us to meddle with it here, but to commit to ye consideration of ye Quarterly Meeting: Ye tenor of it being nearly related to ye truth.

"On behalf of ye Monthly Meeting.

(Signed)   P. JO. HART."

But the Quarterly Meeting only referred it to the Yearly Meeting, making the following note:

"This, above mentioned, was read in our Quarterly Meeting, at Philadelphia, the 4 of ye 4th mo., '88, and was from thence recommended to the Yearly Meeting, and the above said Derick, and the other two mentioned therein, to present the same to ye above said Meeting, it being a thing of too great weight for this Meeting to determine.

"Signed by order of ye Meeting,   ANTHONY MORRIS."

PERCENTAGE OF INCREASE OF NEGRO POPULATION OF PENNSYLVANIA AND OF THE UNITED STATES.

	Whites—Percent.		Negroes—Percent.	
Before the Civil War.	Penna.	U. S.	Penna.	U. S.
1790 to 1800	38.2	35.8	58.4	32.3
1800 to 1810	34.2	36.1	43.1	·37.5
1810 to 1820	29.5	34.2	30.6	28.6
1820 to 1830	28.0	33.9	26.0	31.4
1830 to 1840	28.0	34.7	25.0	23.4
1840 to 1850	34.7	37.8	11.9	26.6
1850 to 1860	26.2	37.8	6.2	22.1
After the Civil War.				
1860 to 1870	21.3	24.8	14.7	9.9
1870 to 1880	21.4	29.2	31.0	34.9
1880 to 1890	22.7	27.0	25.8	13.8
1890 to 1900	19.3	21.2	45.8	18.0
1900 to 1910	....	....	....	....

SOURCE OF FREE COLORED POPULATION OF PHILADEL-
PHIA IN 1860 AND OF NEGRO POPULATION OF
PHILADELPHIA AND PENNSYLVANIA IN 1900.

States in which born	Philadelphia 1860	Philadelphia 1900	Pennsylvania 1900	
Alabama	1	111	415	....
Arkansas	0	18	67	....
California	2	48	43	....
Connecticut	38	108	164	....
Delaware	2,977	2,527	5,944	....
Florida	....	94	184	....
Georgia	58	429	926	....
Illinois	2	64	167	....
Indiana	3	32	134	....
Iowa	....	1	44	....
Kansas	....	9	27	....
Kentucky	13	59	657	....
Louisiana	25	57	151	....
Maine	10	17	26	....
Maryland	1,976	9,474	17,415	11.1
Massachusetts	48	183	294	....
Michigan	....	26	89	....
Minnesota	4	13	13	....
Mississippi	1	54	160	....
Missouri	7	27	127	....
New Hampshire	3	6	5	....
New Jersey	1,047	1,771	2,571	....
New York	138	697	1,199	....
North Carolina	100	3,403	5,206	....
Ohio	17	172	1,696	....
Oregon	....	1	3	....
Pennsylvania	13,724	22,835	70,365	45.1
Rhode Island	9	52	74	....
South Carolina	205	577	1,009	....
Tennessee	3	109	835	....
Texas	....	42	95	....
Vermont	3	10	16	....
Virginia	1,241	16,369	40,870	26.1
Wisconsin	....	36	17	....
District of Columbia	145	1,185	2,067	....
At Sea	1	6	....	....
Not Stated	71	238	774	....
Alaska	....	....	....	....
Arizona	1	1	1	....
Colorado	....	7	16	....
Hawaii	....	....	....	....
Idaho	....	1	1	....
Indian Territory	....	2	5	....
Montana	....	35	11	....

States in which born	Philadelphia 1860	Philadelphia 1900	Pennsylvania 1900	
Nebraska	....	12	14	....
Nevada	....	....	I	....
New Mexico	....	2	I	....
North Dakota	....	11	I	....
Oklahoma	....	5	....	....
South Dakota	....	2	I	....
Utah	....	I	2	....
Washington	....	76	159	....
West Virginia	....	197	1,917	....
Wyoming	....	....	2	....
Porto Rico	....	7	....	....
Americans born abroad	....	29	....	....
Total	21,922	62,253	155,981	....

SOUTHERN STATES TO WHICH PENNSYLVANIA BORN NEGROES HAVE MIGRATED AND VICE VERSA

States	Negroes born in Pennsylvania living in specified Southern States	Negroes born in specified Southern States now living in Pennsylvania	Excess in favor of Pennsylvania	Excess in favor of Southern States
Delaware	848	5,944	....	5,098
Maryland	1,141	17,415	....	16,274
District of Col.	586	2,067	....	1,481
Virginia	450	40,870	....	40,420
West Virginia	311	1,917	....	1,606
North Carolina	137	5,206	....	5,069
South Carolina	32	1,009	....	977
Georgia	65	926	....	861
Florida	94	184	....	90
Kentucky	85	657	....	572
Tennessee	84	835	....	751
Alabama	56	415	....	359
Mississippi	75	160	....	85
Louisiana	118	151	....	43
Arkansas	73	67	...	7
Texas	140	95	...	54

CITIES HAVING OVER 500 NEGROES 1860, AND 1900

Cities	1860	1900
Allegheny City	690	3,315
Braddock Borough	....	558
Carlisle	509	1,148
Chambersburg	524	769
Chester City	417	4,405

Cities	1860	1900
Columbia	648	421
Harrisburg City	1,321	4,107
Homestead Borough	....	640
Lancaster City	29	777
McKeesport City	....	748
Norristown Borough	382	728
Philadelphia City	22,185	62,613
Pittsburgh City	1,154	17,040
Reading City	285	534
Scranton City	1	521
Steelton Borough	....	1,508
Uniontown Borough (Fayette Co)	....	803
Washington Borough,		
(Washington County)	435	984
West Chester Borough	561	1,777
Wilkes-Barre City	....	680
Williamsport City	....	1,142
York City	334	776

DISTRIBUTION NEGRO CITY POPULATION BY WARDS,

1900.

Wards.	Philadel-phia.	Pitts-burgh.	Alle-gheny.	Reading.	Scran-ton.	Wilkes-Barre.	Harris-burg.
1.......	712	161	269	2	3	27	310
2.......	1,319	167	847	10	7	11	467
3.......	1,704	49	752	55	2	...	190
4.......	2,875	50	116	26	1	61	339
5.......	1,251	211	363	13	2	104	99
6.......	110	219	236	44	...	21	550
7.......	10,462	1,208	...	57	15	20	467
8.......	2,464	2,595	1	109	44	63	1,506
9.......	606	55	188	139	130	13	170
10.......	792	3	238	3	4	35	9
11.......	36	1,489	153	17	....	82	.....
12.......	286	844	147	12	...	45	.....
13.......	571	3,025	5	1	25	129	.....
14.......	1,961	676	...	21	43	31	.....
15.......	2,423	405	...	4	8	19	.....
16.......	102	401	...	21	143	19	.....
17.......	125	278	...	...	65	...	.....
18.......	18	83	...	...	16	...	.....
19.......	270	1,326	...	...	1	...	.....
20.......	2,821	1,108	...	...	10	...	.....
21.......	464	1,881	...	...	...	...	.....
22.......	3,676	211	...	...	...	...	.....
23.......	794	27	...	...	...	...	.....

Wards	Philadelphia	Pittsburgh	Allegheny	Reading	Scranton	Wilkes-Barre	Harrisburg
24	2,193	6	...	...	...	...	.....
25	236	23	...	...	...	...	.....
26	2,874	120	...	...	...	...	.....
27	3,171	25	...	...	...	...	.....
28	1,164	62	...	...	...	...	.....
29	3,160	1	...	...	...	...	.....
30	5,242	25	...	...	...	...	.....
31	29	19	...	...	...	...	.....
32	962	160	...	...	...	...	.....
33	766	36	...	...	...	...	.....
34	1,773	...	...	...	...	...	.....
35	364	90	...	...	...	...	.....
36	1,955	43	...	...	...	...	.....
37	284	119	...	...	...	...	.....
38	675	39	...	...	...	...	.....
39	831	...	...	...	...	...	.....
40	689	...	...	...	...	...	.....
41	383	...	...	...	...	...	.....
Total	62,613	17,040	3,315	534	521	680	4,107

NEGRO POPULATION IN COUNTIES HAVING NO LARGE CITY SHOWING DECREASE IN 20 AND 10 YEARS

Counties	1880	1890	1900	20 yrs	10 yrs
Adams	471	319	338	3	....
Bedford	577	587	499	78	88
Bradford	537	599	307	230	292
Butler	128	154	115	13	39
Corbon	8	36	12	....	24
Clarion	99	72	16	83	56
Clinton	286	324	253	33	71
Columbia	145	118	126	19	....
Crawford	493	314	359	134	....
Cumberland	2,167	2,091	1,818	354	273
Erie	322	308	311	21	....
Franklin	2,551	2,019	1,954	597	65
Fulton	129	112	106	23	6
Greene	503	445	313	190	132
Indiana	227	212	160	67	52
Juniata	261	170	172	89	....
Lancaster	2,845	2,603	2,461	384	148
McKean	326	299	302	24	....
Mercer	425	304	351	74	....
Mifflin	215	169	162	53	7
Monroe	155	176	151	4	25

Counties	1880	1890	1900	20 yrs	10 yrs
Montour	107	96	88	19	8
Perry	164	137	82	82	55
Pike	84	107	81	3	26
Schuylkill	358	374	252	106	122
Snyder	19	505	3	16	2
Susquehanna	219	162	141	78	21
Tioga	115	91	85	30	6
Union	133	52	65	68	....
Venango	547	473	522	25	....
Warren ʹ.............	103	75	52	51	23
Wayne	31	33	18	13	15
Wyoming	21	8	14	7	....

AGE DISTRIBUTION OF NEGRO POPULATION IN PENNSYL-
VANIA AND SOUTHERN STATES FROM WHICH
NEGROES EMIGRATE CHIEFLY.

Age Periods	Pennsylvania No.	Per Cent	Virginia No.	Per Cent	North Carolina No.	Per Cent
Under 15	39,947	25.5	267,410	40.5	268.074	42.9
15 to 29	55,697	35.5	189,416	28.7	184.183	29.5
30 to 44	37,971	24.2	101,727	15.4	80,514	12.9
45 to 59	16,099	10.3	62,892	9.5	57,910	9.3
59 and over	6,345	4.0	36,922	5.5	30,803	4.9
Unknown	786	0.5	2,355	0.4	2,985	0.5
Totals	156,845	100.0	660,722	100.0	624,459	100.0

CONJUGAL CONDITION OF NEGROES IN PENNSYLVA-
NIA AND VIRGINIA, THE PRINCIPAL SOURCE OF
NEGRO IMMIGRATION, COMPARED WITH CONJU-
GAL CONDITION OF NEGROES IN THE U. S.

	Negroes of U. S. Number.	P. C.	Virginia Number.	Pennsylvania. Females	Males.	Total
Single	5,346,262	60.5	420,248	40,815	47,584	88,399
Married	2,867,572	32.5	197,968	28,314	28,276	56,590
Widowed	565,396	6.4	39,940	8,046	3,055	11,101
Divorced	33,071	.4	1,115	179	135	314
Unknown	21,693	.4	1,451	143	298	441
Totals	8,833,994		660,722	79,348	77,497	156,845

ILLITERACY OF PENNSYLVANIA NEGROES COMPARED WITH
NEGROES OF OTHER SECTIONS OF THE UNITED STATES
1900

Negroes of	Total 10 Years and Over.	Illiterates.	P. C.
Continental United States	6,415,681	2,853,194	44.5
North Atlantic States	320,176	44,275	13.8
North Central States	404,568	87,914	21.7
Western States	25,862	3,399	13.1
South Atlantic States	2,655,833	1,250,279	47.1
South Central States	3,009,142	1,467,327	48.8
Pennsylvania	28,935	19,532	15.1
New York	84,688	9,180	10.8
New Jersey	57,534	9,882	17.2
Massachusetts	26,573	2,853	10.7
Virginia	478,921	213,836	44.6
North Carolina	437,691	208,132	47.6
South Carolina	537,398	283,883	52.8
Georgia	724,096	379.067	52.4
Alabama	589,629	338,605	52.4
Mississippi	638,646	313,312	59.1
Louisiana	464,598	284,028	61.1

PROPERTY HOLDING AMONG NEGROES.

FROM REPORT OF INDUSTRIAL STATISTICS, 1911.

SUMMARY OF NEGRO PROPERTY HOLDING IN PHILA-
DELPHIA. A REPORT BY R. R. WRIGHT, JR.

Ward	Properties.	Tax valuation.
1	10	$19,700
2	1	2,700
3	20	60,600
5	6	23,400
7	172	584,900
8	36	290,400
9	1	12,000
10	2	17,000
12	1	2,900
13	1	2,300
14	10	32,600
15	25	62,400
19	2	3,400

Ward	Properties.	Tax Valuation
20	24	53,200
21	10	23,000
22	96	215,300
23	13	11,700
24	37	73,900
26	47	93,900
27	37	92,500
28	114	27,600
29	5	11,000
30	168	484,200
31	3	4,300
32	11	22,400
33	4	1,700
34	35	48,900
35	8	6,250
36	84	159,300
37	7	14,500
38	24	50,100
39	2	3,000
40	66	63,325
41	2	1,900
42	7	10,800
44	28	54,900
45	4	3,400
46	14	26,800
47	46	129,100
Totals	1,080	$2,801,275

SUMMARY OF PROPERTIES OF NEGROES OF PITTSBURGH.

Ward.	Taxables.	Assessed value.	Real value.
First	1	$26,400	$26,400
Second	2	26,300	40,000
Third	44	236,520	367,000
Fourth	10	23,370	34,850
Fifth	168	331,920	508,350
Sixth	24	42,840	62,900
Seventh	18	80,530	118,500
Eighth	9	15,830	22,500
Ninth	13	15,860	23,300
Tenth	80	88,700	132,050
Eleventh	24	62,890	95,300
Twelfth	25	50,770	74,500
Thirteenth	51	114,340	175,000
Fourteenth	5	7,120	10,400
Fifteenth	4	3,820	5,400

Ward	Taxables	Assessed Value	Rea Value
Sixteenth	2	4,120	5,900
Seventeenth	6	28,140	42,200
Eighteenth	62	89,560	133,800
Nineteenth	11	14,990	21,700
Twentieth	....	....	....
Twenty-first	6	13,240	19,800
Twenty-second	9	28,550	42,800
Twenty-third	4	12,400	18,400
Twenty-fourth	1	3,000	4,500
Twenty-fifth	25	79,150	115,700
Twenty-sixth	16	27,160	40,680
Twenty-seventh	5	9,540	14,300
Total	643	$1,437,060	$2,153,830
Exemptions	38	....	406,853
Grand total	681	$1,437,060	$2,560,683

PROPERTY HOLDING OF NEGROES IN OTHER PENNSYLVANIA CITIES AND TOWNS

Town or District.	County.	Properties.	Assessed value.	Market value.
Williamsport	Lycoming	93	$50,840	$70,000
Washington	Washington	95	214,450	327,050
Carlisle	Cumberland	81	129,700	309,500
Darby	Delaware	69	72,920	119,300
Scranton	Lackawanna	11	113,000	165,000
Meadville	Crawford	27	15,060	38,100
Lewistown	Mifflin	22	19,375	38,750
Franklin	Venango	20	11,875	31,700
Uniontown	Fayette	21	25,000	33,325
Titusville	Crawford	18	13,040	38,480
Ardmore	Montgomery	24	64,250	96,400
Harrisburg, 2 wards....	Dauphin	41	41,900	66,800
Langhorne	Bucks	26	16,950	22,400
Lancaster	Lancaster	25	54,900	73,000
Canonsburg	Washington	14	46,300	59,800
Robesonia	Berks	1	900	1,200
Norwood	Delaware	8	107,350	115,100
Sharon Hill	Delaware	5	3,075	3,975
Edgemont	Delaware	1	500	650
Lansdowne	Delaware	7	10,850	11,650
Ashton	Delaware	5	4,300	5,725
Prospect Park	Delaware	2	1,400	1,850
Concord	Delaware	9	6,760	6,760
Glenolden	Delaware	2	1,400	2,100

Town or District	County.	Properties.	Assessed value.	Market value.
Lower Chichester	Delaware	8	5,240	7,700
Clifton Heights	Delaware	2	1,600	2,100
Marple	Delaware	4	3,150	4,250
Marcus Hook	Delaware	6	3,300	4,500
Chester, 2 wards	Delaware	14	21,990	28,000
Swarthmore	Delaware	3	1,790	2,975
Ridley Park	Delaware	3	3,200	4,000
Colwyn	Delaware	4	2,850	5,300
Haverford	Delaware	4	4,700	6,250
Springfield	Delaware	4	2,750	3,300
Bristol	Bucks	17	6,650	11,775
Lower Makefield	Bucks	5	1,925	2,550
East Rock Hill	Bucks	4	2,120	3,100
Morrisville	Bucks	6	3,750	5,100
Yardley	Bucks	5	2,000	2,000
Richland	Bucks	2	3,175	4,100
Falk	Bucks	5	2,612	2,475
Wrightstown	Bucks	2	1,300	2,000
South Langhorne	Bucks	1	125	150
Mechanic Valley	Bucks	11	3,150	3,150
Nockamixon	Bucks	1	1,080	1,200
Emilie	Bucks	2	500	1,000
Ruscomburaner	Bucks	2	225	275
West Rockville	Bucks	3	870	1,150
Newtown	Bucks	4	1,350	1,600
Marietta	Lancaster	24	8,100	2,700
Smethport	McKean	5	2,850	4,500
Bradford	McKean	13	18,180	40,750
Mifflintown	Juniata	1	700	1,000
Montrose	Susquehanna	17	2,200	8,240
Sewickley	Allegheny	11	24,150	32,500
Braddock	Allegheny	35	104,475	156,700
Swatara	Dauphin	5	4,760	6,350
Omerlin	Dauphin	7	2,700	3,400
Royalton	Dauphin	2	600	900
Middletown	Dauphin	14	8,470	11,260
Steelton	Dauphin	7	10,800	14,390
Lower Paxton	Dauphin	2	4,200	5,800
Penbrook	Dauphin	2	160	250
Highspire	Dauphin	1	400	500
Catawissa	Columbia	2	725	1,000
Bloomsburg	Columbia	11	3,980	9,950
Tilden	Berks	3	1,740	2,150
Upper Bern	Berks	1	80	80
Wyomissing	Berks	1	100	150
Reading	Berks	18	41,925	62,750
Stroudsburg	Monroe	9	6,275	8,375

Town or District.	County.	Properties.	Assessed value.	Market value.
Lewisburg ....Union		4	2,100	3,500
Kingsley ....Forest		1	40	120
Sunbury Borough .....Northumberland .		1	240	800
Warren ....Warren		1	1,500	3,500
Milton ....Northumberland .		8	3,550	15,150
Courtney ....Washington		4	5,700	10,200
Greensburg ....Westmoreland ..		13	18,600	27,900
Hegins ....Schuylkill		3	3,500	7,800
Connellsville ....Fayette		11	6,150	9,900
Vanderbilt ....Fayette		13	16,250	21,475
Cito ....Fulton		7	2,060	2,860
Three Towns ....Beaver		32	33,600	64,500
Coudersport ....Beaver		2	960	1,500
Huntersville ....Beaver		1	500	650
Elizabeth ....Allegheny		28	24,780	32,900
Doylestown ....Bucks		3	1,600	1,800
		1,072	$1,351,217	$2,316,865

ADDITIONAL PROPERTY OWNERS

Place.	Property holders	Market value
Bedford Springs	20	$10,000
Bradford	10	75,000
Chester	102	100,000
Coatesville	50	150,000
Columbia	25	35,000
Erie	2	15,000
Homestead	28	150,000
Irvine	4	5,000
Johnstown	25	35,000
McKeesport	30	10,000
Morton	22	25,000
Oil City	28	35,000
Tyrone	5	4,500
Waynesburg	12	10,000
West Chester	125	400,000
West Newton	4	....
Wilkes-Barre	36	75,000
York	50	80,000
Totals	578	$1,214,500

SUMMARY

Place.	Number property holders	Assessed value	Market value
Philadelphia	1,080	$2,801,275	$3,735,000
Pittsburgh	643	1,437,060	2,153,830
Eighty-seven towns and cities	1,072	1,351,217	2,316,865
Eighteen towns	578	....	1,214,500
Totals	3,373	$5,589,552	$9,420,195

CHURCH PROPERTY.

A great deal of the property of Negroes is in churches. Among the various influences which the church has had, has been the encouragement of co-operative buying of church properties. Many Negroes learned, for the first time, what a deed meant, or a builders' contract, or a mortgage, etc.. from his participation in church buying and building. The Census Department reported in 1906, that Negroes owned about $58,000,000 worth of church property in the United States, of which fully $50,000,000 worth was unencumbered. As will be seen, Pennsylvania Negroes own more than their share, which is due largely to the fact that in this State Negro churches took root very early and have always been encouraged as one of the influential factors for the better development of the race.

There are about 150 Baptist Churches in the State of Pennsylvania, but only 73 of them reported to the State Baptist Convention, and of these, only 44 reported their value, which was put at $785,230. An average of about $17,850 each. These, of course, were the best properties. The balance of about 100 churches include about fifty which are more or less temporary and own but little property. If the average of these 100 Baptist Churches is $1000, that would give an additional $100,000 of church property, and a total of $885,230, the value of the property of Negro Baptists. There are 196 African Methodist Churches in the State, of which 136 are of the African Methodist Episcopal denomination and 60 African Methodist Episcopal Zion denomination. Of the former 106 reported at the last conference session, a property valuation of $1,067,213. Allowing a valuation of $100 each for the 36 not reported, we have 136 properties of the African Methodist Episcopal Church in the State of Pennsylvania valued at $1,097,213. Of the latter, 46 reported property valued at $553,824, an average of about $12,000 each. If the average value of the remaining 14 African Methodist Episcopal Zion Churches is $1000, the total valuation would be about $567,824.

There were fourteen Presbyterian Churches whose value is estimated at $190,000, and eight Episcopal Churches valued at about $100,000. There are a number of Negro congregations of the Methodist Episcopal Church, the chief ones being in Philadelphia and Pittsburgh. They own about $250,000 worth of property. Other churches are the A. U. M. P., the Church of God, Congregational and C. M. E. Church, and several independent churches who own property valued at about $100,000. This would make the total amount of church property owned by Negroes approximately, as follows:

Baptists	$885,230
A. M. E.	1,067,213
A. M. E. Zion	567,824
Methodist (North)	250,000
Presbyterian	190,000
Episcopalian	100,000
Other denominations	100,000
Total value of church property	$3,160,267

GENERAL ESTIMATE OF PROPERTY.

By the above it is seen that in the cities of Philadelphia and Pittsburgh, the assessed value of property, exclusive of churches, is $4,238,335; that in eighty-seven other cities and towns the assessed value of 1072 properties is $1,351,217, making a total of $5,589,552, having a market value of $8,205,695. To this market value must be added the estimated holdings of Negroes in eighteen other cities and towns with a market value of $1,214,500 and $3,160,260, the value of church property, making a total of $12,580,455 as the value of holdings of Negroes in this State.

If we consider the difficulty of obtaining data, and scan carefully the list of places reported, we must conclude that this estimate is possibly 25 per cent. under the real holdings of Negroes in the State. I would estimate that they own property, the most conservative estimate of whose value is $15,000,000 to $20,000,000.

POPULATION, PROPERTY HOLDINGS, ETC., NOT IN-
CLUDED IN ¡PRECEDING REPORT.

Short sketches of Negroes in Pennsylvania cities and towns, compiled from letters from city and town officials, resident ministers,
teachers, physicians, etc., and personal observation:

ALTOONA, Blair County; population 1900: 38,566 whites, 407
colored. Estimated colored population in 1907 was 1000. Negroes are
scattered more or less, but find it difficult to rent. There are about ?5
home owners, having about $300,000 worth of property; one Negro
is reputed to be worth $250,000, owning some of the most valuable
portions of the city. Chief businesses are: 1 contractor, 1 retail furniture store, occupying about 2500 square feet of space; 1 pool room, 2
restaurants, 7 barber shops, 25 independent teamsters, 4 teamsters
and excavators, 1 tailor, 10 plasterers, 1 dying establishment. Wages
of the women in domestic service from $3.00 to $5.00 per week, and
$1.00 per day. Men get $1.50 per day. Three churches: A. M. E.,
A. M. E. Z., and Baptist, with a total of 138 members. Masons, Odd
Fellows, True Reformers. Mixed school, no Negro teachers; 2 policemen, 1 high school graduate in 1907 now attending Howard University, 1 in 1906.

BEDFORD SPRINGS, Bedford County: 1 colored lawyer, 3
barbers, more waiters, about 25 persons own their homes; one Negro
worth $5000, 1 farmer owns 65 acres. One young woman graduated
in 1906, and now in college, none in 1907, 4 since 1900; several cases
of inter-marriage between Negroes and whites.

BLOOMSBURG, Columbia County: 6067 whites, 97 colored.
There are 4 Negro property owners, one farmer having 30 acres, 3
barber shops, shaving both colored and white; 7 women in silk mills,
others in hotels and domestic service; 1 church, no inter-marriage,
mixed schools, 1 death in 1906, 3 births, 2 still births.

COATESVILLE, Chester County. Population, 1900: 5288 white,
433 colored. Estimated Negro population 1907, 1000. Negroes chiefly day laborers and in domestic and personal service; about a dozen
men in business; chief businesses are a blacksmith shop, groceries,

tailoring, barbering, dressmaking, express and hauling, 1 physician, a graduate of the University of Pennsylvania Medical School; 4 school teachers, 1 postoffice employe, 6 firemen, 1 policeman, 50 property holders, value of property estimated at $150,000; 4 churches. Much immigration from South during recent years; race prejudice has increased; 1 case of inter-marriage.

COLUMBIA, Columbia County. Population, 11,893; 423 colored. Negroes came to this town as early as 1819, most of them being manumitted slaves from Virginia; at a later time some fugitive slaves were among them. After passage of the Fugitive Slave Law in 1850, there was considerable emigration of many of the best Negroes, not less than 75 persons. Columbia was one of the most important places in the Underground Railroad in Pennsylvania, and held among its population some of the most prominent Negroes. Both Stephen Smith, the lumber merchant and philanthropist, and William Whipple lived here. At present there are about 500 Negroes who work chiefly in domestic service and do common labor on traction road, and some few are employed in the rolling mill, which has one colored foreman. Wages for men very from $1.25 per day to $1.50. There are 2 churches: 1 A. M. E., 1 Baptist; a separate primary school having two teachers and 56 pupils—28 girls and 27 boys between the ages of 6 and 14 years. There are three Negro children in the High School, but no graduates. The businesses are all small, and consist of 2 barber shops, 3 teamsters, 1 small notion store, 1 small grocery, 1 itinerant meat dealer and 2 boarding houses. There are lodges of Odd Fellows and True Reformers and Household of Ruth. The Metropolitan Life Insurance Society and the Baltimore Mutual do a good business among the Negroes. The Negroes live chiefly in small one- and two-story houses, made of rough boards, on alleys from 12 to 20 feet wide; some of these houses are worn out and about to fall, while others are newly painted or whitewashed, and appear neat. A few families live in brick houses on Fifth street. There are about 25 property holders with property valued at about $35,000. The community has made practically no progress in a generation.

ELIZABETH, Allegheny County. Total population in 1900 was 1866. About 20 families own properties valued from $1500 upward. One man has a large grocery and employs 2 persons. Two teamsters, 2 pupils in High School; no graduates.

ERIE, Erie County. 52,483 whites and 250 colored. 2 ice cream manufacturers and 2 barber shops are the chief businesses. Negro men are waiters, porters, laborers in stores and foundry; women work in private families. There is 1 policeman, 1 young woman graduated from High School in 1907, now bookkeeper in ice cream factory. There are two farmers, 1 owning 59 acres; 1 Negro is said to be worth $75,000. There are 6 cases of inter-marriage among the races, Negro men marrying white women in every case. More emigration than immigration. Emigrants go chiefly to rolling mill centre at Youngstown, Ohio. 1 A. M. E. Church, 30 members; 1 lodge of Masons.

FRANKLIN, Venango County. Population: 7043 whites and 274 colored. Negroes work chiefly in steel mills and oil refinery, averaging $1.50 per day; some are waiters, porters and general laborers; women are domestic servants. There are 12 property holders; 1 girl graduate of High School in 1906 studying music; 1 young man graduated in 1907 and is studying pharmacy. There is one storekeeper, 4 churches: 1 A. M. E., 1 A. M. E. Z., 1 Free Methodist, 1 Wesleyan Church. True Reformers and Masons have lodges.

GREENSBURG, Westmoreland County. Population, 1900: 6374 whites, 134 colored. Business: 1 restaurant, 1 tailor and dyer, 1 barber, 1 shining parlor. Negroes in domestic service chiefly. 7 persons own homes.

HARRISBURG, Dauphin County, Capital of Pennsylvania. 46,044 whites, 2107 Negroes, 10 Chinese, 6 Indians. Estimated Negro population in 1907, 6000. Negroes live chiefly in three or four "settlements" of four or five blocks each. The oldest is within one block of the State Capitol and the depot of the Pennsylvania Railroad, about South, Short, Walnut, State, Cowden and Filbert Streets, and adjacent alleys. Jews and Negroes live side by side. Other Negro settlements are about Balm Street. There are: 1 undertaker, 1 steam fitter, 6 restaurants, 4 caterers, 1 tailor, 1 peanut and coffee roaster, 1 contractor, 6 expressmen, 1 wrapper manufacturer, 1 notions and dry goods store, 7 barbers, 2 hand laundries, 1 shoe repairer, 1 chiropodist, 1 insurance society, 1 pool room, 8 coal, wood and ice dealers, 1 ladies' tailor and dealer in second-hand clothing, 1 Building and Loan Association. Chief occupation for both men and women is domestic service. There are about 25 Negroes employed as janitors, messengers and clerks in the State House, at salaries from $50 per month to $1200 per year; 5 Negroes are in postoffice, and 31 in city offices, and 5 on the police force. There are 3 physicians, 1 lawyer, 1 dentist and 10 teachers; 2 A. M. E. Churches, 1 A. M. E. Zion Church, Baptist Churches, 1 Presbyterian and 1 Episcopal Churches. There are schools composed entirely of Negroes. Four cases of inter-marriage are reported. Immigration has been heavy in recent years. There are 3 nurses, 2 stenographers and typewriters, 10 graduates from High School in 1906. There were 637 arrests in 1905; 77 births and 109 deaths; about 175 marriages.

HOMESTEAD, Allegheny County. Population, 1900, 11,903 whites, 651 colored; estimated Negro population, 1907, was 800; sub-urb of Pittsburgh; built up around the iron and steel industry, in which Negro workingmen earning from 90c to $6 per day. A few men do common labor at $1.60 to $1.50 per day; and some are porters, butlers and domestic servants. Women earn as domestics from $3.50 to $4.50. Negroes have come to Homestead chiefly since the strike of 1892, when a number of them were brought there as strike breakers. Prior to this time Negroes were few and worked chiefly in lumber and brick yards. A few Negroes are helpers on open-hearth furnaces, earning from $4 to $6 per day. The chief busi-nesses are: 3 groceries, 6 barber shops, 6 teamsters, several carpen-ters, masons, 1 undertaker, 2 doctors, 2 men in post office, 1 mail clerk and 1 carrier, 2 policemen, 1 graduate from high school in 1907; about 28 persons own homes; 1 Negro said to be worth about $100,-000; 14 pieces of property, bank stock, stock in coal corporation. There is one land company, and one small co-operative grocery store started in 1903.

IRVINE, Warren County; population, 1900, 307; about 70 Ne-groes, 4 property holders; 4 barber shops; several coal miners; 2 small churches, A. M. E. and A. M. E. Zion.

JOHNSTOWN, Cambria County, 35,613 whites, 323 colored. Chief occupations are janitors, waiters, porters; the two largest hotels employ Negro waiters. About 25 property holders. Negroes have begun to buy because of difficulty in securing homes. Several Negroes own more than 1 piece of property and rent to others of their race. There are 8 barber shops, 2 hotels, one in the business part of the town between the Majestic Theatre and the Columbia Opera House; 1 transfer company, 1 restaurant, 1 lodging house, 5 expressmen, 1 contractor (painter), does the work for the Cambria Steel Com-

15

pany; 1 tar and gravel roofer, employing 10 men; 1 sign painter, 1 contractor for excavating, now working on railroad with Negroes and Hungarians; 1 newspaper; 1 real estate dealer, 1 National Real Estate and Investment Company, incorporated at $10,000 in 1905, at $5 per share; has branch offices in Alabama, Kansas, Florida and South Carolina and Georgia. Johnstown has had only one Negro High School graduate. She is now teaching in Washington, D. C. There are 2 colored women's clubs; 1 Negro member of the Civic Club; Coachmen's and Porter's Club; lodges of Masons, Eastern Star, Mystic Shriners, Odd Fellows, Household of Ruth, Knights of Pythias, Court of Calanthia, Good Samaritans, 3 churches, 1 Baptist, 1 A. M. E., 1 A. M. E. Zion. Several cases of intermarriage.

LEWISTOWN, Mifflin County; total population, 4451; 132 Negroes; 7 property holders; 3 barber shops, 2 of which shave whites only; 1 teamster, 1 dressmaker, 1 notion store; some Negroes in steel works and hotels; 1 electrician, 2 churches, with 27 members; 5 cases of intermarriage; 1 lodge of Odd Fellows.

McKEESPORT, Allegheny County. Population, 1900. But little immigration from the South; 10 business men, 2 ministers, 1 physician. Property valued at $80,000; 2 churches, 5 high school graduates, 10 pupils now in high school. Negroes "are thrifty and many of them are buying property because the tendency is not to rent to them in desirable locations." Prejudice against Negroes has increased. One Negro on police force said by the chief of police to be "very good."

MEADVILLE, Crawford County, 10,110 whites and 181 colored; a college town, 1 church.(A. M. E.); no graduates from high school, 10 property holders; chief work, domestic service, railroad work, 1 barber, 1 carpenter; value of church and parsonage, $10,000.

MONONGAHELA, Washington County. Population, 1900, 4827 whites, 346 colored. There are 6 barber shops, 4 teamsters, 1 paver, several dressmakers, brick and stone masons; mixed school; no Negro teacher; 1 graduate from high school, 1906, and none in 1907; no intermarriages.

MONESSEN, Westmoreland County; 2197 total population 1900; about 250 Negroes in 1907. About 150 men work chiefly for Pittsburgh Steel Company, of whom 28 are wire drawers, earning about $4.00 per day of 11 hours; others are firemen, boiler tenders, etc. Negroes started here in 1902, when 32 wire drawers got free passes

from Joliet, Ill., and a guarantee of $4.00 per day to come here to
work; 6 of the original 32 still remain. There are 2 churches: A. M.
E. and Baptist; 1 Negro doctor, 3 barber shops, shaving whites only.

NEW CASTLE, Lawrence County. Population, 1900, 27,868
whites and 471 colored. About 800 Negroes in 1907. Negroes chiefly
porters, butlers, hod carriers, laborers in steel mills; a few plasterers;
6 barber shops; 1 pool room, 2 restaurants, 4 churches, 2 Baptist,
A. M. E., and A. M. E. Zion; 1 physician; no graduates from high
school, 1906 or 1907. True Reformers, Odd Fellows and Masons
have lodges; some immigration.

OIL CITY, Venango County. Population, 1900, 13,072 whites
and 182 colored. Men work in machine works, and with oil company at $1.50 to $2.50 per day; some waiters, laborers, bartenders
and porters. About four-fifths of the people own their homes; 2
cases of intermarriage; 1 A. M. E. Church.

OXFORD, Chester County. Population, 1900, 2032. Near Lincoln University. There are 3 ministers, 1 teacher, 12 business men.
Some immigration and some emigration in past years. Prejudice has
not increased. "The condition of the Negro here is not so inviting,
the few in business make no mark in the business world, the several
are doing fairly well on a small scale."

PHILADELPHIA, Philadelphia County. Population, 1900,
1,229,673 whites, 62,613 Negroes. Negro population now (1907) about
80,000. Negroes lived most largely in the 4th, 7th, 8th, 15th, 22d,
24th, 27th, 29th, 30th wards, but are generally scattered over the city.
Voting population was, in 1900, 20,095, of whom 2190 Negroes were
illiterate; 416 persons owned houses, of which 198 were encumbered.
In 1907 there were 802 pieces of property owned, the taxable value
of which was $2,438,675; Negroes have over $3,000,000 in banks; more
than 800 persons in business; 40 incorporated businesses; savings
banks. The chief occupation is domestic service, in which more than
95 per cent. of the female and 65 per cent. of the males were engaged
in 1900. There is, however, an increasing number of Negroes in the
professions, trade and transportation and in manufacturing and
mechanical pursuits. There are 80 churches, with approximately
28,000 members; of these 31 are Baptists, 17 are A. M. E. Churches,
8 Methodist Episcopal Churches, 6 Episcopal Churches, 5 A. M. E.
Zion, 4 Presbyterian, etc. The schools are mixed. There are about
50 teachers, teaching Negroes chiefly. Negroes attend school fairly

well. There have been graduates from the high and normal schools each year during recent years. There are lodges of Masons, Elks, Odd Fellows, True Reformers and other secret orders. Negroes are emigrating to the city in large numbers,. chiefly from Virginia, Maryland, North Carolina; about 150 cases of intermarriage.

PITTSBURGH (including Allegheny), Allegheny County. Population, 1900, 451,512, of whom Negroes comprised 20,355 (Pittsburgh, 17,040; Allegheny, 3315). Negroes are chiefly in 8th and 13th wards, along Wylie, Bedford and Centre avenues; but are also in every ward in the city; the movement of the population has been eastward for several years; many of the most prosperous Negroes live in the East End of Pittsburgh. In 1900 there were 259 homes owned, of which 146 were encumbered. Considerably over a million dollars' worth of property must be owned today. More than 300 Negroes are in business employing about 1000 Negroes. The chief businesses are barber shops, restaurants, hotels, excavating and hauling. Negroes are largely employed in the steel mills and some have very responsible places. Negro puddlers are used exclusively in the Park's Mills (The Black Diamond); Negro rollers are employed in the Old Clark's mills, now owned by the Carnegie Steel Company, of the United States Steel Corporation. There are 5 lawyers, more than a dozen physicians, dentists and pharmacists, but no teachers. There are 175 Negroes in the employ of the Federal, county and city government, of whom 25 are policemen and about 40 in the post office. There are nearly 40 churches, the Baptist having the largest number and the largest memberships. Immigration is very heavy, especially from Virginia and North Carolina.

PITTSTON, Luzerne County; about 12,530 whites and 26 colored in 1900; in 1906 about 150 colored; 1 family owns home. Negroes chiefly in domestic service and unskilled labor; coachmen and waiters; 1 Negro has peanut stand, 2 teamsters, 1 novelty manufacturer, 1 A. M. E. Church, 1 lodge, Odd Fellows; no intermarriage.

SCRANTON, Lackawanna County. Population, 1900, 101,487 whites and 539 colored. Principal businesses are teaming, 1 man running 12 teams, employing 40 persons; 1 grocery, 1 hotel of 40 rooms, 2 barber shops. Men are largely coachmen, messengers, waiters, a few coal miners; women chiefly domestics, 2 graduates from high school in 1907, 1 teaching in West Virginia, the other in a business college; 1 lawyer, 2 churches, A. M. E. and Baptist; lodges, Masons, Odd Fellows, Elks, True Reformers.

STEELTON, Dauphin County, suburb of Harrisburg. Population, 10,575 whites, 1571 colored. This town is built around the steel industry. Negroes are chiefly on Adams and Ridge streets, largely segregated. Only a few own homes. The principal businesses are: 1 general store, 2 small confectionery and notion stores, 1 tobacco store, 2 restaurants, 2 pool rooms, 4 express and hauling, 4 barber shops, 2 rag and junk dealers, 1 manicurist, 1 undertaker, 2 carpenters, 1 plasterer, 1 newspaper, 1 building and loan association, 1 cleaning and pressing establishment. The chief occupation is laboring in the steel mills, where about 500 Negroes are employed. There are some foremen, and one machinist. Women do but little work. There are 2 Baptist Churches and 1 A. M. E. Church, having an aggregate membership of about 700 persons; there is one physician, a graduate of Lincoln University and Howard University; 5 teachers in public schools. The Negro pupils are taught chiefly by Negro teachers; no graduates in 1907 from high school. There are three Negro policemen, 1 detective, 1 clerk in the Steel Company's store, 1 member of the City Council; 25 Negroes own property, Negroes first entered steel mills as strike breakers. Immigration has been very heavy in past ten years, chiefly from Virginia, Maryland and North Carolina.

TYRONE, Blair County. Population, 1900, 115 Negroes, 54 males and 61 females, and 5731 whites. Negroes are chiefly porters, laborers; 5 property holders, 1 farmer owns 70 acres. There are five barber shops, one hairdresser, 1 A. M. E. Church at Hollidaysburg; a few miles away one Negro does a large confectionery business. Hollidaysburg had 116 Negroes in 1900.

UNIONTOWN, Fayette County. Population in 1900, 6537 whites, 807 colored; now (1907) about 1200 colored; about 15 home owners, averaging $1000 each. Businesses include 2 small grocers, 2 restaurants, 4 barber shops, 3 of which for whites only; 1 employment agency, 4 dressmakers, 2 boarding houses, 1 bricklayer and carpenter. Men work principally in the coal mines and coke manufactory. Wages range from $1.15 to $3.50 per day. All hotels have Negro waiters. Women chiefly in domestic service. There are 4 farmers in neighborhood, having from 10 to 40 acres. There are 4 churches, 2 Baptists, and 1 A. M. E. and 1 A. M. E. Zion; mixed schools; no Negro teachers; 1 physician and 1 electrical engineer. There were 4 Negro graduates from the high school in 1907 and 2 in

1906. About 350 Negro pupils in school. Lodges of Knights of
Pythias, Odd Fellows, Good Samaritans and True Reformers are in
the city. Considerable immigration in past two years, from Virginia,
North Carolina and Maryland; 1 Negro policeman.

WASHINGTON, Washington County. Population, 1900, 6677
whites and 993 colored. Estimated Negro population in 1907 was
1500. Businesses are: 1 grocery, 3 restaurants, 8 barbers, boarding
houses, 1 contractor, 1 plasterer, 1 tailor, 2 hairdressers, 2 caterers.
There are 4 churches, A. M. E., A. M. E. Z., Baptist and M. E.;
1 lawyer, 1 physician, 3 teachers under a white principal. Colored
children in separate room from whites in public school; 1 high school
graduate (male), 1907, 2 in 1906; 1 former graduate is a physician
in Virginia; a few cases of intermarriage; large immigration from
Virginia and West Virginia. Men work chiefly in tin-plate manufac-
tory and coal mines, earning from $4.50 to $7.50 per day. About 150
persons own property, one owning 7 houses, valued at $10,000; an-
other having property valued at $5000. Church property valued at
$40,000. People live in good houses, scattered in all parts of the
city.

WAYNESBURG, Greene County. Population, 1900, 62,390
whites and 154 colored. Men work in tin-plate mills for $1.50 to $5
per day; finishers being able to earn the latter amount; about one-
third of the Negroes own their homes; but not as much property is
owned as formerly; one Negroe owns property worth $20,000. There
are 3 barber shops, 3 teamsters, 1 carpenter, 1 plasterer, 1 A. M. E.
Church, 1 lodge of Masons; no graduates; no intermarriage.

WEST CHESTER, Chester County. Population, 1900, 7739
whites, 1785 colored. Estimated Negro population, 1907, 2000; chief
occupations of men are common labor, work in brickyards and mills;
of women, domestic service; wages, $1.25 to $3.00 per day for men;
$2 to $5 per day for women. 45 Negroes in business, 6 restaurants,
1 hotel, 8 barbers, 1 real estate dealer, 1 blacksmith, 1 excavating contractor, 2 shining parlors, 1 colt trainer, 1 contractor, 1 caterer, 2
hairdressers, 2 boarding houses, 1 grocery, 3 expressmen, 3 fish and
vegetable dealers, 4 junk dealers, 5 dressmakers, 1 bakery, 1 paper
hanger. There are also 1 stone mason, 2 bricklayers, 1 engineer,
sveral fireman and brickmakers. The Negro business people employ
from 58 to 75 persons. In this hotel 9 are employed regularly. There
are 6 teachers, 2 post office employes, 1 physician, 8 ministers, 1 po-

liceman. Property is estimated to be worth $600,000. But little immigration during recent years; not much prejudice. Negro school put under Negro principal a year ago.

WEST NEWTON, Westmoreland County. Population in 1900, 2467. Negroes now estimated at 200 (1907); 4 property holders; 2 barber shops, serving only whites; 1 restaurant, 2 engineers. Mining is the chief work of the Negroes; a few work in radiator and boiler works; a few teamsters, coachmen and hotel workers. Women wash and sew chiefly; 1 church (A. M. E.); no lodge. Population is decreasing on account of scarcity of coal. The church membership has decreased by 50 per cent.

WILKES-BARRE, Luzerne County. Population, 1900, 51,036 white, 685 colored. Negro population in 1907 estimated about 1000. No physician, 3 ministers, 2 post office employes, 1 clerk and 1 carrier, 1 Court officer with whites, good; Negroes own between $75,000 and $100,000 of property; one stock clerk in wholesale store, 1 stenographer with large coal company; majority of men work in hotels, clubs and daily unskilled labor; women in domestic service; 23 business men, 6 barber shops, 1 hotel, several express men and general haulers, 2 tile setters, 1 weekly newspaper, 2 churches, 1 mission, 1 lodge of Odd Fellows; but little immigration from South.

WILLIAMSPORT, Lycoming County. Population, 1900, 27,613 whites, 1144 colored; about 40 property holders, one of whom owns eight houses. Negroes are not segregated, but scattered over the city. Chief businesses: 1 steam laundry, employing 10 persons; 3 restaurants, 4 paper hangers, 4 paper hangers and painters, 2 carpenters, 3 plasterers, 1 bricklayer, 2 grocery stores, 1 hotel, 3 colored barber shops and about a dozen teams. Negroes work in silk braid factory, 1 foreman; laborers in the lumber mills; waiters, porters, etc. There are 4 churches, aggregating 640 members; 1 A. M. E., 1 A. M. E. Z. and 2 Baptists; 2 lodges of Odd Fellows, 1 of Masons, 1 of True Reformers; 1 policeman, 1 constable, 2 men in post office, 1 letter carrier, 1 lawyer; no teachers; mixed schools; 2 graduates from high school, 107, and 1 graduate, 1906; 3 cases of intermarriage.

YORK, York County. Population, 1900, 32,929 whites, 778 colored. Negroes live scattered over the town, some in quite desirable places, with clean brick houses, with small porticos, others in the side streets. There are about 50 property holders, some owning one, two, three, four and as high as five houses in addition to their homes.

Within the last ten years it has become very difficult for colored
people to rent houses on the better streets; as a result, they are
forced to buy if they would live in the desirable parts of the city.
The value of property in York is about $100,000. There are 6 barber
shops, 3 of which shave whites only; 2 restaurants, 1 caterer, 3 teamsters, 1 hair dresser, 2 boarding houses, 2 dressmakers, 1 inurance
agent. Negroe are engaged largely in domestic service and unskilled
labor. Wages for men run from $25 to $40 per month, for women,
$3 to $3.50 per week. The York Manufacturing Company (iron
works) has about 100 Negroes employed; pay ranged from $1.50 to
$2.50 per day. In some establishments Negroes hold positions of
importance. The York Dental Supply Company has a Negro to
burn artificial teeth; one of the iron companies has a Negro engineer and a Negro draughtsmen. There are 4 churches, 1 A. M. E.,
with 90 members; 1 A. M. E. Z., with 250 members; 1 Presbyterian,
40 members, and 1 Baptist. There were 136 Negroes in public
school, June, 1907, and 2 in business college. There were 4 teachers
and 1 physician. Negro children go to a separate primary school.
Nine Negroes have graduated from high school in past ten years;
one is a physician, another a Presbyterian minister, another a graduate in law, now in the Government service in Chicago; 1 died while
studying medicine; 2 are teachers, 1 a barber, 1 in training school
for teachers and 2 are at home. There have been Negro teachers in
the schools for a half century. There has been immigration during
the past ten years, chiefly from Virginia, Maryland and North Carolina, but this has been very nearly balanced by emigration to Harrisburg and larger cities. The Negroes are optimistic, and report
no ill-feeling among them and whites.

Bibliography

A BRIEF HISTORY of the Movement to Abolish the Slums of Philadelphia (Pam).

ACT OF INCORPORATION, Causes and Motives of the African Episcopal Church of Philadelphia, 1810.

ADDRESS TO THE PEOPLE OF COLOR in Penna., 1838, by the Abolition Society, Joseph Parrish, Isaac Barton, Needles, etc.

AGG—Proceedings and Debates of the Convention of the Commonwealth of Pennsylvania to Propose Amendments to the Constitution, Commenced and Held at Harrisburg on the 2d day of May, 1837. Reported by John Agg, 13 vols., Harrisburg, 1837-1838.

"AMERICAN WEEKLY MERCURY."

A MECHANIC—To Tradesmen and Mechanics, etc., of Pennsylvania. Dec. 4, 1773.

AN ADDRESS Before the Pennsylvania Augustine Society for the Education of People of Color, Sept. 30, 1818. Constitution of the Society of Prince Saunders.

A NARRATIVE OF SOME OF THE PROCEEDINGS of the North Carolina Yearly Meeting on the Subject of Slavery—Greensborough, N. C., 1848.

AN INQUIRY INTO THE CONDITION and Prospects of the African Race in the United States. Phila., 1837.

"ANNALS OF ACADEMY POLITICAL AND SOCIAL SCIENCE."

ANNUAL REPORTS of American Colonization Society.

APPEAL OF FORTY THOUSAND COLORED CITIZENS, Threatened With Disfranchisement, to the People of Pennsylvania, 1838 (Pam).

ARMSTEAD—Tribute to Negroes, 1848.

ARMSTRONG, EWDARD—Record of Court at Upland in Pennsylvania.

ARNETT, B. W.—The Centennial Budget, of the A. M. E. Church, for 1888-1884. 651 pp.

ARNETT, B. W.—The Budget, Containing Annual Reports of the General Officers, etc. 1885-6. 375 pp.

ARNETT, B. W.—The Budget, 1891. 241 pp.

ARNETT, B. W.—The Budget, 1901. 78 pp.

ARNETT, B. W.—The Budget of 1904. 373 pp. Philadelphia.

ASHER, JEREMIAH, Autobiography, Philadelphia, 1862.

ASHMEAD, H. S.—History of Delaware County.

A STATISTICAL INQUIRY into the Condition of the People of Color of the City and Districts of Philadelphia—Philadelphia, 1849.

ATLANTA UNIVERSITY CONFERENCE REPORTS, 1896 to Date—Atlanta, Ga.

A TRIBUTE TO THE MEMORY OF THOMAS SHIPLEY, the Philanthropist—Robt. Purvis, 1836.

ANDERSON, MATTHEW, Presbyterianism and Its Relation to the Negro—Philadelphia, 1897.

BARMEISTER—Comparative Anatomy and Psychology of Negro, 1853.

BASSETT, E. D., Handbook on Hayti, Philadelphia.

BASSETT, J. S.—Slavery in State of North Carolina.

BATTLES—History of Bucks County, 351-2.

BEAN—History of Montgomery County, 302.

BIAS, J. J.—Synopsis of Phrenology, Philadelphia, 1859.

BLACKSON, LORENZO—Autobiography, Philadelphia, 1861.

BLAINE, JAMES G.—Twenty Years in Congress.

BLODGETT, JAMES H.—Wages of Farm Laborers in the United States, Bulletin No. 26, Miscellaneous Series, U. S. Department of Agriculture.

BOLLES, ALBERT J.—History of Pennsylvania, Philadelphia.

BOSTON, MASS, GRAMMAR SCHOOL COMMITTEE—Report of a Special Committee of the Grammar School Board. Abolition of the Smith Colored School. Boston, 1849. 71 pp., 8 vo.

BOWDEN, JOSEPH—History of the Society of Friends: 2 vols.

BRADFORD, SARAH H.—Harriet, the Moses of Her People. 171 pp. New York, 1901.

BRAGG, G. F.—The Attitude of the Conference of Church Workers Among the Colored People; a pamphlet; 1907.

BROOKS, CHAS. H. (Grand Secretary of the Order)—The Official History and Manual of the Grand United Order of Odd Fellows in America. A Chronological Treatise, etc. 274 pp. Philadelphia, 1902.

BROOKS, C. H.—Manual and History of the Grand United Order of Odd Fellows, Philadelphia, 1864.

BROUSSEAN, KATE—L' Education des Negres, 1904—Felix Alcan.

BRUCE, P. A. B.—Economic History of Virginia in the Seventeenth Century, 1896, McMillan.

BRUCE, P. A. B—The Plantation Negro as a Freeman, 1899, McMillan.

CAMPBELL, ROBERT—A Pilgrimage to My Motherland; An Account of a Journey Among the Egbas and Yornbas of Central Africa—Philadelphia, 1861.

CAREY, M. & BIOREN J.—Laws of Pennsylvania, 1700-1802—Philadelphia, 1803.

CATTO'S SEMI-CENTENARY DISCOURSE, Philadelphia, 1856.

CATTO. W. T.—History of the Presbyterian Movement. Phila., 1857. A Semi-Centenary Discourse and History of the First African Presbyterian Church, Phila., May, 1857, From Its Organization, Including a Notice of Its First Pastor, John Gloucester; also Appendix Containing Sketches of All the Churches in Philadelphia.

CATTO, W. Y.—History of the Presbyterian Movement, Philadelphia, 1858.

CELEBRATION of the Ninetieth Anniversary of the Pennsylvania Society.

CENSUS OF THE UNITED STATES, First to the Eleventh. Washington, 1790-1898.

CHARITIES—The Negroes in the Cities of the North, Oct. 7, 1905.

CHAPPELL, CHAS. W.—Negro Business Directory of Pittsburgh and Vicinity. 1907-1908.

CINCINNATI CONVENTION of Colored Freedmen of Ohio. Proceedings January 14-19, 1852. Cincinnati, 1892. 8 vol.

CLARKSON—History of American Slave Trade, Wilmington, 1815.

COLLECTION OF REPORTS of Charitable Institutions for Colored Persons (Ridgway Library).

COLLEGE-BRED NEGRO. Atlanta University Publication No. 5. 115 pp. 1900.

COLORED ENLISTMENTS, Philadelphia (Pam. Philadelphia Library Co.).

COLORED PEOPLE IN PHILADELPHIA, Philadelphia (Pam. Phila. Library Co.).

COLORED REGIMENTS, Philadelphia (Pam. Phila. Library Co.).

CONDITION OF THE PEOPLE of Color in Ohio. With Interesting Anecdotes. Boston, 1839. 48 pp. 12 mo.

CONSTITUTION of the Association (National) of Colored Women. Tuskegee. 7 pp. 1898.

CONSTITUTION of the National League of Colored Women of the U. S., Washington, 1892.

CONSTITUTION and Act of Incorporation of the Pennsylvania Society for Promoting the Abolition of Slavery and for the Relief of Free Negroes Unlawfully Held in Bondage, and for the Improving of the Condition of the African Race, etc., Phila., 1820.

CONSTITUTION of the American Society of Free Persons of Color for Improving Their Condition. Philadelphia, 1831.

CONSTITUTION of the Free Produce Society of Pennsylvania. Phila., 1827.

CONSTITUTION OF PENNSYLVANIA. Harrisburg, 1835.

COPPIN, L. J.—Catherine S. Campbell Beckett.

COPPIN, LEVI J.—The Relation of Baptized Children to the Church, Philadelphia, 1891.

CRAIG, NEVILLE B.—The Olden Time, etc., 2 vols. Pittsburgh, 1846.

CROMWELL, J. W.—The Early Negro Convention Movement, Occasional Paper No. 9, of the American Negro Academy, Washington, 1904.

CUTLER, J. E.—Lynch Law, 1905, Longams.

DAILY LOCAL NEWS—West Chester, Past and Present; Centennial Souvenir With Celebration Proceedings. 1799-1899.

DALLAS, R. C.—Growth of Maroon. London, 1803, Vol. 1.

DALLAS, A. J.—Laws of Pennsylvania, 1700-1781. Phila., 1797.

DAVIS—History of Bucks Co.

DELANEY, MARTIN ROBINSON—Condition, Elevation, Emigration and Destiny of the Colored People of the United States., etc. Philadelphia, 1854.

DENNIKER, J.—The Races of Man. 611 pp. New York, 1904.

DEXTER, FRANKLIN B.—Estimate of Population of Colonies.

DINWIDDIE, EMILY W.—Housing and Conditions in Philadelphia.

DIXON—Life of Penn, Phila., 1851.

DOUGLASS, WILLIAM—Annals of St. Thomas' Church. Philadelphia, 1862.

DOUGLASS—Personal Narrative of Mrs. Margaret Douglass, Imprisoned in Norfolk for the Crime of Teaching Free Colored Children to Read. Boston, 1854.

DU BOIS, W. E. B.—The Philadelphia Negro, 1899. Ginn Co.

DU BOIS, W. E. B.—The Suppression of the Slave Trade, 1896.

DU BOIS, W. E. B.—The Souls of Black Folk, 1903, Longmans. McClurg Company.

DU BOIS, W. E. B.—Negro Farmer, Special U. S. Census Report.

DU BOIS, W. E. B.—The Negroes of Farmville, Va. (U. S. Bureau of Labor Bulletin, January, 1898).

EDUCATION AND EMPLOYMENT Statistics of the Colored People of Philadelphia (MS. in Library of Historical Association), Dr. E. O. Emerson, Vital Statistics of Philadelphia in American Journal of Medical Sciences, July, 1848.

EDWARDS, BRYAN—History of the West Indies.

ELY—The Labor Movement in America.

EMERSON, DR. E. O.—Vital Statistics of Philadelphia (in America Journal of Medical Sciences, July, 1848).

EXPULSION OF FREE NEGROES—Vol. 2—1860.

ECONOMIC POSITION of the American Negro, The—Reprinted from Papers and Proceedings of the Seventeenth Annual Meeting of the American Economic Association, December, 1904.

FERRIS, BENJ.—History of the Original Settlement on the Delaware, etc. Wilmington, 1846.

FIVE YEARS' ABSTRACT of the Transactions of the Pennsylvania Society for the Promotion of the Abolition of Slavery. Phila., 1853.

FLEMING, W. L.—Civil War and Reconstruction in Alabama, 1905, McMillan.

FORTUNE, T. T.—Black and White, 1884, Fords, Howard and Hurlbert.

FRANKLIN, BENJAMIN—An Essay on the African Slave Trade, Phila., 1790.

FREEDMAN'S SAVING BANK—Bankers' Magazine.

FREEDMAN'S SAVING BANK—Old and New.

FRIENDS—A Brief Statement of the Rise and Progress of the Testimony of the Religious Society of Friends Against Slavery and the Slave Trade. Philadelphia, 1843.

FRIENDS—A Brief Sektch of the School for Black People and Their Descendants, Established by the Religious Society of Friends in 1770. Philadelphia, 1867.

FRIENDS—Brief Statement of the Rise and Progress of the Testimony of Friends Against Slavery, 1671-1787. Phila., 1843.

FRIENDS—Germantown Friends Protest Against Slavery, 1868. (Facsimile copy.) In Adger Collection, Home for Aged and Infirm Colored Persons, Phila., 1880.

FRIENDS—The Appeal of the Religious Society of Friends in Pennsylvania, New Jersey, etc., on Behalf of the Colored Races. Phila., 1858.

GAINES, W. J.—African Methodism in the South. Atlanta, 1890.

GARNETT, HENRY HIGHLAND—The Past and Present Condition and the Destiny of the Colored Race. Troy, 1848. 20 pp.

GARNER, J. A.—History of the Reconstruction in Mississippi, 1901, McMillan.

GOODWIN, M. B.—History of Schools for the Colored Population in the District of Columbia. U. S. Bureau of Education. Special Reports on District of Columbia for 1869. pp. 199-300.

GOODELL, WM.—America's Slave Code, New York, 1853.

GOVERNOR OF PENNSYLVANIA on Slavery, 1855.

GREGOIREO—Inquiry Concerning the Intellectual and Moral Faculties and Lierature of Negroes, Followed by an Account of 15 Negroes and Mulattoes Distinguished in Science, Art and Literature. Brooklyn, 1810.

GRIMKE, A. H.—Right on the Scaffold of the Martyrs of 1822. Occasional paper No. 7 of the American Negro Academy, Washington, 1901.

GUTHRIE, JAMES M.—Camp Fires of the Afro-Americans, Philadelphia, 1899.

HAMMOND, M. B.—The Cotton Industry, 1897, McMillan.

HAMPTON NEGRO CONFERENCE Reports, Hampton Institute, Va.

HARPER, F. E. W.—Forest Leaves, Baltimore, 1855.

HARPER, F. E. W.—Iola Leroy: A Novel. Third Edition, Phila., 1892. 280 pp.

HARPER, F. E. W.—Miscellaneous Poems, Boston, 1854.

HAZARD, SAMUEL—The Register of Pennsylvania, Philadelphia, 1828-36.

HERBERT, H. A.—(Ed) Why the Solid South? 1890, Woodward (Baltimore).

HICKOK, CHAS. T.—The Negro in Ohio. 1802-1870. A thesis, etc. 182 pp. Cleveland, 1896.

HISTORY of the Insurance Company of North America, With the Account of the African Insurance Co., Organized in Phila., 1810.

HISTORY OF BRADFORD COUNTY.

HISTORY OF BUCKS COUNTY.

HISTORY OF PENNSYLVANIA HALL, Which Was Destroyed by a Mob on the 17th of May, 1838. Phila., 1838.

HISTORY OF THE YELLOW FEVER in Philadelphia, in 1797. 2d Phila., 1798.

HOFFMAN, F. L.—Race Traits and Tendencies of the American Negro, 1896, McMillan.

HOWARD, JAS. H. W.—Bond and Free, Harrisburg, 1836.

HOWARD, JAS. H. W.—Pennsylvania at the National Business League, Harrisburg, 1908.

HOWARD, O. O.—Autobiography. 2 vols. N. Y., 1907.

HULL HOUSE Maps and Papers, New York, 1895.

HURD, J. C.—Topics of Jurisprudence Connected With Freedmen; Inquiry into the Conditions of the Negro in the United States. By an American. Philadelphia, 1839.

JANNEY, SAMUEL M.—History of the Religious Society of Friends, Philadelphia, 1859-67.

JAY, WILLIAM—Inquiry into the Character and Tendency of the American Colonization Society and American Anti-Slavery Societies, 6th Ed. New York, 1838.

JONES, ABSALOM—A Thanksgiving Sermon—On Account of the Abolition of the African Slave Trade, etc. Phila., 1808. (Pam.)

JONES, ROBT.—Fifty Years in the Lombard Street Central Presbyterian Church. Philadelphia, 1894.

JONES—The Religious Instructions of Negroes in the United States, by Chas. Jones, Savannah, 1842.

JOURNAL OF THE HOUSE OF REPRESENTATIVES of Pennsylvania, from Nov. 28, 1876-Oct. 2, 1781. Philadelphia, 1782.

JOURNAL OF THE HOUSE, Pennsylvania, 1862-1801.

JOURNAL OF THE HOUSE, Pennsylvania, 1802.

JOURNAL OF THE SENATE, Pennsylvania, 1802.

JOURNAL OF THE SENATE, Pennsylvania, 1790-1802.

JUPITER HAMMOND'S ADDRESS to the Negroes in the State of New York. Philadelphia, 1787.

KELSEY, CARL—The Negro Farmer.

LAIDLAW, WALTER—(Ed) The Federation of Churches and Christian Workers in New York City. First and Second Sociological Canvassers. New York, 1896-1897.

LAWS OF THE COMMONWEALTH of Pennsylvania from October 14, 1700, to March 20, 1810. Philadelphia, 1810.

LAY, BENJ.—Against Keeping Slaves.

LAY, BENJ.—Slave Keepers, Apostates.

LOVE, E. K.—History of the First African Baptist Church, Savannah, 1889.

LIVERMORE, GEO.—Historical Research Respecting the Opinions of the Founders of the Republic, Boston, 1862.

LYTLE, M. S.—History of Huntingdon County, Penna.

McDOUGALL, M. J.—Fugitive Slaves.

McKNIGHT—History of Jefferson County, Penna.

MATTHEWS, HARVEY—An Account of the Malignant Fever Prevalent in Philadelphia, etc. 4th edition. Phila., 1793.

MAYO, SMITH R.—Statistics and Sociology, New York, 1896.

MEMOIRS—Historical Society of Pennsylvania, Vol. 1, 405.

MERRIMAN, G. S.—The Negro and the Nation, 1906, Henry Holt Co.

16

MINUTES of the American Moral Reform Society, Phila., 1836.

MINUTES of the First Annual Convention of the People of Color, Philadelphia, 1831. (Pam.)

MINUTES of the Second Convention of the Free People of Color, Philadelphia, 1832.

MINUTES of the Fourth Convention of the Free People of Color, 1834.

MINUTES of the Fifth Convention of Free People of Color, Phila., 1835.

MINUTES of the Philadelphia Councils Committee, Appointed Sept. 14, 1793, to Alleviate the Suffering, etc.

MINUTES of the Proceedings of a Convention of Delegates from the Abolition Societies, etc., Philadelphia, Jan. 1st to 7th, 1794.

MINUTES of the Proceedings of the Special Meeting of the Fifteenth American Convention for the Promoting of the Abolition of Slavery and Improving the Condition of the African Race. Philadelphia, Dec. 10-15th, 1818.
The same, the Eighteenth Session, Oct. 7, 1823.
The same, the Nineteenth Session, Oct. 4, 1825.
The same, the Twentieth Session, 1828.

MINUTES of the Convention of Pennsylvania, Which Commenced Nov. 24, 1789, for the Purpose of Reviewing, Altering and Amending the Constitution of This State. Phila., 1789-1790.

MITCHELL, J. T., & FLANDERS, HENRY, Commissioners—The Statutes at Large of Pennsylvania from 1682 to 1801, Compiled Under the Authority of the Act of May 19, 1887.

MONTGOMERY, M. L.—Handbook of Berks County, 1762-1883.

MOORE, J. J.—History of the A. M. E. Z. Church. York, Pa., 1880.

MOORE—Slavery in Massachusetts.

MOSSELL, N. F. MRS.—Forerunners of the Afro-American Council, Howard Magazine, Washington, April, 1900.

MOSSELL, MRS. N. F.—The Work of Afro-American Women, Philadelphia, 1894. 178 pp.

MOTT, A.—Biography of Colored People, Philadelphia. (Pam. Phila. Library Company.)

MURPHY, E. G.—The Present South, 1904, McMillan.

NARRATIVES of the Proceedings of the Black People During the Late Awful Calamity in Philadelphia in the Year 1793. By Absalom Jones and Richard Allen.

NEEDHAM, J. F.—Journal of Proceedings of the 48th General Meeting of the Grand United Order of Odd Fellows, Phila., 1907.

NEEDLES, EDW.—An Historical Memoir of the Pennsylvania Society for Promoting the Abolition of Slavery. Philadelphia, 1848.

NEEDLES, EDW.—Ten Years' Progress, or a Comparison of the State and Condition of the Colored People in the City and County of Philadelphia from 1837 to 1847. Philadelphia, 1849.

NELL, WILLIAM C.—Services of Colored Americans in the Wars of 1776 and 1812. Reprinted, Philadelphia, 1894.

NELL, W. C.—The Colored Patriots of the American Revolution, etc. Boston, 1855.

NICKOLLS, R. B.—A Letter to the Treasurer of the Abolition Society, London, 1788.

OBSERVATIONS ON ENSLAVING. Germantown, 1760.

OBSERVATIONS ON ENSLAVING NEGROES. Germantown. Printed by C. Sower, 1759.

OLEARY, MATTHEW—Observations on Rush's Inquiry into the Origin of the Late Epidemic Fever in Philadelphia. Phila., 1793.

PAYNE, DANIEL A.—History of the A. M. E. Church, Nashville, 1891.

PEARCE, EDW. LILLIE—The Negroes at Port Royal; Report to S. B. Chase, Secretary of Treasury, Boston, 1862. 36 pp.

PENN, I. G. AND J. W. E. BOWEN, Editors—The United Negro, His Problems and His Progress. Containing the Addresses and Proceedings of the Negro Young People's Congress (Christian and Educational), held Aug. 6-11, 1902. Atlanta, 1902.

PENNSYLVANIA COLONIAL RECORD, Philadelphia.

PENNSYLVANIA GENERAL ASSEMBLY: Charter to William Penn and Laws of Province, 1682-1700.

PETERS, RICHARD—Fugitive Slave Case of Edward Prigg vs. Commonwealth of Pennsylvania. January, 1842.

PHILADELPHIA IN CARTOON.

PHILADELPHIA IN 1824.

PHILADELPHIA NEWSPAPERS—Dailies, Bulletin (evening), Inquirer, North American, Press, Public Ledger, Record, Telegraph (evening), Times (evening).

PHILADELPHIA NEWSPAPERS—Colored, The Christian Banner, The Courant, The Philadelphia Tribune, The Pilot, McGirt's Magazine (monthly), The A. M. E. Review (quarterly), The Christian Recorder.

PICKARD, MRS. KATE E. R.—"Kidnaped and Ransomed: Peter Still and His Wife, 'Vina.' "—Syracuse, 1856.

PIERCE, P. S.—The Freedmen's Bureau, 1904. State University of Iowa.

PLATT, O. H.—Negro Governors. In papers of the New Haven Colony Historical Society. Vol. 6. New Haven, 1900.

PROCEEDINGS OF CONVENTION of Colored Freedmen of Pennsylvania, Phila. (Pam.)

PROCEEDINGS of the National Negro Business League, Annually, 1900-07.

PROUD, ROBT.—History of Penna., 1681-1742.

PURVIS, ROBT.—Remarks on the Life and Character of James Forten. (Pam.)

RATZEL, F.—History of Mankind. 3 vols., New York, 1904.

RELATION OF STATE to Colored Population. Vol. 11, 1832.

REPORTS—Bureau of Charities; Bureau of Health, Phila. Annual Reports. The Children's Aid Society.

REPORT—Annual, of the Commissioner-General of Immigration, Washington.

REPORTS—Eastern Penitentiary.

REPORTS—Frederick Douglass Hospital, Phila.

REPORTS of the Commissioner Appointed for the Purpose of Securing to Colored People in Philadelphia the Rights to the Use of the Street Cars, Phila. (1865, Pam.)

REPORT of the Committee on the Comparative Health, Mortality, Length of Sentences, etc., of White and Colored Convicts. Phila., 1849.

REPORT of the Committee of Senate Upon the Relations Between Labor and Capital, and Testimony Taken by the Committee. 5 vols. Washington, 1885.

REPORT of Major General O. O. Howard, Commissioner, Bureau of Refugees, Freedmen and Abandoned Lands, etc. 30 pp. Washington, 1869.

REPORT of the U. S. Industrial Commission, Vol. 14.

REPORTS of the Home for Aged and Infirm Colored Persons.

REPORTS of the Philadelphia Association for the Protection of Colored Women.

REPORTS of the Starr Center (Social Settlement).

REPRESENTATIVE AMERICAN NEGROES—The Negro Problem, 1903. Jos. Pott & Co.

RICHARD ALLEN (First Bishop of A. M. E. Church)—The Life, Experience and Gospel Labors of the Rt. Rev. Richard Allen, etc. Written by himself. Phila., 1833.

RICHARD ALLEN AND JACOB TAPSICO—The Doctrine and Discipline of the A. M. E. Church. Phila., 1819.

RIIS, JACOB—The Making of an American. McMillan.

RUPP, I. DANIEL—History of Lancaster County. Lancaster, 1844.

RUPP, I. DANIEL—History of Berks and Lebanon Counties, 1844.

SANDIFORD, RALPH—Observations on Negro Slavery.

SAUNDERS, PRINCE—A Memoir; Presented to the American Convention for the Promotion of the Abolition of Slavery. Phila., 1818.

SECESSION PAMPHLETS—Washington and Jackson on Negro Soldiers, Vol 10.

SHADWELL, ARTHUR—Industrial Efficiency, Vol. 1.

SHARFF AND WESTCOTT—History of Philadelphia.

SIEBERT, WM. H.—Underground Railroad. 478 pp. New York, 1898.

SINCLAIR, W. A.—The Aftermath of Slavery, Small, Maynard & Co., Boston, 1905.

SMEDLEY, R. C.—The Underground Railroad. Phila., 1833.

SMITH, T. W.—The Slave in Canada. In the Collection of the Nova Scotia Society. Vol. 10. Halifax, N. S., 1889.

SMITH, W. B.—The Color Line, 1905, McClure, Phillips & Co.

SOCIAL AND INDUSTRIAL Condition of the Negro in Massachusetts. 319 pp. Boston, 1904.

SOME EFFORTS OF NEGROES for Social Betterment. Atlanta University Pub., No. 3. 66 pp. 1838.

SPARKS, JARED—Work of Benj. Franklin, 1. 314, 315.

SPEARS, JNO.—The American Slave Trade, Scribners, 1901.

SPIERS, FREDERICK W.—The Street Railway System of Philadelphia, etc. Johns Hopkins University Studies. Series 15, Nos. 3 and 5, Baltimore, 1897.

STARR CENTER—History of a Street, Phila., 1901.

STATE CONVENTION of Colored Men of South Carolina.

STATISTICAL INQUIRY, A—Into the Condition of the People of Color of the City and Districts of Philadelphia, 1849. 44 pp. 8 vo.

STATUTES-AT-LARGE of the State of Pennsylvania, Phila.

STILL, WILLIAM—Underground Railroad Records. Hartford, Conn., 1886.

TALBOT, EDITH—Samuel Chapman Armstrong, 1904, Doubleday, Page & Co.

TANNER, B. T.—An Apology for African Methodism, Baltimore, 1867.

TANNER, B. T.—An Outline of History and Government, for A. M. E. Churchmen, Phila., 1884. 206 pp.

THE ADDRESS of the Southern and Western Conventions; With Notes by a Citizen of Pennsylvania. Cincinnati, 1845.

"THE AFRICAN REPOSITORY," III, 26.

"THE FRIEND," vol 29.

THE NEGRO in the Cities of the North. Charities. Vol. 15, No. 1. New York, October, 1905.

THE NEGRO EQUALED BY FEW EUROPEANS, Translated from the French, to Which Are Added Poems on Various Subjects, Moral and Entertaining; by Phyllis Wheatley. 2 vols. Phila. Wm. Woodward, 1801.

THE NEGROES OF FARMVILLE, VA.—In U. S. Bulletin of the Dept. of Labor, Number 14.

THE NEGROES OF LITWALTON, VA.—In U. S. Bulletin of the Dept. of Labor, No. 37.

THE PROCEEDINGS and Debates of the General Assembly of Pennsylvania, September 4, 1787-October 4, 1788. Taken in shorthand by Thomas Lloyd. 4 vols. in one. Phila.

THE THIRTEENTH ANNUAL REPORT of the Colored Orphans' Association, Phila., 1849.

TYSON, JNO. R.—The Social and Intellectual State of the Colony of Pennsylvania Prior to 1743.

TUSKEGEE COTTON PLANTERS in Africa. J. N. Calloway. Outlook.

TOBIN, FATHER—A Model Catholic Community of Colored People.

THE NEGROES OF SANDY SPRING, MD.,—In U. S. Bulletin of the Dept. of Labor, No. 32.

THE NEGROES OF XENIA, OHIO—In U. S. Bulletin of the Dept. of Labor, No. 48.

THE PRESENT STATE and Condition of the Free People of Color in the City of Philadelphia and Adjoining Districts, etc. Philadelphia, 1838.

THE STUDY OF THE NEGRO PROBLEMS. Annals of the American Academy of Political and Social Science. Phila., 1898.

THOMAS, ALLEN CLAPP—The Attitude of the Society of Friends Toward Slavery, etc. (Reprinted from Vol. 8, American Society of Church History, New York, 1897.)

THOMAS, W. H.—The American Negro, 1901, McMillan.

TILLINGHAST, J. A.—The Negro in Africa and America, 1902, McMillan.

TRADES OF THE COLORED PEOPLE, Phila., 1838.

NATIONAL CONVENTION OF COLORED MEN and Their Friends. Troy, N. Y. 1847. 38 pp. 8 vol.

NATIONAL CONVENTION OF COLORED MEN. Syracuse, N. Y., Oct. 4-7, 1864. Boston, 1864. 62 pp. 8 vol.

NATIONAL CONVENTION OF COLORED MEN in America, 1869. Proceedings. Washington, 1869. 42 pp. 2 vo.

NEGRO LANDHOLDERS OF GEORGIA—In U. S. Bulletin of the Dept. of Labor, No. 35.

OHIO ANTI-SLAVERY CONVENTION. Putnam, Ohio. Report on the Condition of the People of Color, etc. 1835. 24 pp. 8 vo.

PROCEEDINGS of the Select Committee of the U. S. Senate to Investigate the Causes of the Removal of the Negroes from the Southern States to the Northern States. Washington, 1879-1880.

U. S. LIBRARY OF CONGRESS; Select References.

VARIOUS AUTHORS—From Servitude to Service, 1905. Unitarian Assn.

VASS, S. N.—Progress of the Negro Race, Raleigh, N. C., 1906.

VAUX, ROBT.—Memoirs of Benj. Lay and Ralph Sandiford, Phila., 1815. T. W., 1228.

VILLAGE IMPROVEMENT Among the Negroes. R. L. Smith, Outlook.

WALKER, DAVID—Appeal in Four Articles, Together With a Preamble, to the Colored Citizens of the World, etc. 66 pp. Boston, Mass., 1829.

WASHINGTON, B. T.—The Future of the American Negro, 1897, Small, Maynard & Co.

WASHINGTON, B. T.—Tuskegee and Its People, 1905, Appleton's.

WASHINGTON, B. T.—Up From Slavery, 1901, Doubleday, Page & Co.

WASHINGTON, B. T.—Working With the Hands, Doubleday, Page & Co.

WASHINGTON, GEORGE—On Colored Troops.

WATSON, JNO. F.—Annals of Philadelphia, Phila., 1830.

WAYMAN, A. W.—My Recollections of A. M. E. Ministers, Phila., 1882.

WEBSTER, NOAH—Effect of Slavery on Morals and Industry, Hartford, 1793.

WESCOTT, THOMPSON—Persons Who Took the Oath of Allegiance.

WHEATLEY, PHYLLIS—Poems on Various Subjects, Religious and Moral; Dedicated to the Countess of Huntingdon, Phila., 1801. Published by Wm. Woodward, Baltimore.

WHITE, WM. S.—The African Preacher, Phila., 1849.

WILLIAMS, GEO. W.—History of the Negro Race in America from 1619-1880. New York, 1883.

WILLSON, JOSEPH—Sketches of the Higher Classes of Colored Society in Philadelphia. Phila., 1841.

WILLSON, JOSEPH T.—The Black Phalanx, Hartford, 1889.

WOOLMAN, JOHN—Considerations on Keeping Negroes, Phila., 1762.

"WORKMAN SOUTHERN," Hampton, Va.

WRIGHT, CARROLL D.—Slums of Great Cities; Seventh Special Report of the United States Department of Labor. Washington, 1894.

WRIGHT, R. R., JR.—Housing and Sanitation in Relation to Mortality of Negroes in Hampton Bulletin. Vol. 1, No. 3. Sept., 1893. Also Southern Workman, Sept., 1906.

WRIGHT, R. R., JR.—Article, Mortality of Negroes in Cities. Atlanta University Publications. The Health and Hygiene of Negroes, 1906.

WRIGHT, R. R., JR.—Migration of Negroes, in Annals of the Academy of Political and Social Science, May, 1906.

WRIGHT, R. R., JR.—Negro Rural Communities in Indiana, in Southern Workman, March, 1908.

WRIGHT, R. R., JR.—"Social Work and Influence of the Negro Church;" in Annals of Academy of Political and Social Science, Nov., 1907.

WRIGHT, R. R., JR.—"The Newspapers and the Negroes;" Occasional paper No. 20 of Starr Center, Oct., 1907. Reprinted in McGirt's Magazine, Nov., 1907, and in the A. M. E. Review, Jan., 1908.

WRIGHT, R. R., JR.—Philadelphia Colored Directory, 1908.